OF PALM WINE,
WOMEN AND WAR

The **Institute of Southeast Asian Studies** (**ISEAS**) was established as an autonomous organization in 1968. It is a regional centre dedicated to the study of socio-political, security and economic trends and developments in Southeast Asia and its wider geostrategic and economic environment. The Institute's research programmes are the Regional Economic Studies (RES, including ASEAN and APEC), Regional Strategic and Political Studies (RSPS), and Regional Social and Cultural Studies (RSCS).

ISEAS Publishing, an established academic press, has issued more than 2,000 books and journals. It is the largest scholarly publisher of research about Southeast Asia from within the region. ISEAS Publishing works with many other academic and trade publishers and distributors to disseminate important research and analyses from and about Southeast Asia to the rest of the world.

OF PALM WINE, WOMEN AND WAR

The Mongolian Naval Expedition to
Java in the 13th Century

DAVID BADE

INSTITUTE OF SOUTHEAST ASIAN STUDIES

Singapore

First published in Singapore in 2013 by
ISEAS Publishing
Institute of Southeast Asian Studies
30 Heng Mui Keng Terrace
Pasir Panjang
Singapore 119614
E-mail: publish@iseas.edu.sg
Website: http://bookshop.iseas.edu.sg

The responsibility for facts and opinions in this publication rests exclusively with the author and his interpretations do not necessarily reflect the views or the policy of the Institute or its supports.

ISEAS Library Cataloguing-in-Publication Data

Bade, David W.
    Of palm wine, women and war : the Mongolian naval expedition to Java in the 13th century.
    Revised edition of the author's work entitled: Khubilai Khan and the beautiful Princess Tumapel : the Mongols between history and literature in Java. Ulaanbaatar : A. Chuluunbat, 2002.
    1. Java (Indonesia)—History—Mongol Invasion, 1293.
    2. Java (Indonesia)—History—Mongol invasion, 1293—Historiography.
    3. Mongols—Indonesia—Java—Historiography.
    4. Javanese literature—History and criticism.
    5. Kublai Khan, 1216-1294—In literature.
    I. Title: Khubilai Khan and the beautiful Princess Tumapel
DS646.27 B131 2013   2013

ISBN 978-981-4517-82-9 (soft cover)
ISBN 978-981-4517-83-6 (e-book, PDF)

Cover photo (top): Scenes Sanggramawijaya defeated Mongolia after defeating Jayakatwang forces in staging the colossal dance drama Throne Wilwatikta by STUPA community in Yogyakarta Cultural Park Auditorium, 5 December 2012. This dance drama tells the story of the establishment of the kingdom of Majapahit by Narrarya Sanggramawijaya helped Duke Wiraraja of Sumenep by defeating forces Jayakatwang and Mongolia.
Source: TEMPO/STR/Suryo Wibowo, Indonesia.

Cover photo (bottom): Relief from Candi Jago, constructed near Malang, east Java, in 1280 in memory of a deceased king, Wisnuwardhana, by his son Kertanagara. The temple bears reliefs from a Buddhist text, Kunjarakarna, in which the main deity is Vairocana. This relief may depict Vairocana and a female deity in a garden. Courtesy of Professor John N. Miksic

Typeset by Superskill Graphics Pte Ltd
Printed in Singapore by Oxford Graphic Printers Pte Ltd

For my daughter Khulan
Охин Хуландаа зориулав

Contents

Preface to the revised edition

The first edition of this book (entitled *Khubilai Khan and the Beautiful Princess of Tumapel: The Mongols Between History and Literature in Java*) was written and published under a number of constraints. A deadline for publishing that gave me seven months to finish it, technical difficulties that led me to eliminate all diacritics except umlaut and acute accent, and most of all an inadequate knowledge of Chinese and no knowledge of Javanese, Balinese or Sundanese. In this revised edition the diacritics remain absent except in Stuart Robson's essay as it would have entailed an enormous labor to track down all the original materials to identify where and what diacritics had been used, and my knowledge of the relevant languages has advanced only slightly: I am still indebted to translators and their translations. And that, I have come to realize, is a far greater problem than I had previously imagined.

A number of important publications have appeared in the years since 2002, including Heng's monograph on Sino-Malay trade and Yamaguchi's paper on Wolio genealogies. In addition to new publications, I have continued my search for relevant materials of older vintage, and this new edition not only makes use of Gaubil's *Histoire de Gentchiscan...* and Robson's translation of the *Desawarnana*, both works that I was unable to obtain in 2002, but also Robson (1979, 2000), Schurmann (1956), Mills and Ptak's translation of Fei Xin's Hsing-ch'a sheng-lan, Damais (1958), Reid (1996), Gonda (1976) and others.

One of the most important discoveries I made in the years since the book's first publication was the work of the Oxford philosopher and linguist Roy Harris, especially his 2004 monograph *The Linguistics of History* and the more recent *After Epistemology* (2009). *The Linguistics of History* raised many questions about the writing and understanding of history, not the least of which is the role of translation, not only accross languages, but also across cultures, times and spaces. Tan Ta Sen's recent book *Cheng Ho and Islam in Southeast Asia* brought the issue of translation forcefully to the fore, but perhaps more importantly he brought attention to the importance of the questions we ask of texts and histories. Since the first edition of the book it is this matter of questioning that has come to have an increasing importance for me. The writings of R.G. Collingwood and Eugen Rosenstock-Huessy underwrote the first edition, and this revision has benefited from an intense period of studying the works of Roy Harris, whose writings of the past 35 years demonstrate the most relentless pursuit of questioning of foundations that I know of, and of Belgian philosopher Michel Meyer who has argued that questioning rather than ontology must serve as the basis for philosophy.

My most unexpected discovery followed upon a reading of Stuart Robson's 2001 essay on the *Kidung Harsawijaya*. Stuart Robson is Adjunct Associate Professor in the School of Languages, Cultures and Linguistics, Monash University. I wrote to Robson asking whether he knew of any plans to translate either of the kidungs treated in my book, and in his response he mentioned that he had written his B.A. honor's thesis on the sources of the Mongol invasion of Java, a copy of which he subsequently sent to me. What he did in that thesis was to look at all the available sources with the intention of seeing what they could tell us, rather than following the only other existing approach which was to unquestioningly accept the story that fit a national ideology or an imagined other. It was sheer pleasure to read, and I am honoured that Prof. Robson has agreed to revise and publish in this volume a work that he had nearly forgotten about as only a school exercise of his youth.

In addition to the acknowledgements in the first edition, I offer my thanks to Stuart Robson for his contribution to this book and to my education, to Yamaguchi Noriko for translating some Japanese material for me, and to Geoff Wade not only for his translation of the relevant section of the *Yu pi xu zi zhi tong jian gang mu*, but for believing that this book deserved a new edition and a wider audience. Thanks also to Hawe Setiawan whose research in Indonesian libraries on my behalf was a wonderful gift from a stranger that has made the book more like the book I wanted to write but could not write on my own. And most of all my thanks to Burmaa Kaylin, Duudii guai, Chuka and Garmaa, without whom this book would never have been written, much less published.

David Bade
June 15, 2011
Joseph Regenstein Library
University of Chicago

Preface to the first edition

A number of years ago the books *Banjaran Singhasari* and *Banjaran Majapahit* crossed my desk as part of my work in the library. Their account of the Mongol army in Java in 1293 was very different from that which I had read in the passing remarks of historians of the Mongols, and I looked around a bit to see what else I could find. At the time, I could not get very far because of my lack of knowledge of old Javanese. The topic has remained in the back of my mind for eight years as I worked on Polish and Czech-Slovak bibliographies of Mongolian studies. I left the wonderful Southeast Asian collection at Northern Illinois University where I had access to everything I needed for studying Java, but very little for studying Mongolia, and moved on to the University of Chicago in 1995. When Professor Bira invited me to read a paper at the 8th International Congress of Mongolists in 2002, I pulled out the paper of 1994, my notes, photocopies and all that I could remember of the topic, and decided there should be enough material to make a decent short paper for the congress.

The most important text — the *Pararaton* — is now available in English, the translation having appeared in 1996, while the *Desawarnana* in English, and English and Dutch summaries of the *kidungs* have been around for many years. The interest in this incident among Indonesian and Javanese historians has been limited to just those aspects of the story and the texts written about it which are relevant to issues of Javanese medieval history, society and culture; very little has been written on the Java campaign by Mongolists, and apart from Rossabi's brief comments in his *Khubilai Khan*, the Javanese version of that campaign has never appeared in publications on the Mongols. The more I worked on the paper, the more interested I got, and the longer it became. The length increased even more when I decided to include translations and summaries of the relevant texts, since those texts are not readily accessible in Mongolia.

I have not written a philological treatise on the texts, nor have I attempted to make this an exhaustive historical study. It is intended as an introduction. The only book written on the Mongols in Java to date is based almost entirely on the account found in the *Yuan shi* and addresses very different questions from those which I found myself asking.

There are several reasons for my writing this book. One is to introduce the Javanese version of the events of 1293 to Mongolists in much the same way that Groeneveldt introduced the Chinese version with his translations of the relevant sections of the *Yuan shi*. The existence of two markedly divergent historiographical traditions itself raises fascinating questions and the translations and summaries presented herein are intended as a preliminary gathering of materials until the time comes when all of the relevant texts will be available in a language more accessible to Mongolists than Old Javanese. I hope that better qualified students will take up the questions which I and others have raised, will themselves raise more questions, and bring the whole Javanese tradition into the arena of Mongolian studies alongside the works of Odoric of Pordenone, Wassaf, the Papal correspondence and the *Yuan shi*.

Another reason for writing is simply the joy of finding an entire tradition of historiography relating to the Mongols which is so unlike that which I have encountered elsewhere. The fact that these Middle Javanese versions of the Mongol campaign have been revived and taken center stage — literally! — in Indonesia in the late 20th century adds a literary and international aspect to the historical interest of the Javanese materials.

And finally I have a personal reason, a reason which has nothing to do with historians and philologists. I wrote the book as a gift for my Mongolian friends, especially those to whom the book is dedicated, in gratitude and appreciation of their friendship.

My thanks to Bill Alspaugh, Shintia Argazali, Tim Behrend, Abigail Cohn and Ete Olson for bio-bibliographical assistance, and to Robert Bird, Wayne Cristaudo, Judith Pfeiffer and Evrim Binbas for comments and suggestions.

David Bade
University of Chicago
July 2002

A note on transcription

Chinese words appear in pinyin in the text which I have written; in quotations they appear as they are in the original publication.

For all other languages, all diacritics other than umlaut and accent have been omitted everywhere except in the paper by Stuart Robson. Items in the bibliography appear in the script of the original publication rather than in transliteration.

Introduction: Views from the other side

Why views from the other side? Because no Mongol views have survived into our time.

> When they had landed on the elected coast they gained possession of the island which is 200 parasangs in length and 120 parasangs in breadth through spreading fear of the fury of their sword ... His Majesty [Khubilai] did not permit that certain death should excercise his power here, but put his son [Kertanagara's son in law Wijaya] on the steps of the high throne. He bestowed on him a ceremonial dress of honor, and conferred on him much grace, and, against the payment of tribute and taxes in the shape of pearls and gold, he left the island in his hands. (Wassaf, translated in Spuler, 1988, pp. 168–69)

Wassaf thus describes the Mongol invasion of Java in what is perhaps the closest to an official Mongol version as is extant, having been written for the Mongol Ilkhans of Persia in the early 14th century. The Yuan dynastic history compiled under the Ming gives a very different account, as do the accounts written in Java. Even so, Wassaf's account — and all other accounts of the Java campaign — differ greatly in tone from his own and other accounts of the Mongol campaigns in western Asia and elsewhere. Although Wassaf claims that the Mongols "gained possession of the Island ... through spreading fear of the fury of their sword", he concludes his account with the claim that Khubilai "did not permit that certain death should excercise his power here," but installed a new king on the throne — Javanese, not Mongol — "conferred on him much grace" and left the kingdom in his hands. Compare the preceding description with his account of the Mongol siege of Baghdad and Ibn al-Athir's account of the Central Asian campaigns:

> The people were killed, both from inside and outside, or were carried away wounded ... In this way was Baghdad besieged and terrorized for fifty days. ... [T]hey razed to the ground the walls ... and filled in the moat which was as deep as the contemplation of rational men. Then, they swept through the city like hungry falcons attacking a flight of doves, or like raging wolves attacking sheep, with loose rein and shameless faces, murdering and spreading fear; ... The massacre was so great that the blood of the slain flowed in a river like the Nile, red as the wood used in dyeing... those hidden behind the veils of the great harem ... were dragged like the hair of the idols through the streets and alleys; each of them became a plaything in the hands of a Tatar monster; and the brightness of the day became darkened for these mothers of virtues. (Wassaf, translated in Spuler, pp. 116–21)

> For several years ... I put off reporting this event. I found it terrifying and felt revulsion at recounting it... O would that my mother had never borne me, that I had died before and that I were forgotten! ... The report comprises the story of a ... tremendous disaster such as had never happened before, and which struck all the world... They killed women, men and children, ripped open the bodies of the pregnant and slaughtered the unborn. (Ibn al-Athir, translated in Spuler, pp. 29–30)

No such events are recorded for the Java campaign. Not by the Mongols, not by the Javanese, nor in Chinese sources such as the *Yuan shi*. The fear and horror which appears in accounts by European and Asian witnesses and chroniclers of the Eurasian campaigns does not appear in Wassaf's — nor Rashid al-Din's — account of the Java campaign. Some of the Javanese accounts describe battles which are noisy, violent and bloody, but with one exception the victims are the enemy soldiers, not the whole population. The Javanese authors neither "found it terrifying" nor "felt revulsion at recounting it", and in the Chinese sources, the worst of the matter was the wrath of Khubilai towards his own officers upon their return.

The earliest published Javanese account of the Mongols in Java appeared in 1817 in Raffles' *History of Java*. It contains the following remarks about the "King of Tatar, called Sri Laksemana", i.e. Khubilai, during his visit to Java:

> *Jáya Kátong,* previous to the invasion of *Browíjáyá,* had promised his guest, the King of *Tátar,* whose name and title was *Srí Laksemána,* to give him his adopted daughter (wife to *Browíjáyá*) in marriage. This was however delayed. Several times did *Laksemána* press *Jáya Kátong* to fulfil his promise, but he never received a positive answer.

> *Laksemána* therefore being informed that *Browíjáyá* of *Májapáhit* had attacked *Kedíri,* forthwith sent a letter to him, saying that he would co-operate with the people of *Májapáhit,* provided *Browíjáyá* would be on good terms with him. ...

> In the heat of the action *Jáya Kátong* and *Laksemána* met, and a fierce encounter took place between these chiefs. *Jáya Kátong* threw his javelin at *Laksemána,* but missed him; and *Laksemána,* in return, struck him on the breast with his poisoned spear, and killed him on the spot. ...

> *Browíjáyá* then eagerly went into the *kadáton,* and was received by his faithful wife. They embraced with tears of joy; and *Browíjáyá* was so enraptured at recovering her, that without taking further notice of the *kadáton,* he returned with his wife to *Májapáhit.* He invited the King of *Tátar* to visit him. On his arrival *Browíjáyá* received him with every attention, and made him a present of a beautiful virgin.

> *Laksemána* remained for some time at *Májapáhit,* during which *Browíjáyá* gave him two or three grand entertainments. He afterwards embarked on board of his own vessel and returned to his kingdom of *Tátar.* (Raffles, quoted from the 2nd ed. of 1830, pp. 115–16)

Imagine that.

What the Javanese chose to record, how the Javanese record compares to the Chinese record, why they may have written thus, and what these various accounts mean for our — and their — understanding of the Mongol campaign to Java are of interest both as history and as a glimpse into the human act of meaning-making itself and the ways in which we know who we are.

Part I contains a discussion of Meng Qi's mission and a narrative of the expedition to Java. Part II, on historiography, is comprised of three sections: 1) Chinese histories, 2) Javanese texts, and 3) Western accounts and modern scholarship. The various sections of Part III explore the significance of the two complementary traditions and the notions of unity, universality, justice, peace, kingship, love, war and women implicit in or absent from them. The texts of the various sources appear in selections in English translation or summaries in the appendices which complete the book.

PART I

A History: The Mongol Campaign in Java

Beginnings are difficult for everyone but God, since for the rest of us every beginning is preceded by and results from prior events. Should an account of the Mongol invasion of Java begin with Khubilai's order to send a naval force? Or with the Javanese king Kertanagara's branding of the envoy Meng Qi? Should it not begin with the history of Chinese-Javanese relations or biographical portraits of Kertanagara and Khubilai, noting those characteristics which lead each of these kings to acts of aggression?

To establish the facts of the invasion in so far as that is possible there is no need to leave the narrow period of their occurrence; to evaluate the narratives through which we learn of those events, to interpret them, to understand how the narrated events relate to prior events, why things happened thus and not otherwise in these histories, it is necessary to look back to the actors and the worlds in which they lived. An infinite regression is unnecessary for many facts can be left out of account, such as the composition of the muddy water Wijaya threw into the eyes of Mundarang. Since the narrative in this section is not intended as an exhaustive study but as a background from which to view the various histories and stories told and written about and around it over the last 700 years, only a few facts will matter, and they will matter because of the questions they raise and my interest in them. The composition of Wijaya's mud and many other matters shall be left for other authors with other interests and other questions.

Why Java?

> In general, the underlying reasons for the expedition have been little examined, and Mongol "imperialism" has seemed a satisfactory explanation. To be sure it is advisable to place the expedition in the context of the global project which sought control of the maritime trade routes after having taken command of the continental routes; Marco Polo tells us explicitly that when all the other nations of the southern seas had submitted, Java refused to enter the system. But one can without doubt seek greater precision. The recent expedition of Kertanagara against Malayu disturbed the ancient equilibrium which had prevailed for centuries; the hegemony of Sriwijaya which as a rule had always been on good terms with China was suddenly gone... (Lombard, p. 38)

While early writers apparently had no difficulty accepting and understanding such an expedition, the Javanese campaign has puzzled modern historians — those few who have given it much thought — and provoked a number of explanations. In addition to the "imperialist" and "equilibrium" explanations noted by Lombard, recent historians have offered a number of explanations for the campaign: an attempt to control the spice trade; the desire to eradicate the remnants of the Song army, some of whom may have fled to Java; an effort by Khubilai to legitimate his reign; Khubilai's need to impress his Chinese subjects; an attempt to deflect internal disatisfaction through the creation of external enemies; a combination of Khubilai's depression, alcoholism and megalomania; a "spiritual war" waged by the Javanese king Kertanagara against Khubilai. The main Chinese and Javanese sources mention none of these reasons and offer very simple explanations: the *Yuan shi* gives as reason that a Mongol envoy was mistreated by Kertanagara, ruler of the Kingdom of Singhasari in Java; the Javanese sources all state that the Regent of Madura Wiraraja requested Mongol military assistance. Rossabi remarks on the account given in the *Yuan shi* as follows:

> Khubilai's sudden outbursts against foreign territories make sense only in the context of the domestic failures of the 1280's. His

difficulties within China presaged similar catastrophes abroad. A lack of control characterized both domestic and foreign policies. ... The justification for some of these dramatic turn-arounds lacks credibility. The sources imply that the extraordinary naval expeditions were mounted simply to punish foreigners who harmed Mongol envoys. There was clearly much more at stake in these expeditions. (Rossabi, 1988, pp. 206–07)

Rossabi is undoubtedly right when he says that there was more at stake, but "what was at stake" will be examined only after a narrative of the expedition and the reasons given by the early writers on those events. We begin with the Chinese version, in the second month of the year 1292, and proceed backwards and forwards as the need for understanding requires.

The Chinese version: Meng Qi's mission to Java

When the emperor Shih-tsu (Kublai) pacified the barbarians of the four quarters of the world and sent officers to the different countries over the sea, Java was the only place he had to send an army to.

In the second month of the year 1292 the emperor issued an order to the governor of Fukien, directing him to send Shih-pi, Ike Mese and Kau Hsing in command of an army to subdue Java; ... (Groeneveldt, 1880, p. 21)

That is how the *Yuan shi* begins the story of the Java campaign in Book 210. This book does not begin immediately with the Java campaign; two paragraphs precede the quotations above. In these opening paragraphs of the book the location of Java is given and a very brief description of the customs, produce and people. The customs are unknown, the many rare and valuable things from Java bring high prices in China, and the people are strange and ugly. (Ibn Battuta (1958–2000, v. 4, p. 885) described the people otherwise: the men are handsome and brave, while the "women ride horses, understand archery and fight just like the men.") The Chinese historian, having informed the reader of the valuable items and ugly people in Java immediately notes that the emperor had to send an army there. The commanders of the army, the number of soldiers requested, where they should be collected, how many ships will launch and the provisions taken: these are the first matters to be noted.

Next we are informed of the reason for the campaign, since the coexistence of many valuable goods and ugly people in a far off land does not in itself justify conquest. The explanation for the campaign is put in the emperor's own words from his final audience with the generals in charge of the expedition:

> When you arrive at Java you must clearly proclaim to the army and the people of that country, that the imperial Government has formerly had intercourse with Java by envoys from both sides and been in good harmony with it, but that they have lately cut the face of the imperial envoy Meng Ch'i and that you have come to punish them for that. (Groeneveldt, 1880, pp. 21–22)

In Book 131 of the *Yuan shi*, in the biography of Ike Mese (Yi-hei-mi-shi), there appears a different message from Khubilai, perhaps more comments from the same imperial speech:

> When you have arrived in Java, you must send a messenger to inform me of it. If you occupy that country, the other smaller states will submit from themselves, you have only to send envoys to receive their allegiance. When those countries are brought to obeyance, it will be all your work. (Groeneveldt, 1880, p. 30)

Who was this "Meng Ch'i" mentioned above?

Gaubil offered the following account of Meng Qi "translated" from an unspecified Chinese original:

> After some time he [Khubilai] had sent to the King of *Kouaoua* a official named *Mengki*. It does not say what *Mengki* did, nor what was the incident that made the King of *Kouaoua* act so terribly. The king took *Mengki* and with a hot iron marked him on the face as was often done to common thieves. After being thus affronted *Mengki* was

sent away. The Chinese were indignant at seeing a Great Mandarin of their nation dishonored by a Prince treating them like barbarians, and they implored Khubilai to exact vengeance. *Khubilai made an uproar over the insult done to one of his envoys, and ordered a large flotilla of warships and others to assemble in Tsuentcheou in Fokien.* The Provinces of *Kiamsi*, of *Fokien*, and of *Houkouang* furnished 30000 resolute men, and they had no trouble arming the flotilla, the Chinese being eager to furnish everything necessary, the Mandarins of the nation being much interested and resolved to make foreign lands see at least that they were very sensitive to a dishonor done to a Minister of the son of Heaven. (Gaubil, pp. 217–18)

Here we have a problem that will follow us throughout our study: Gaubil's version "taken from the Chinese history and translated" — without any specific indication as to which history was translated — differs radically from Groeneveldt's translation of the corresponding section of the *Yuan shi* made a century and a half later. Gaubil's history seems to have been based on the *Yuan shi*, at least in large part, but there is considerable variation between his version of the Mongol expedition to Java and Groenveldt's, and Gaubil clearly engaged in much interpretation and interpolation. Both "translations" have been utilized almost exclusively by later scholars, few having taken the trouble to consult the Chinese text themselves. The same problem appears again in another text frequently used by western sinologists, the *Histoire générale de la Chine, ou Annales de cet empire, traduits du Tong-kien-kang-mou*, Mailla's "translation" of the *Tong jian gang mu*.

In Mailla's edition there is a more detailed discussion of Meng Qi's mission to Java:

The emperor had sent envoys to many nations in order to request them to put themselves under his protection and to pay tribute. Meng Qi, one of his ministers who was sent to Java, was not well received there. The king of Java was offended at Meng Qi's proposal and branded him in the face with a hot iron as is done to common thieves, and scornfully sent him on his way. (Mailla, 1777, v. 9, pp. 450–51)

Irwin (1974) demonstrated that the text Mailla used for his translation was the Kangxi edition of 1708 supplemented by the Manchu translation/version of the same work. Geoff Wade has translated the passage from that same Kangxi edition (a copy of which is in the University of Chicago Library) and came up with the following:

> Earlier, Meng Hong, the Assistant of the Right had been sent as an envoy to Java, but [those of] Java had branded his face. (for the full text, see the Appendix)

Mailla (or his continuators) apparently drew on the *Yuan shi* or Gaubil's *Histoire* to supplement his translation, and Gaubil drew on sources other than the *Yuan shi*; exactly which sources does not seem to be a matter on record. As I have found no other sources providing information on Meng Qi (Meng Hong in the *Yu pi xu zi zhi tong jian gang mu*), I am inclined to believe that the differences between Gaubil and Groeneveldt and between Mailla and Wade are due in each case to the former's attempt to elucidate and elaborate upon the text they were translating. (For further discussion of these matters, see Part II below.)

What exactly happened to Meng Qi, when and why this happened are not really clear; whether he was actually branded in the face as the *Yu pi xu zi zhi tong jian gang mu* states, slashed, cut, beaten, or merely treated in a rude or hostile manner has been debated. Whatever happened, his treatment was condemned by Khubilai. The date of the incident is not given in the Chinese sources; Groeneveldt (1880) suggested "1280 but probably later", and Rockhill (1914) thought that the incident involved the envoy Mêng K'ing-Yüan and happened during the mission sent by Khubilai in late 1281 for the purpose of asking Kertenagara to send a family member to the Yuan court. He offered this suggestion because the biography of the Mongol general Meng Qi makes no mention of a mission to Java nor of his being branded. This suggestion entails treating the name given in the *Yuan shi* as mistaken and the incident happening a full decade prior to Khubilai's response. Earlier writers had offered other dates: in his edition of the *Pararaton*, Brandes (1897, p. 86) suggested a date before 1280 or even before 1275; in the 2nd edition edited by Krom after the death of Brandes (Brandes 1920), the date 1289 was suggested, following Kramp who had argued for that date based on a statement in the biography of Shi-bi in Book 162 of the *Yuan shi* (Kramp, 1903, pp. 359–60). Campbell (1915, v. 1, p. 58) claimed that the mission arrived in 1290, while Franke (1932–1950, v. 5, p. 232) regarded the branded Meng Qi and the famous general as one and the same and dated the incident in the year 1291. Most later historians (e.g. Rossabi and Slametmuljana) have followed Kramp and assumed a date of 1289, but there seems to be no evidence which would decisively indicate any of these dates: 1289 has been oft repeated but remains unproven. We shall repeat it, without proving it, with the understanding that it is a widely accepted probability and not a certainty. Khubilai's missions to Java in 1279, 1280, 1281 and 1286 are mentioned and dated in Books 10–14 of the *Yuan shi*; the mission of Meng Qi is mentioned in Book 210 but nowhere are we told when it occurred.

Neither the biography of Meng Qi in Book 160 of the *Yuan shi* nor the early Javanese sources make any mention of this incident. But before considering the Javanese perspective, Meng Qi requires further investigation.

Why did Khubilai send Meng Qi to Java? While Mailla's sources apparently claimed that Meng Qi was one of those ministers whom Khubilai sent abroad to ask for submission and tribute, other possibilities have been suggested. The reason for Meng Qi's mission to Java must be understood as having been the same as for the later military campaign for if the reasons for the military campaign were other than those for sending Meng Qi, then the latter was actually irrelevant, a later justification for a war fought for other reasons. The three principal reasons given for the military expedition are: trade, tribute (submission), and diplomatic response to Javanese expansionism. To investigate how these explanations might apply to Meng Qi's mission as well as the war of 1293 will be the first detour.

Meng Qi was on a trade mission

Trade with the southern islands had long occupied Chinese merchants and the Chinese government established a shipping office for the southern trade in Canton in 971. This trade was at its peak during the Song dynasty, and in the 12th century a serious problem arose as the empire's cash reserves were being exported for "useless goods." The *Song shi* records that the Censor Chen Qulu blamed "the extravagance of its people in purchasing such luxuries as perfumes, ivory and rhinoceros horns, and to the sea-trade generally" (Rockhill, 1914, p. 423) for draining China of its currency. While numerous measures were taken during the 11th and 12th centuries to curtail the influx of luxury items and stem the outflow of cash, the Mongols reversed these measures after 1277, opened more southern ports to foreign trade and began issuing paper money. Within a few years, restrictions were again placed on the exchange and use of cash, and in 1284 a new trade policy was instituted: government funded and regulated traders were chosen to engage in trade for the realm, with the government receiving seven tenths of the profits. The use of private capital was forbidden, as was the export of copper cash in 1286. The *Yuan shi* mentions two occasions on which Khubilai was approached for the purchase of large pearls; he refused both offers, and in the second instance "told his officers to keep the money for the poor." (*Yuan shi*, in Rockhill, 1914, p. 426)

The nature of this trade in the early years of Mongol rule in China is aggressive but neither hostile nor military. Khubilai sent "a golden badge for Wa-ni, king of Kulam, on whom the Emperor conferred the title of Fu-ma or "Imperial Son-in-Law." (Rockhill, 1914, p. 438) Rockhill notes that trade missions from the island kingdoms became more numerous "as a result of the missions of Yang Ting-pi and of the friendly reception given the foreign envoys to Court in 1282." The *Yuan shi* records that in 1284 ministers from kingdoms in Sumatra, Ceylon, "Li-lun" and "Ta-li" — the latter two states unidentified by Rockhill — brought articles of tribute "in compliance with the commands brought them by an official named Pa-ko-lu-ssu sent by the Governor of Fu-kien" as well as letters from the rulers of those places. Khubilai sent numerous missions to the south "to learn more of them and to bring him of their strange birds and beasts, their jewels and their learned men," (Rockhill, 1914, p. 439) and twice — 1282 and 1287 — sent Ike Mese to acquire sacred relics of the Buddha from Ceylon.

The crisis experienced by the Indianized states of Southeast Asia from the 13th to the 15th centuries, the period of great changes in cultural and political life noted by Cœdès, makes up the background for the Mongol embassies and military campaign to Java. Noting that the Mongol conquest (presumably he means conquest of much of Asia, but not of Java) did not provoke this "profound shaking, mutation" of Asia, Lombard points to commerce as the prime mover of that world and time. Cœdès had sought to explain this crisis by attributing it to a growing number of indigenous peoples adopting Indian civilization thereby leading to a dilution of the "pure" Sanskrit culture, the pure culture then being represented by a dwindling number of the aristocracy. Lombard objects:

> That interpretation of a progressive change, according to a process that was basically internal, of a supposedly "pure" culture in its origin but which was degraded through contact with local civilization, is not entirely satisfactory, even when it does account in part for the facts. It is tempting to ask if one of the main causes is not to be found in the intensification of large scale commerce. (Lombard, v. 2, p. 32)

Rossabi notes two of the most important factors underlying trade policy under the Yuan and distinguishing Yuan economic policy from earlier Chinese governments. The first of these is the Mongol regard for artisanry: "Like his forebears, Khubilai cherished artisans. Unlike the traditional Chinese, he accorded craftsmen a high status. Because the Mongols had few craftsmen of their own, they relied on foreigners for the craft articles they required." (Rossabi, 1994, p. 448)

This interest in and valuation of artisanry, as well as scholarship, medicine and technology was noted by all travelers to Khubilai's court and is evident in the reports of the missions of Ike Mese to Ceylon and the goods brought as tribute. The second factor was the lack of any negative valuation of traders: "Chinese dynasties had imposed numerous restrictions on merchants because the Confucian scholar-officials disapproved of trade. Khubilai did not share this bias, however, and in fact accorded merchants high status." (Rossabi, 1994, p. 449) Rossabi later quotes Marco Polo: "I believe there is not a place in the world to which so many merchants come" (Rossabi, 1994, p. 450, quoted from Moule and Pelliot, *Marco Polo*, vol. 1, p. 235). The growth and extent of trade under Khubilai has led some historians to suggest that the whole series of missions to Java, from those in 1281 to the ill-fated mission of Meng Qi and the military campaign of 1292–1293 were all about control of the spice trade in the southern archipelago. Rossabi in the article just cited describes the Java mission of Meng Qi and subsequent military expedition thus:

> In 1289, Khubilai sent an ambassador named Meng Ch'i to seek the submission of Java. The Javanese king, Kertanagara, fearful that the Yüan court wished to take away his control over the spice trade in Southeast Asia, responded by branding the face of the unfortunate envoy. Khubilai used this incident as a pretext to initiate a military expedition against Java. (Rossabi, 1994, p. 487)

Trade relations between Java and China are well documented prior to the ascension of Khubilai and the Yuan era; at some point — perhaps only with the arrival of Meng Qi — those friendly relations were severed. If Meng Qi (or an earlier envoy) had been sent as the customary envoy of the new dynasty, then not just trade but tribute relations and political status vis a vis the Yuan dynasty were severed with Kertanagara's rebuff.

The explanation that Meng Qi and later the army was sent to Java in an ongoing struggle to control the spice trade was advanced early in the 20th century and was repeated by various historians through Rossabi and more recent works which have relied on his biography of Khubilai. It is also present in literary texts of the 20th century, beginning with the *Babad Majapait*, a Sundanese poem first published in 1935, but appears nowhere in any earlier Javanese sources. Although trade is probably always a "contest" in the sense of merchants competing against each other, fighting pirates and dealing with tax officials all along their routes in order to make a profit, there is no evidence that there was a 'trade war' much less a state-sponsored military struggle to control the spice trade. There was a spice trade, and in a later century Andrew Corsalis (quoted in Kuwabara, 1935) claimed that China's trade with the southern sea region was principally trade in spices. An especially intense desire for incense brought prices of that commodity fabulously high in China. Undoubtedly local kings all over the archipelago wished to benefit as much as possible from that trade whether through taxation, control of shipping routes or simply encouragement of trade. States throughout the region promoted trade and held state monopolies on goods bought and sold within their borders. That China and other countries were engaged in trade promotion and diplomacy is well documented (see e.g. Heng, 2009); military manoeuvres (apart from the struggle with piracy) to capture and control as much of that trade through force is plausible but undocumented — unless, of course, that is what the expedition to Java was all about.

The documents which do exist (e.g. Ibn Battuta, Marco Polo, the *Yuan shi*) and the archeological record (Heng, 2009) tell of traders from throughout the region, trade embassies, government monopolies within China, regulation of merchants, and pirates. The South China Sea and the waters north of Java were both full of pirates and unsafe for merchants. North of Java merchant ships were regularly intercepted by smaller boats lying about waiting for them. These boats forced all whom they could to bring their cargo into Java. Gustaaf Schlegel writing in 1870 even thought that the entire Java campaign was nothing other than an adventure in piracy carried out by the merchants of Canton and had nothing to do with the government of Khubilai.

Piracy was a problem not only around Java but all the way to Korea. Schurmann noted that

> In addition to the ships and crews which the Mongols obtained with the fall of the Sung, a number of maritime specialists and pirates entered their service ... The most striking individuals were the former pirates Chu Ch'ing and Chang Hsüan, who went over to the Mongols with a large number of ships and sailors. (Schurmann, p. 109)

Those two pirates, Zhu Qing and Zhang Xuan, operating in South China under the Southern Song, had both gone into the service of the Mongol Khaan by 1276 with their "more than 500 vessels and several thousands of mariners" (Schurmann, 1956, p. 126). Schurmann noted that Zhu was sent by the Yuan court to fight against pirates in 1280 and 1281, and that both Zhu and Zhang "were ordered to accompany A-t'a-ha-yi in the great maritime invasion of Japan", while in 1284 these three headed the fleet in the campaign against Champa, and in 1292 (1291 according to Schurmann) Zhu and Zhang participated in the Java campaign (Schurmann, 1956, pp. 126–27).

Regarding the Mongols of the Empire period in general Ruotsala wrote "Nevertheless, what drove the Mongols on was mainly economic factors. To begin with their motivation was robbery and later on more sophisticated forms of exploitation" (Ruotsala, 2001, p. 109) and if one accepts Ruotsala's remark, then the issue of pirates in the southern seas and the piracy of the merchants of Canton are part of a larger picture of an economy of expropriation and robbery that existed throughout Asia at the time. In any case, piracy, whether or not the events of 1292 and 1293 may be so regarded, was rooted in neither a mystical nor a political program for power and domination but rather characterized maritime economic conditions both before and after as well as during the reigns of Khubilai and Kertanagara.

There is some evidence that the Yuan government may have tried to exert some kind of control over maritime trade simply to stem the outflow of money. Heng (2009, p. 164) noted that "Javanese epigraphy indicates that by the thirteenth century Java had officially adopted Chinese copper cash as the currency to be used in low-value official transactions" and Zhao Rugua's remarks suggest that the Yuan officials were worried enough about the loss of money through trade to consider trying to control maritime trade as a matter of monetary policy. By controlling the Javanese ports, the money would be in Chinese hands at both ends of the trade route and thus slow the depletion of the treasury. However, prior to 1289 the last edict prohibiting the export of copper cash had been in 1234 (Hirth and Rockhill, 1966, pp. 81–82) and the Mongols carried out their commercial transactions using paper money, so monetary policy can hardly be accepted as a sufficient explanation for the mission of Meng Qi and the invasion of Java.

Not one of the sources which specifically discuss Khubilai's sending of Meng Qi or the naval expedition, neither the *Yuan shi* nor any of the pre-20th century Javanese or Persian accounts, makes any reference to economic factors as a reason for Meng Qi's visit. The *Yuan shi* does record aggressive trade policy decisions beginning in the years 1278 and 1279. Kuwabara mentions three passages which all indicate that Khubilai wanted the south sea islanders including the Javanese to come and trade with China, but not that he wanted submission or war:

> In the eighth moon of the fifteenth year of Chih-yüan, A.D. 1278, the Emperor commanded So-tu and P'u Shou-keng and other officials in Fu-chien province, that as the foreign peoples of the south-eastern islands are filled with the most loyal devotion to the righteous cause of our nation, they should make the traders going to those islands proclaim to the foreign peoples our gracious intention that, if they come, they would be cordially treated and allowed to travel and trade anywhere in our country as they please. (Kuwabara, 1935, p. 80)

> When the Emperor Shih-tsu subjugated South China, he, with an intention of extending his power beyond the seas, promoted So-tu to the post of left vice-minister of the provincial government at Ch'üan-chou, and commanded him to invite the southern barbarian peoples. (ibid., p. 81)

> [In A.D. 1279] P'u Shou-keng asked his emperor that a proclamation be issued to encourage the barbarian peoples of the southern seas to come to the Chinese ports. But this was not granted. (ibid.)

All three of these passages record Khubilai's attitudes toward the nations of the southern seas during Kertanagara's reign in Singasari. In the first case the foreign peoples are invited to come to China and promised cordial treatment. In the second passage Khubilai is described as wanting to extend his power across the seas and for that reason he invited foreign embassies to come to China. In the last passage, when requested to encourage the southern nations to come to China, Khubilai refused. Rockhill and Kuwabara concur that the problem in the last passage was not Khubilai's changing attitudes toward the southern peoples, but a struggle between the Yuan state and private merchants within China. Suo-du and Pu Shou-geng "may have been too eager on their own profit to be mindful of the government revenue" (Kuwabara, 1935, p. 81). Lombard also notes that in China of the Song or Ming, as in Majapahit and later Thailand "commerce was organized for the benefit of the state; it was not a matter of "free" trade, but of an activity confined to the functionaries and which should profit the public treasury" (Lombard, v. 2, p. 39; for a detailed discussion of Yuan commercial policy and restrictions on trade in the Malay Archipelago, see Heng, 2009).

Perhaps as important as the states' control of trade and the issue of monetary equilibrium was the predominance of Arabs and other Middle Easterners — the Ortaq group — in the maritime trade, a predominance established long before Marco Polo's visit. Lombard even suggested that it was the Islamic elite in China, the rich merchants of Fujian who "pressed the councillors of Khubilai to undertake the large-scale military expeditions to Japan, Champa, Vietnam and Java." (Lombard, v. 2, p. 32) Earlier Hirth had noted "The ocean-trade of almost every port in these waters, which may be said to reach from the coast of Morocco in the West to that of Japan and Corea in the East, was in the hands of Arab merchants" (Hirth, 1896, p. 57). As noted above, Khubilai did not give in to their demands in 1279.

The claim made by Rossabi and others that Khubilai was trying to wrest control of the spice trade from Kertanagara can hardly be accepted for two reasons: 1) Kertanagara did not control the spice trade, and 2) if Khubilai were competing in a spice war with anyone, it would have been with the Arab merchants living in his own kingdom and elsewhere, not with the Javanese. Both Meng Qi and the army may have been sent to Java by Khubilai under pressure from the Fujian dwelling Arab merchants, but no evidence has been offered to prove it.

Explaining the Khubilai-Kertanagara conflict as a simple trade war or even a not-so-simple trade war to shore up the currency of the realm is a hypothesis which deserves further study, for it is likely that a desire for trade did figure in Khubilai's decisions. Yet the desire for trade is not the same as nor should it always be reduced to "trade war" or the desire to control regional trade, and Heng (2009) argues that even prior to the Yuan period commercial and diplomatic affairs were being pursued independently by the Song court. There are suggestions in the Javanese sources which support the interpretation of Khubilai's intentions as desire for trade rather than desire for control: according to the *Kidung Panji Wijayakrama* during the period of Wijaya's exile in Majapahit — after the death of Kertanagara — all the world came to Majapahit to trade due to the illustrious goodness and generous treatment given to all by Wijaya. The Chinese sources in turn describe in detail the great wealth to be found in Java.

There is also a passage in the *Kidung Panji Wijayakrama* which states that Wiraraja offered Jayakatwang a gift of spices from China, and in the *Pararaton* another passage states that when Wiraraja decided to ask the King of Tatar for assistance, he sent his letter "by way of the Tatar boat which is here for trade" (*Pararaton*, p. 111). Since the ban on private maritime shipping instituted in 1284 was not revoked until 1294 (Heng, 2009, p. 65), the ship mentioned in the Pararaton had to have been there trading on behalf of the Yuan government. These two incidents argue against Meng Qi's mission as a mission to reestablish trade since they demonstrate that Mongol-Javanese trade was not interrupted between the mission of Meng Qi and the arrival of the Mongol army. The branding of Meng Qi and the failure of his mission apparently did not alter commercial relations. Heng in fact argues that the Yuan court did not "view tribute missions and diplomatic intercourse as necessary for furthering commercial exchanges" (Heng, 2009, p. 108).

Meng Qi was a diplomatic envoy, demanding vassalage and tribute

This is the reason suggested by the *Yu pi xu zi zhi tong jian gang mu* as Mailla presented it (though not as Wade translated it). Although Chinese records give evidence of tribute missions from Java to China for centuries prior to the Yuan period, Marco Polo claimed that at the time of his visit to Java in 1292 the island was subject to one king only and paid tribute to no one. As noted above, the *Yuan shi* records that Khubilai was of another opinion, telling his officers that "the imperial Government has formerly had intercourse with Java by envoys from both sides and been in good harmony with it" (Groeneveldt, 1880, p. 22) and Rockhill records the embassy of 1286 in which family members of the rulers of ten southeast Asian states arrived for an audience with Khubilai and presented articles of tribute (Rockhill, 1914, p. 441). The previous tributary relation between China and Java was considered to be still in effect and the establishment of the new dynasty was the occasion of a new but not a different kind of relationship. According to this interpretation, Meng Qi was simply an envoy reaffirming the traditional status of Java vis-a-vis China. This is the explanation offered by Kramp in 1903 who cites the accounts of the missions of 1281 and 1286 with their demands for Kertanagara to appear before the Khaan in person. The same explanation is accepted by Cœdès in the 3ʳᵈ edition of his *Indianized states of Southeast Asia* where no other reasons are offered for the expedition:

> Kritanagara must have felt himself strong enough, and above all far enough away from China, to resist the demands of the Mongols, who from 1279 had been insisting that a member of the royal family be sent to the court of Peking. The missions of 1280 and 1281 came to nothing. In 1289 it seems that the envoy of Kublai was mistreated by the Javanese, and to avenge this insult the Great Khan decided in 1292 to send to Java an expedition... (Cœdès, 1968, p. 198)

The Javanese texts which tell of the Mongol invasion do not mention Meng Qi, but they almost all include the statement that Wiraraja of Madura was a friend of the 'King of Tatar' (Khubilai). Perhaps this is how the Javanese over time came to understand or remember their 'vassalage' and tributary status vis-a-vis China and the Yuan?

The nature of tribute in Chinese foreign relations in all periods was not a straightforward political matter. Kuwabara claimed that "The words *chin-feng* mean literally 'to bring tribute' but in reality meant 'to open trade'" (Kuwabara, 1928, p. 42). States desirous of the lucrative trade with China could engage in trade at the ports or be profitably rewarded by bringing tribute to the court. The trade nature of tribute has often been noted, often emphasized and for some historians (e.g. Kuwabara in the citation above) the tribute relation is nothing but a kind of trade relation. The trade aspect of tribute is revealed in many particulars such as the fact that the Emperor was expected to reward his vassals and the tribute bearers expected to return to their homes laden with gifts from the Khaan. Yet the tribute relation can only be regarded as simply a kind of trade relation if one ignores many aspects of that relation, and the history of those relations.

A more refined view of the relation between international trade and tributary relations in Asia has been offered by Lombard. He suggested that the changing significance and power of the merchants (whom he refers to as the "new elites") in the port cities led to the freeing of these ports from their dependence and subordination to the agricultural interior and gave rise to a new political structure, the sultanate. This new political structure developed in Sumatra towards the end of the 13th century, appearing later in Java. One indication of this change of political centers from interior to coastal regions may be found in the role played by the governor of Madura and the Madurese in the struggle between Wijaya and Jayakatwang. "One is tempted to see in the decisive intervention of Wira Raja the first sign of the emergence of maritime interests in the political sphere" (Lombard, v. 2, p. 325). Such an understanding would give even more weight to the Javanese tradition of Wiraraja's claim to being a friend of the King of Tatar, a relationship that Robson (1962) considered impossible.

Concerning a later era of Chinese international relations (Ming and Ching dynasties) Hamashita wrote:

> The fundamental procedures required to maintain the tribute relation were the investiture of local rulers and the visit to see the Emperor, when recognition of the tribute group itself confirmed the recognition of the rulers. The relationship was characterized as one of mastery and obeisance, and the "loyal" countries, areas and tribes concerned were expected to pay tribute to China regularly. (Hamashita, p. 11)

Furthermore, the tribute system "was in symbiosis with a network of commercial trade relations." (ibid., p. 13) The tribute system evolved, according to Hamashita, from an early sinocentric system of tribute relations, into a regional network of multiple tribute relations in which China remained the center, and finally into a modernized multilateral "tribute-trade" system in which China was no longer the origin and terminus of all regional trade:

> [T]he relationship between tribute goods and "gifts" was substantially one of selling and purchasing. In fact, it is quite legitimate to view tribute exchange as a commercial transaction. ... Seen from an economic perspective, tribute was managed as an exchange between seller and buyer, with the "price" of commodities fixed. ... The key to the functioning of the tribute trade as a system was the huge "demand" for commodities outside of China and the difference between prices inside and outside of China. (ibid., p. 17)

While the tribute system in East Asia may have developed away from a formal political system into a primarily economic system, the view from the Chinese court continued to be that participation in the tribute system signified political submission. Voegelin remarks that the mission sent by Saint-Louis in 1249, led by Andrew of Longjumeau, yielded a result which "was not quite what the King had expected it to be, for the Regent Ogul-Gaimish had considered the sending of an embassy as an act of submission, and reacted accordingly." (Voegelin, p. 381) Even among western scholars such as the 18th century Jesuit Amiot the tribute relation clearly entailed political submission. The description of the island of Java given in the *Mémoires concernant l'histoire, les sciences, les arts, les mœurs, les usages, &c des Chinois par les missionaires de Pékin* (v. 14, 1789) is found under the heading "Introduction a la connoissance des peuples qui ont eté ou que sont actuellement tributaires de la Chine" [Introduction to the knowledge of the peoples who have been or who are now tributaries of China] and is listed in the table of contents under the heading "Introduction a la connoissance des peuples Chinois." [Introduction to the knowledge of the Chinese peoples]. The peoples of Java, because of their tributary status, are discussed as peoples under Chinese rule.

Nearly five hundred years after Andrew of Longjumeau's mission the same political understanding lay behind the Kiakhta Treaty (1727), a point made by Amiot in one of his contributions to the above mentioned *Mémoires* of 1789 and reaffirmed by Hamashita:

> Compared to the one-sided nature of the tribute system in which China was clearly dominant, the exchange of letters under the Kiakhta arrangement appears evenhanded. But China did not really see Russia in equal terms because the mandate of the Colonial Office was to *control* the affairs of the Mongols. (Hamashita, p. 22)

On the other hand, formal submission and vassalage status were not always required. While the Mongolian campaigns in the rest of Asia — Burma, China, western and central Asia — are renowned for the demands and ultimatums which set them in motion, the *Yuan shi* contains some interesting examples in which the usual did not happen in the southeast Asian archipelago. Chapter 210 of the *Yuan shi* includes a brief note about a discussion among Khubilai's ministers concerning the vassalage of the country of San-xu-guo, apparently a group of three small islands near Taiwan which can not now be more exactly identified:

> In the 30th year of Chih-yüan (1293 A.D.), under the reign of Shih-tsu (Khubilai Khan), orders were given that a mission should be despatched to the country to invite vassalage from it. Bayan, in the office of the Vice-Minister, and others, however, thus replied: 'We have discussed the matter with the intelligent persons. The country has a population of less than 200 families, some of which come at times to Ch'üan-chou for trading purposes. Last year, when our warships passed the country on their way to Liu-chiu, the countrymen supplied provisions to our expedition and also lodged our officers. They have certainly no design against us, so please let there be no despatch of a mission to them.' And the Emperor followed the advice. (quoted in Sei Wada, "The Philippine Islands...", pp. 144–45)

Three significant matters are indicated here: 1) the country was not officially a vassal of the Yuan court; 2) no mission asking for such status was sent;

3) relations were friendly and there were no hostilities on either side. Vassalage was neither needed nor demanded. It may well be that the small population of the archipelago was the most important factor in the people of San-xu-guo having neither designs on Mongol China nor willingness to oppose the visiting ships, as well as in Khubilai's decision not to bother with a formal request for submission.

Another mission sent to the people of the island of Taiwan in 1292 (with an interpreter from San-xu-guo) suffered the deaths of three men due to lack of communication (the people of Taiwan could not understand the man from San-xu-guo) and returned to China without achieving its goal. From this latter incident, also recorded in the *Yuan shi* (Wada, p. 145), it is clear that however frequently they are recorded, neither the hostile nor the friendly behaviour of the people of Taiwan or San-xu-guo nor the punitive expeditions of Khubilai Khan were entirely predictable and automatic. Instead of demanding submission of San-xu-guo and an immediate and destructive punitive expedition in Taiwan, what we find is evidence of Khubilai's willingness to harken to different council and choose no action, to offer no response to offence.

If Meng Qi were sent to Java to demand tribute and submission, he would have been carrying out a mission much like those sent to foreign nations from the time of Chinggis on. According to the interpretation of the Mongol viewpoint offered by Voegelin, the consequences of submission would be that those offering their submission would become members of the Empire, the divinely willed and only legitimate government on earth; refusal to submit would mean rebellion against that same government and required punitive measures. While that seems to be largely true, the exceptions noted above in Taiwan and San-xu-guo suggest that in the southern seas these rules did not always apply.

For the rulers of 13th century Java, the absence of Mongol navies in the southern seas would have made of any submission or acknowledgement of vassalage a mere formality with economic but not military consequences. It is not difficult to understand Kertanagara's treatment of Meng Qi if it is assumed that he did not believe that Khubilai would send a military expedition to Java. But if Meng Qi arrived in Java in 1289 as most historians now accept, Khubilai had already engaged in many years of campaigning against the kings of Burma, Annam and Champa, campaigns which ended with these latter two kings declaring their allegiance to Khubilai. Rossabi notes that they recognized "that the Mongols would continue to plague them unless they offered *pro forma* acquiescence to the great khan. They therefore began to send tribute, and the Mongolian expeditions against them ended in the late 1280s" (Rossabi, 1994, p. 487). Had Kertanagara known of those recent campaigns, would he have risked offending the Khaan's envoy? Did Kertanagara know of the destruction of the Mongolian navy during the two Japanese invasions of 1281 and 1284? Robson argued "There is no evidence that the Javanese knew of this" (Robson, 1962, p. 23) and that therefore Berg's theories, which require that Kertanagara know about these campaigns as well as Mongolian plans to avenge the treatment of Meng Qi, are not based on any evidence. Berg argued not only that Kertenagara knew of these campaigns but that Kertanagara was himself engaged in a campaign of expansionism and felt himself ready and able to expand his activities northward in direct conflict with Khubilai's activities there.

Meng Qi was a diplomat responding to a Javanese campaign of anti-Mongol expansionism

A third explanation which has been offered for the arrival of Meng Qi on Javanese soil is that Kertanagara the king of Singhasari was engaged in a bold and aggressive military campaign to unite the whole archipelago and mainland southeast Asia — or at least some part of it — in a confederation of powers or even under his kingship to counter Khubilai's expansion into southeast Asia. That Kertanagara was a strong king with some aspirations of conquest is clear. Apart from the consolidation of his lands in eastern Java, his chief military concern (according to Krom) was the conquest of Sumatra. Berg states that the *Desawarnana* mentions four military campaigns undertaken by Kertanagara: two against other Javanese in 1270 and 1280, the war against Sumatra (Malayu) in 1275, and an invasion of Bali in 1284. Phalgunadi mentions expeditions to conquer Pahang (Malaysia), Sunda (West-Java), Balkailapura (Borneo) and Gurun (New Guinea) in addition to Malayu (Sumatra) and Bali (Phalgunadi, p. 9); he notes that these expeditions are not mentioned in the *Pararaton*, but are corroborated by the *Desawarnana*. It was while Kertanagara's soldiers were campaigning in or ruling over southern Sumatra that Khubilai's expeditionary forces arrived, only to find that Kertanagara had already been killed by the neighboring king of Daha (Kadiri), Jayakatwang.

The arguments for this explanation were developed by C.C. Berg along with his interpretations of the nature of Kertanagara's religious practices and political ambitions. By dismissing certain elements of the Javanese accounts of Kertanagara's life and reign, juggling dates and places, and giving highly unusual readings of various passages, Berg proposed a theory of Kertanagara's aims, religious and political, which received a wide hearing after 1950. Repeated in many histories (such as Hall's), they appear in Mongolian historiography for the first time in Rossabi's biography of Khubilai. The key elements in this picture are Kertanagara's fear of Khubilai, his adoption of Tantric Buddhism — like Khubilai — in order to be spiritually equal to the Mongol Emperor, and an aggressive campaign of military conquest which he supposedly undertook to gain allies and power with which to meet Khubilai far to the north rather than in Java.

One of the pillars of Berg's argument concerns Kertanagara's adoption of Tantric Buddhism as a defence against Khubilai's spiritual power:

> Kertanagara's regnal period coincided with a period of expansion of the Mongolian empire under Kubilai Khan. Before starting the conquest of South China, Kubilai … embraced Tibetan Buddhism, and the Tibetans accepted him as their overlord. Since Kertanagara introduced a similar form of Buddhism in Java, we may guess that he followed Kubilai's example in order to acquire the same degree of power so as to be able to protect his country against Kubilai's raiders. (Berg, 1965, p. 99)

It is important to note that for the proponents of this theory, Khubilai's dedication as a Jina-Buddha in 1264 and 1269 is taken as an indication that he had adopted a new program of conquest and expansion. Kertanagara was afraid of Khubilai, so he got religion, and a similar one at that. The crucial evidence that this conversion was related to fear of Khubilai comes from a particular interpretation of one passage in the *Desawarnana*, canto 45, stanza five. Bosch comments on Berg's interpretation as follows:

According to Berg this means: "In 1275 he (king Krtanagara) gave the order for an expedition against Malayu, which would submit, or had submitted, to him in fear of his deification (*kadewamurttin*) earlier (*nguni*)" (Kert. 4 sq.). Berg takes this to mean that the king was deified in 1275, i.e. consecrated to Bhairawa-Buddha by his priests, and so enabled to proclaim an imperialist programme... Malayu was as it were paralysed by terror and awe for the king's deified condition ... (Bosch, p. 19)

In fact what Berg suggested was that Kertanagara's religion was actually a mask or means for political ambitions. If that were true, then his attitude — with or without religion — was much like that demonstrated by Khubilai when he instructed the officers in charge of the Java campaign: "If you occupy that country, the other smaller states will submit from themselves, you have only to send envoys to receive their allegiance." Berg does not cite this passage from the *Yuan shi*, but the similarity is clear. Is it not simpler to suggest that when Khubilai says "If you occupy that country, the other smaller states will submit" he is merely referring to submission in the face of superior military power? There is no indication of any religious dimension; however much Khubilai may have felt that he was acting on Heaven's will, he always responded to non-submission with his armed forces, not with prayers and a delegation of Buddhist monks. Yet Berg goes further, adding to the story that Khubilai embarked upon his conquests after having been consecrated in tantric Buddhist rituals, and that it is this religious practice which Kertanagara follows and which empowers him in his own mind *and in the neighboring kings' minds* for the military policies and victories that should follow: having heard of Kertanagara's spiritual powers, the other smaller states will submit.

Another indication that a mystical-political-military alliance is the aim of Kertanagara's policies is found, according to Berg, in a certain Buddhist sculpture which was sent by Kertanagara to the king of Malayu in 1286. This sculpture and its gift-meaning is only understandable if regarded "as a symbolic invitation to join an alliance against Kubilai on the basis of Buddhism and connubium." (Berg, 1965, p. 99)

Slametmuljana accepts some parts of Berg's thesis, and claims that Kertanagara's expedition to Malayu (southern Sumatra) had two aims: 1) to expand Singhasari's territory; and 2) "to prevent Kubilai's growing influence into the regions of Southeast Asia." (Slametmuljana, 1976) He claims that the kingdom of Suwamabhumi in south Sumatra had from its inception enjoyed good relations with China, and for that reason Kertanagara felt compelled to get there first. He also translates an inscription known as the *Amoghapasa Inscription* from which we read about the above mentioned statue:

> Hail! In the month Bhadrapada of the Sakayear 1208 (August-September 1286)... the Amoghapasa Lokeswara statue together with fourteen other statues as its companions is brought from Java to Suwarnabhumi. These gifts of Prince Wiswarupakumara are to be placed in the region of Dharmasraya. For that purpose His Majesty Sri Kertanagara Wikrama Dharmottunggadewa orders ... to accompany them. Hopefully all inhabitants of Malayu ... will enjoy these gifts. (Slametmuljana, 1976, p. 26)

Yet Slametmuljana continues by noting that Khubilai's response to this conquest of Suwarnabhumi was to make "no efforts to approach her ruler or to send military troops to expel the Singasari army." Perhaps now Khubilai was afraid of Kertanagara? No, for in 1289 (according to Slametmuljana) Khubilai sent an envoy "demanding that King Kertanagara recognize the emperor as his suzerain and send tribute to China." (Slametmuljana, 1976 p. 26) That envoy was Meng Qi.

A modified statement of this position appears in Lombard's discussion of the Mongol campaign. Lombard notes that the deeper reasons for the campaign have seldom been sought, most commentators mentioning Mongol "imperialism" or control of maritime trade routes and pressing no further. His suggestion takes up Berg's hypothesis of Kertanagara's campaign against Khubilai, and turns it on its head. The refusal of Kertanagara to continue the friendly and open relations which had characterized Chinese-Javanese relations for centuries and his military expedition against Malayu (the Pamalayu) were not policies directed against Khubilai but were in fact destabilizing the entire region. Javanese traders were not operating in accordance with Chinese commercial law and the southward flow of money was a serious problem for the Yuan treasury. Kertanagara was not engaged in a personal vendetta against Khubilai, spiritually or militarily, but by acting against the patterns of the past, he forced others to act as well.

As if in a mirror, Heng turned Lombard's analysis upside down and argued that Chinese commercial policy under the Yuan was acting against the patterns of the past and forcing adjustments in the Malay Archipelago.

> With the advent of Yuan rule in 1279, the restriction on the length of stay abroad imposed on Chinese shipping during the Song appears to have been revoked. Under such conditions, Chinese shipping could now remain outside China for extended periods, and a number of Chinese shippers began to base their operations in Island Southeast Asia. (Heng, 2009, p. 129)

With the Mongol Empire reaching from the Persian Gulf to the North China Sea, maritime communication became an important element in imperial government, yet the effects of improved maritime networks would not be limited to public administration and would reach out beyond the empire:

> As a result of the expansion of its geographical range into the Indian Ocean, Chinese shipping appears to have begun to take over the Malay region's role of transshipping products from the Indian Ocean littoral and Middle East to China, and vice versa. (Heng, 2009, p. 64)

It was in this situation that Kertenagara attacked and conquered Srivijaya. Meng Qi was somewhere in the middle of all this, sent to Java by the Mongol Khaan to negotiate something with a king who was in no mind to negotiate whatever that was.

Meng Qi, for whatever reason he was sent, got branded

Whether or not Kertanagara was engaged in a seventeen year long war of military conquest, imperialist dreams, and spiritual warfare instigated by and directed against Khubilai, he branded or otherwise sorely mistreated Meng

Qi after his arrival and sent him back to the Mongol court. Although Meng Qi's purpose in traveling to Java is not recorded in the *Yuan shi* that account does state that after the Mongols had defeated Jayakatwang in 1293 "Tuhan Pidjaya was sent back to his dominions in order to make preparations for sending tribute" and that upon returning to China "The emperor's officers made a list of the valuables, incenses, perfumeries, textures etc. which he brought and found them to be worth more than 500.000 taels of silver.... golden and silver articles, rhinoceros-horns, ivory and other things." Of the several reasons proposed as explanations for Meng Qi's journey to Java, the reestablishment or affirmation of vassalage and payment of tribute is the only reason found in the Chinese histories, and the tributary relationship connected as it was to both trade and political submission can adequately account for the matters noted above. Meng Qi was probably sent to Java to encourage trade, reaffirm vassalage, punish Kertanagara and warn him against further military expansion. All of these matters must have engaged the Yuan court to some degree at the time; whether Khubilai was concerned more with one than another aspect of Java's status and Kertanagara's activities is not a matter on record. The most important fact is that Meng Qi was sent to Java as the official representative of Mongol authority, and that he was scorned and rejected.

Why Meng Qi was mistreated is another matter. Was this rash act provoked by Meng Qi himself, the result of a misunderstanding (like the three soldiers in Taiwan), or deliberately performed by Kertanagara because of his feelings of military or spiritual superiority? On this point the Chinese sources say nothing. Modern Indonesian historians incline to the opinion that Khubilai through Meng Qi demanded too much — submission and vassalage from a king who felt he not only did not need to submit but even had designs on the same territories — while the old Javanese sources make no mention of the incident at all. Modern Javanese and Sundanese literary treatments — historical dramas and 'babads' (poetic chronicles) — place the blame equally on the trade restrictions, impoliteness and foolish diplomacy of Kertanagara and on the "impolite and arrogant" Meng Qi. The following is the account found in the *Banjaran Singhasari*, an historical drama written and produced under Indonesian government sponsorship for performance on the 700th anniversary of the end of Singosari in 1992:

Shri Khan [Khubilai] was shocked to hear that
    The merchants may not voyage anymore,
    He quickly asked his envoy,
    Meng Khi accompanied by his soldiers,
    To meet with the king,
    Shri Baginda Kertanegara,
    The King of Nusantara.

    Their voyage went smoothly,
    They arrived in Java,
    And met the King,
    Prabu Kertanegara.
    Impolite and arrogant [i.e. Meng Khi],
    Bare-chested and loud,
    He shocked and astonished those who heard him.

    Shri Kertanegara's face,
    Reddened like a wora-wari flower,
    Red like fire,
    Unable to restrain his anger,
    Wild-eyed and sweaty,
    As if his chest had been kicked,
    His chair trembled.

    He quickly went to the weapons store,
    Where his sword hung,
    It flickered when drawn from its sheath,
    Like a hungry tiger,
    He attacked the envoy,
    Meng Khi the anger maker.

Meng Khi (Meng Qi) is here called the anger maker because he brought to Kertanagara Khubilai's request for free trade. Another 20th century work first published in 1935, the Sundanese poem *Babad Majapait*, also concerns the foundation of Majapahit. It records a similar yet less critical attitude towards Kertanagara's actions:

Then the nation of Singosari
befriended the nation of the Tatars
from the land of the Chinese Empire,
asking for the favor
of the Ruler of the Tatars
whose renowned name was Khubilai
since in fact from the earliest of times
of previous kings they enjoyed
a close relationship of unceasing friendship.

Yet these two kingdoms
were not of the same mind
because Khubilai Khan
beheld Tumapel as a subject
since such was the opinion of his heart
he felt unsatisfied to accept the
Khan's wishes to
immediately come across to surrender
Himself properly as a subordinate.

When he did not send his representative
with an official as the messenger
then Khubilai Khan
sent a messenger immediately
who, carrying orders for Kertanagara
went to the land of Java,
appeared before the honourable King
bringing the orders from his Khan
directly before His Majesty of Singasari
the sovereign Lord Kertanagara.

But the King of Singasari
did not feel himself under orders
to serve Khubilai,
would not consider subjection.
Often in their correspondence

presents from Java
were offered in friendship
without the proper submission
which Khubilai desired,
thus were they unacceptable.

The Tatar Khan would not accept
nonfulfillment of his wishes
and sent again delegations,
several envoys,
and still He was not pleased
until finally the King,
the Honorable King Kertanagara
because of the repeated delegations
responded in a fit of rage

When the envoy named Meng Ki arrived
he was seized and branded
prominently on his forehead
then ordered to return,
to go back towards his homeland again.
When he arrived
he appeared before the great Khan,
reported the whole matter
and the Khan could not bear his anger
when he saw the branded forehead.

Whereas the Chinese historians develop their narrative of the war in Java from the incident concerning Meng Qi, the Javanese accounts offer a completely different genesis and meaning for the arrival of the Mongols, Meng Qi being entirely absent from them.

The early Javanese versions: By invitation only

For the Chinese chroniclers an envoy was abused, the incident angered Khubilai and the result was that armed forces set sail for Java on a mission to punish Kertanagara. That version sounds much like the stories that abounded during the reign of Khubilai's father and grandfather; the early Javanese versions are interesting primarily for their being unlike any other accounts by peoples who met with Mongol armies.

Meng Qi was neither sent nor abused; rather, Khubilai came to Java by urgent invitation

The medieval Javanese versions as recorded in the *Desawarnana, Pararaton, Kidung Harsawijaya* and *Kidung Panji Wijayakrama* lack any reference to Meng Qi. The immediate and sole reason offered for the presence of Mongol soldiers in Java is that Khubilai was a friend of Wiraraja, and Wiraraja asked him to come to Java to destroy Wijaya's enemy — the usurper Jayakatwang — and place Wijaya on the throne as the rightful royal heir in exchange for a lovely princess or two. The Javanese accounts vary in their chronology, names, places and certain other matters; their main concern is with the royal action and succession, including the role and fate of the Javanese princesses: Kertanagara's refusal to heed the advice of his older and wiser ministers, demoting and unjustly treating them, followed by the ill will which arose and eventually led to his overthrow and death; the flight of Wijaya and the installation of the usurper Jayakatwang as ruler over Java; the friendship of Wijaya and Wiraraja; the princess in captivity for whose rescue a messenger was sent to Khubilai requesting military assistance, and so on.

While it is possible to regard much of the material in these stories as 'romance' and unhistorical — as many historians have and continue to regard them — it is precisely the romantic elements of these stories which reveal most clearly the divergent viewpoints which produced the great differences between the Javanese and Chinese narratives, differences which deserve far more attention than they have received. By comparing the two traditions it is possible not only to question the historicity of the Javanese sources but also to investigate the Chinese accounts from an entirely different viewpoint. The events subsequent to the departure of Meng Qi and prior to the arrival of the Mongol army, known only from the Javanese sources, provide a background for a far more compelling interpretation of Wijaya's later turn against his allies from Mongolia. It is to those events that we now turn.

Wijaya's own account of Jayakatwang's coup: the inscription of Kudadu

The earliest Javanese account is found in the 1294 inscription of Kudadu, issued by the new king and founder of Majapahit — Wijaya — shortly after the departure of the Mongols. The inscription was issued to commemorate a grant of land to Kudadu's village chief in reward for his kindness and assistance to Wijaya (called Nararya Sanggramawijaya in the inscription). Its first section contains a description of Wijaya, who has taken the reign name of Kertarajasa Jayawardhana:

> ...on this day has come down the order from His Majesty the all-heroic praised ruler, the valiant exalted king, the bringer of destruction to his enemies, the ruler with great laws, whose character is of one greatly gifted, strong, virtuous, beautiful and dutiful, lord over the whole island of Java, protector of right for all the good-intentioned, descended from the lineage of Narasingha, the embodiment of the quintessence of right rule, born the exact likeness of the son of Narasingha, the man whose royal privilege was to marry the daughters of Kertanagara, and who as king was annointed with the name Kertarajasa Jayawardhana... (Brandes, *Pararaton (Ken Arok)...*, p. 80)

The text of the inscription continues with a description of Jayakatwang's coup, the attack on the palace at Singhasari (Tumapel), the flight of Wijaya and the assassination of Kertanagara by Jayakatwang. (For Robson's complete translation into English, see Appendix 1 below). Briefly it relates Kertanagara's belated response to the threat from Jayakatwang:

> When King Jayakatwang's troops reached the village of Jasun-Wungkal, King Kertanagara sent His Majesty [Wijaya] and Ardaraja to fight the enemy. His Majesty as well as Ardaraja were sons-in-law of King Kertanagara, but Ardaraja was also a son of King Jayakatwang. When His Majesty and Ardaraja leaving Tumapel arrived at Kedunt Peluk, His Majesty met first the enemy. After

the battle the enemy fled while suffering a great loss. Afterwards His Majesty's army moved to Lembah (valley), but no enemy was in sight...

[When] he reached Rabut Charat, where he saw the enemy coming from the west, he commanded his troops to fight them. Again suffering a great loss, the enemy fled. Seemingly they disappeared forever. However, from east of Hanyiru the enemy hoisted red and white-coloured flags. Seeing them, Ardaraja laid his weapon down and ran shamelessly to Kapulungan in treason, which caused the destruction of His Majesty's troops; but His Majesty remained loyal to King Kertanagara. ... The next day at dawn he was chased by the enemy. (Slametmuljana, 1976, p. 36)

Although the Kudadu inscription includes a narration of the attack by Jayakatwang, the sequence of folly, insult and intrigue which led up to his revolt are not mentioned, nor does the narrative refer to any events after Wijaya's stay in Kudadu, including the arrival, battles and departure of the Mongol army. Because the inscriptions are largely in agreement with the later accounts, they support a more serious engagement with those later texts. It is in those texts alone that we find the extraordinary story leading up to the invitation to the King of Tatar (Khubilai) to come to Java and make war on Jayakatwang.

Kertanagara's military campaign in Sumatra (the *Pamalayu*)

The date of Kertanagara's assumption of power in Singhasari has been variously established as 1254 (Phalgunadi, using the date of his consecration as crown prince), 1266 (Cœdès and Slametmuljana, based on the inscription of Pakis), 1268 (the death of Kertanagara's father, Jaya Wisnuwardhana, according to some historians), 1270 (Jaya Wisnuwardhana's death according to Slametmuljana) and 1272 (the death of Jaya Wisnuwardhana as recorded in the *Pararaton*). Both the *Pararaton* and the *Desawarnana* state that the kingdom of Tumapel was ruled jointly by Jaya Wishnuwardhana and Narasingamurti, Wijaya's father. At the time of Kertanagara's consecration as crown prince

(1254), his father Jaya Wishnuwardhana changed the name of Tumapel to Singhasari, by which name it has been known ever since. According to the *Kidung Harsawijaya*, when Narasinga felt death approaching (he died in 1268 or 1269), he asked his ministers to make Kertanagara the temporary ruler of Singhasari until his own son Wijaya would be old enough to rule. Whether there were two rulers — Wijaya's and Kertanagara's fathers — in Singhasari at that time, or one king and his *Ratu-anga-bhaya* (highest adviser) is a matter of contention; Slametmuljana (1976) notes that Narasingamurti was *Ratu-anga-bhaya* in the *Pararaton*, and that the "facts revealed by the inscriptions do not corroborate" a dual-kingship.

The date for the beginning of Kertanagara's campaign to subdue Sumatra is widely accepted as 1275. (Except for Berg, who suggested that the decision to conquer Sumatra was made in 1275 but the army was not actually sent until 1292.) According to the *Pararaton* and the *Kidung Harsawijaya*, his decision to send his army to Sumatra, leaving Singhasari nearly defenceless, was vigorously opposed by his senior advisors who were wary that Jayakatwang the vassal king of Kediri (Daha) would take advantage of any situation in which the kingdom had no defence. One such senior advisor was named Banyak-Wide who went by the title Arya Wiraraja; he was described by Krom as "one of the most unsavory characters in Javanese history" (Krom, p. 352). The *Pararaton* introduces Wiraraja just before giving the text of the letter which he sent to Jayakatwang. "There was rivalry between king Kertanagara and King Jayakatwang the ruler of Daha. He [Jayakatwang] was the enemy of king Kertanagara. ... He [Wiraraja] was a close friend of king Jayakatwang."

Instead of heeding his older ministers' advice, Kertanagara reacted by being suspicious of his highest ministers: Mpu Raganata was demoted (he was described by Slametmuljana (1976, p. 24) as "the most feared and respected man in the country due to his wisdom" in a phrase which tells so much about Javanese culture); Wiraraja was sent off to be superintendent in a remote settlement in Madura; Cantasmrti retired and became a hermit in the forest. Kertanagara ignored and dismissed his senior advisors while following a plan of conquest urged upon him by younger men.

Kertanagara's military expedition, known as the *Pamalayu*, has been interpreted as the beginning of a policy of expansion and military conquest to preempt or contest further Mongolian expansion in Asia. According to this view mentioned earlier in regard to the mission of Meng Qi, Khubilai's continued campaigns against the Southern Song and the invasion of Japan in 1274 were a worry to Kertanagara who responded by seeking allies. A united archipelago, allies in peninsular and continental southeast Asia, a military power capable of withstanding or even preventing a Mongol attack: this was the meaning of Kertanagara's *Pamalayu*. The principal architect of this theory, C.C. Berg, also argued that Khubilai's conversion to Tibetan Buddhism and subsequent consecration were instrumental in Kertanagara's conversion to a form of Tantric Buddhism: these two kings were already in the 1260's and early 1270's engaging in spiritual warfare, fighting holy fire with holy fire; Kertanagara was also preparing for the day when they would need to fight unholy fire with unholy fire, perhaps naphtha.

Kertanagara's campaign in southern Sumatra was successful, but took almost as much time and resources as Khubilai's campaign against the Song: the *Amoghapasa Inscription* of 1286 records gifts sent by Kertanagara to Sumarvabhumi in the hope that "all inhabitants of Malayu ... will enjoy these gifts" (Slametmuljana, 1976, p. 26). While this suggests some measure of successful conquest by that time, the armies sent on the *Pamalayu* would not return to Java until after Kertanagara's death and the departure of the Mongols in 1293.

Wiraraja's revenge

With his decision to send his army off on a long-term campaign and the mistrust and demotions which followed, Kertanagara estranged his wisest and most trusted ministers while at the same time making himself and his kingdom vulnerable to attack. But it was not the Tatar Khan — Khubilai — who attacked Singhasari in 1292. The above mentioned minister Wiraraja, whom we later discover was a friend of the Tatar Khan (according to the Javanese accounts), was the architect of the destruction of Singhasari. The version of these events found in the Balinese manuscript discovered and translated (or summarized?) by Raffles presents a brief and unflattering description of Kertanagara and the state of his kingdom on the eve of his destruction:

During the reign of *Sáng Srí Síwabúda* [Kertanagara] the state had very much declined. Every district was going to ruin, in consequence of which the *páteh*, named *Mángku Rája Náta* [Mpu Raganata], addressed himself to the prince, reminding him of the manner in which his forefathers used to treat the people, and which the welfare of his kingdom required of him to follow. To this, however, the prince would not listen, and as a punishment to the *páteh* for his presumption, he immediately ordered him to quit *Tumápel*.

Sang Sri Síwabúda had a man in his service named *Wíra Rája*, whom, in consideration of his useful services, he had made ruler over the eastern part of *Madúra* called *Súmenap*. On being informed that the king intended to accuse him of a crime of which he was innocent, and considering himself in danger, sent a messenger to *Sri Jáya Kátong*, sovereign of *Kedíri*, to say, 'that as the kingdom of *Tumápel* was almost in a state of confusion, he might attack and conquer it without difficulty'. (Raffles, 1830, v. 2, p. 113)

The *Pararaton, Kidung Panji Wijayakrama* and *Kidung Harsawijaya* all tell the story of Wiraraja's betrayal by means of a thinly veiled message to Jayakatwang urging military action against Kertanagara, each in slightly different terms. The *Pararaton* gives the text of the message sent as a secret letter:

The secret letter said: "My lord, I respectfully tell you, if His Majesty has any consideration and desire to hunt in the former field, now His Majesty has the chance to so hunt. It will be the best and the most opportune moment. There is no danger. There are no tigers, wild buffaloes, or snakes even. There is only one tiger, but it is toothless. (Phalgunadi, p. 99)

Both the *Kidung Panji Wijayakrama* (Berg's edition) and the *Kidung Harsawijaya* offer longer versions of this message. In the *Kidung Harsawijaya* Wiraraja sends his son Wirondaya to Jayakatwang. Wirondaya is a name not mentioned in either the *Pararaton* — in which no son is mentioned — or the *Kidung Panji Wijayakrama*, where Wiraradja's son is given the name Rangga-Lawe by Wijaya. Slametmuljana translates the message relayed by Wirondaya as follows:

> I have to inform His Majesty you are comparable with a hunter, who has to make use of every good opportunity and place. The right time has just come. Please make use of it. At this moment the field is dry, no grass grows. The leaves are falling down, scattered all over the ground. The hills are small and the ravines are not dangerous occupied by one lonesome, tame tiger, that is not to be feared. The buffaloes, the cows and the rees are hornless. It is good to hunt on them while grazing. Of course there is no danger. The only tiger staying there, is an old and toothless one: he is Mpu Raganata. (Slametmuljana, 1976, p. 27)

In spite of being friends with Khubilai as he later claims, Wiraraja did not send his messengers (whether his son or another) to the Mongol capital but to Jayakatwang at Daha (Kediri). Nor did Khubilai respond militarily to Kertanagara's *Pamalayu* anytime soon after 1275, when the kingdom was unguarded and Kertanagara's plans apparently clear. Whether Khubilai was too busy elsewhere, not paying attention, or felt no threat cannot be ascertained. Khubilai was certainly busy on many fronts, establishing his rule over the whole of China after the fall of the Southern Song, campaigns against Burma, Champa, Annam, and Japan, suppressing rebellions in Tibet and Manchuria, and constantly harrassed by Khaidu and Khadan. The mission of Meng Qi may have been a response to the *Pamalayu*: the probable date of his arrival in Java — 1289 — would follow shortly after the consolidation of Singhasari rule over southern Sumatra around 1286. Yet without further evidence, the question cannot be decided. Khubilai's army did not set sail for Java until after the return of Meng Qi, and that incident alone is given in the *Yuan shi*. None of the Javanese writers link Kertanagara's actions and ambitions with the arrival of the Mongols. Instead, for the Javanese writers, it was Wijaya's plight which led to Wiraraja's request for Mongolian intervention in Javanese affairs.

Wijaya fights, finds the elder princess and flees with her to safety (Wijaya makes love, not war)

Jayakatwang received the message and in the *Kidung Harsawijaya* questions Wirondaya about it after he has delivered it. When Wirondaya (or whoever) delivered the message is not stated. If the message came immediately after the army's departure on the *Pamalayu*, Jayakatwang must have waited 17 years to attack. On the other hand, if the message reached him sometime in 1292, then it was Wiraraja who waited 17 years before seeking revenge. The length of time between action and response on either reckoning is so great as to make one wonder if there were not other matters which intervened. The mission of Meng Qi at this point would make matters more comprehensible: Wiraraja, learning of the incident, perhaps suspected or even hoped for a Mongol reprisal. The branding of Meng Qi may even have offended him personally as being unkingly behaviour (the *Banjaran Singhasari* offers this interpretation); though he himself appears continually as a schemer and betrayer, he is also the advocate and ally of Wijaya, the most noble king of them all. However the 17 year interval is understood, and what may have happened during that time, the years did pass and it was only in 1292 that Jayakatwang acted on the hint from Wiraraja and attacked Singasari.

Jayakatwang launched the attack with an army divided into two sections: one a noisy decoy coming from the north and designed to draw out what palace defences there were; the second marching silently along a southern route which would attack the palace after Wijaya had gone with his soldiers to battle the noisy northern army. Kertanagara, who had taken no precautions, still had no idea what was happening. When at last he was warned about the arrival of the northern army, he refused to believe the reports. It was not until the refugees and the wounded began arriving that he allowed Wijaya to go to battle against the noisy invaders. When Wijaya left the city to engage the enemy to the north, the southern army, having waited silently for his departure, entered the palace where they found Kertanagara drinking and making merry in the women's quarters. According to the *Pararaton* it was at that moment that a demoted minister, Mpu Raganata — the "toothless old tiger" — shouted to Kertanagara that "it would be shameful that a king should be killed by his enemies in the women's quarters." Caught with his pants down and his spiritual powers in remission, Kertanagara, along with

Mpu Raganata and those few of his ministers who remained in the palace were all killed there by Jayakatwang's forces.

Kertanagara's death is mentioned in another inscription, the *Candi Singasari* inscription issued by Queen Tribhuwanatungadewi in 1351, a petition made for the building of a shrine in honor of Kertanagara's minister Mpu Raganata. Mpu Raganata's comment to Kertanagara in the women's quarters provides an argument against Berg's theory. For Berg, the sex and drinking were a part of the tantric rituals and spiritual warfare through which Kertanagara hoped to defeat Khubilai. Judging from his remark to the king, Mpu Raganata could not have regarded Kertanagara's actions as "spiritual warfare" but rather as a shameful dereliction of duty. Krom remarks of Kertanagara that he was a "combination of the dilettante-scholar and wanton bon-vivante" like Claudius of Rome (Krom, p. 342). In either case, whether he was praying or playing, his reign had come to an end.

Wijaya had already routed the northern army when a messenger came to tell him that Kertanagara had been killed and the palace taken. When he understood that a second army had arrived behind him, he decided to go back and do battle again. They returned but had to retreat; the great warrior from Daha (Kediri) Kebo-Mundarang pursued Wijaya into a rice field and was standing over him ready to strike him when Wijaya splashed mud in his eyes and escaped. The *Pararaton* describes Kebo-Mundarang's response to Wijaya's mud-slinging:

> When Kebo-Mundarang was about to pierce him [Wijaya] with a lance, suddenly Raden Wijaya threw up the earth and raised such a storm of dust and mud that smeared Kebo-Mundarang from his chest upwards to his face. Kebo-Mundarang recoiled with horror and exclaimed: "Wow! God is really with you, noble man. (Phalgunadi, p. 101)

Kebo-Mundarang fled with his fellow soldiers and Wijaya rewarded his companions for their help, tearing up some of his clothes and distributing the pieces among them. He then consulted them on what to do next. Both of these actions were characteristic of Wijaya and apparently of great significance to all those who would later tell the tale. His companions advised a renewed attack since that would be the least expected action. Their surprise attack was successful; the soldiers from Daha were all celebrating and had taken no precautions. "The army of Daha was scattered and most of the soldiers were hit with the lances of their own companions in the confusion, while fleeing in the darkness." (Phalgunadi, p. 101) Then night fell, and the battle stopped. During the night Wijaya was resting near a fire previously made by the Daha soldiers who had run in confusion after the attack. Wijaya had commanded his men to warm themselves there when he saw by the fire the elder of the two princesses of Tumapel, daughter of Kertanagara and his bride-to-be. She had slipped away when she realized she was going to be taken captive. Wijaya asked his men whether they should try to go inside and look for the younger princess but they advised him to take the elder princess away to safety immediately. The *Pararaton* provides a beautiful narration of this retreat:

> Sora respectfully said: "Do not do so my Lord! Your sister, the elder princess, has been found, but how many of your followers are left now!"
> Raden Wijaya answered: "I do agree with you!"
> Then Sora spoke again: "The right thing to do, my Lord, is that you should retreat. But if you insist on a fierce attack and it turns out to be successful, that is the best thing. You can get your sister the younger princess back. But if it is unsuccesful, it will be like the white-ants flying to the flame."
> Then Raden Wijaya retreated and carried his sister in his arms. Throughout the night they moved forward to go to the north. Later on in the morning, they were chased again by the army of Daha. They met them to the south of Talaga-pager, where some of his followers were kept waiting to fight and stop the army of Daha from chasing them. Gajah-Pagon was stabbed in his thigh. Even then he forced himself to move. (Phalgunadi, p. 103)

Wijaya and the elder princess fled with a few of his followers, each carrying the princess in their arms by turns. While wandering in the forest Wijaya's followers suggested that they leave the forest and seek refuge with Wiraraja in East Madura. They left the jungle and went to Pandakan where the wounded Gajah-Pagon remained in order to heal; Wijaya and the others went on to Datar. According to the *Pararaton* at this time they were no longer being pursued by the Daha soldiers; the Kudadu inscription on the other hand, states that they were still being pursued by Jayakatwang's soldiers. Significantly, in the Kudadu inscription Wijaya tells this portion of his own story briefly without mentioning the princess:

> The next day at dawn he was chased by the enemy. Some of his troops fought, some were killed, some fled to take refuge. He retreated with only a few followers, desperate and defenceless. Following a deliberation with his companions, his proposal to rush to Terung to ask the village chief, Wuru Agraja, who had been appointed by the late King Kertanagara to gather the inhabitants of the villages east and southeast of Terung, was unanimously accepted. In the night he left for Kulawan, for he was afraid that he should be followed by the overwhelming enemy. Nevertheless in Kulawan he met the enemy, whom he succeeded to avoid by running north-wards in the direction of Kambangsri. But there too was the enemy, who immediately chased him. Instantly he ran together with his companions, crossing the large river northwards. Many among his companions were drowned; some captured and some stabbed with pikes. Those who succeeded in reaching the other bank, scattered themselves all over the place. Only twelve companions remained to protect him. At noon he came to Kudadu hungry, tired and sad. (Slametmuljana, 1976, p. 37)

The absence of any mention of the elder princess at this point in the Kudadu inscription is as glaring as the absence of Meng Qi in all the later Javanese works, and unlike the absence of Meng Qi, her absence cannot simply be dismissed as an omission of later poets — this is Wijaya's own story.

Wijaya and his companions were hidden and protected at Kudadu until they left to make their way to the residence of Wiraraja in Madura. The incidents in the town of Kudadu are also described in the *Kidung*

Panji Wijayakrama where the place is called Pandak, and in the *Pararaton*, where the name of Kudadu is given as Datar. The Daha soldiers meanwhile returned to Kediri (Daha) with the youngest princess of Tumapel and gave her to Jayakatwang.

On the way to seek refuge with Wiraraja, they are forced to spend the night in an irrigated rice field. "He spent the night on a narrow edge of a small dike enclosing irrigated rice-fields, which had been just harrowed. There Sora laid himself on the ground facing downwards. Raden Wijaya and the princess sat on his back." (Phalgunadi, p. 105) Episodes such as this have apparently been considered nothing more than later romantic insertions by many historians since they are left out of the histories that have been written. Even Slametmuljana who is more convinced of the value of the *kidungs* than many other writers leaves this lovely incident out of his *Story of Majapahit*. The Kudadu inscription does not mention the incident and is given the highest rating for historical accuracy; in whatever matters the *kidungs* depart from the inscriptions in recounting the events of this trek into exile, they are disregarded. What might we be missing by excluding them from our reflections?

Wijaya in exile founds Majapahit and plans the rescue of Ratna Sutawan (Pusparasmi), the younger princess of Tumapel, now captive in Kediri

The company arrives at Sumenep and stops to rest in a pavillion outside Wiraraja's palace. As Wijaya approaches the audience-hall to meet with Wiraraja, Wiraraja sees him and responds with surprise, returning momentarily back inside his residence. Wijaya has his doubts, but then Wiraraja returns with the queen and his family, each carrying betel leaves which they offered, the queen to the princess and Wiraraja to Wijaya.

Wijaya and Wiraraja discuss Wijaya's hopes and plans. Wiraraja is promised half the kingdom if with his assistance Wijaya achieves his goals, to which Wiraraja replies: "As you wish, my Lord. In any case, you will be the ruler." (Phalgunadi, p. 107) How long Wijaya remained with Wiraraja is not stated in exact terms, but "for a long time." After this period, Wiraraja proposes to Wijaya that he pretend to apologize, go stay in Daha as Jayakatwang's subject for some time, and when he has gotten into his confidence, to ask for the forest of Trik. During his stay, he would actually be spying and establishing connections with those loyal to him. True to character, Wiraraja writes a secret letter to Jayakatwang begging him to accept the apologies and submission of Wijaya. Jayakatwang, ignoring Wiraraja's past treachery, accepts Wijaya and accords him preferential treatment.

In the *Kidung Harsawijaya*, the troops of Singhasari returned from the *Pamalayu* while Wijaya was staying in Daha, bringing with them two princesses of Malayu whom Wijaya would later marry. These additional princesses are also mentioned in the *Desawarnana* and the *Pararaton*, although in the latter, the soldiers return after the departure of the Mongols. The *Pararaton* as well as the *kidungs* contain variations on what happened during Wijaya's stay in Daha. Common to all these accounts is a tournament in which the men of Daha engage in various contests and war games with Wijaya and his men, the latter winning even when Wijaya is removed from the games with the reason that the men of Daha will not fight to win against such true nobility as Wijaya.

The *Panji Wijayakrama* includes another romantic episode, in which Wijaya recognizes the younger princess of Tumapel (Singhasari) — Ratna Sutawan, called Pusparasmi in the *Kidung Harsawijaya* — and her two handmaidens during the tournament. Wijaya, thinking that she has been taken by Jayakatwang as his wife, believes he has lost his beloved forever, then finds out instead that she had refused Jayakatwang's proposals, threatening to kill herself if he touched her. Instead of marrying her, Jayakatwang has adopted her as his daughter. Wijaya paints a picture for her and by means of one of her handmaids they exchange gifts.

The forest of Trik was then given to Wijaya, the Madhurese cleared it, named it Majapahit, and began settling it before Wijaya's arrival. Wijaya then asked Jayakatwang to be allowed to stay awhile in Majapahit, his request was granted, and he left to settle there, leaving Ratna Sutawan (Pusparasmi) and her handmaidens grieving since they had no inkling of his plans. Wijaya had been able to gain the allegiance of the chief men of Daha (as well as the soldiers returning from the *Pamalayu* according to the

Kidung Harsawijaya) and when he arrived in Majapahit he sent a messenger to Wiraraja inviting him to join together and attack Jayakatwang. Wiraraja replied to the messenger with a different plan.

Wiraraja sends for the King of Tatar

> Tell your master that the emperor of Tatar is a friend of mine. I will take the princess. Go back to Majapahit, messenger! After your return I shall send a letter to Tatar by way of the Tatar boat which is here for trade. I have a boat too and I will order it to get prepared to join them on their way to Tatar. I will invite the Tatar Khan to attack Daha. If the king of Daha is defeated, the beautiful princess of Tumapel whose beauty has no equal all over the land of Java will be offered to the Tatar Khan. That will be my trap for the Tatar Khan. Tell this to your master. Then I will join him in attacking Daha. (Phalgunadi p. 111)

(The word "Tatar" in every instance in this paragraph is used in the original Javanese of the *Pararaton*; Phalgunadi translates it the first time as "emperor of Tatar (China)" and thereafter simply as "China". I have edited his translation slightly here and elsewhere.)

Once again, for the third time, Wiraraja councils deception and betrays a friendship. Was Wiraraja a friend of the Mongol Khaan? Berg dismissed the possibility of any historical truth to Wiraraja's plan for, in his words, "Ook het verhaal van Par[araton] 23, ... hetwelk de Mongolen-invasie als een good idee van Wiraraja voorstelt, is uiteraard cum grano salis te genieten" [The narrative in the Pararaton 23... which presents the Mongol invasion as one of Wiraraja's good ideas, must of course be taken with a grain of salt] (Berg, 1953, p. 226). Robson argued that Wiraraja could not have invited the Mongol Khaan on the following grounds:

> What I consider conclusive proof that Wiraraja did not invite the king of Tatar is supplied, if my deductions are correct, by the fact that the Emperor ordered the governor of Fukien to collect troops

> for the expedition in the second month of 1292, while Tumapel fell to
> Jayakatwang only in April–May, 1292. In view of this Wijaya could
> not have moved to Majapahit before the end of the year, by which
> time the expedition had already sailed. (Robson, 1962, p. 23)

I know of no Chinese or Mongolian records in which such a person can be identified. It is possible that Wiraraja as an important official under Kertanagara had had dealings with Yuan officials at an earlier time, perhaps even an encounter with Meng Qi. In his message he also mentions the Tatar ship trading in his ports even as he makes his plans. While it is hardly likely that he would have actually met Khubilai unless he had been part of one of the earlier tribute missions, it is entirely plausible that he was acquainted with Yuan officials or merchants from China, perhaps a large number of them if he had been involved in trade and tribute negotiations for very long under Kertanagara.

Regarding Wiraraja, there are three alternatives: 1) the whole episode is a romantic fiction, Wiraraja neither knowing the Tatar Khan nor inviting him to make war on Jayakatwang; 2) Wiraraja knew someone from somewhere and asked him or them to take an invitation to the Khaan; 3) the messenger who carried Wijaya's offer of submission, a map of the kingdom and request for assistance as stated in the *Yuan shi* may have been none other than Wiraraja, suggesting that the *Yuan shi* and Javanese accounts, different as they are, actually refer to the same request. The choice of one over the other of these possiblities cannot be made on the basis of currently available evidence but only on the basis of a judgement concerning the historical reliability of the Javanese accounts and the manner of interpreting them. The *Yuan shi* cannot settle the issue because the reason given there for the Mongol expedition is not incompatible with additional reasons, including a letter from Wiraraja. The third alternative mentioned here will be discussed in more detail later.

The *Kidung Harsawijaya* contains an interesting variation on the offer of a princess to the King of Tatar: the princess offered is neither of the princesses of Tumapel, but Ratna Kesari, the daughter of Jayakatwang. The reason for this variation is not hard to imagine: by offering the enemy king's daughter with neither his nor her knowledge, Wiraraja is acting in character and being deceitful; Wijaya is not offering his own wives in exchange for military assistance thereby appearing more honourable; and the later Tatar request for Wijaya's wives after the suicide of Ratna Kesari justifies not only the Tatar demands but also Wijaya's refusal: he had promised a princess, but not his own wives.

In the *Panji Wijayakrama* Wiraraja meets with Wijaya and tells him about Khubilai's response to his request for military assistance in exchange for the princesses. The two princesses from Tumapel were so renowned for their beauty that the Khaan immediately accepted the offer and promised to come at exactly the time which would fit Wijaya's plans. Wijaya then put Wiraraja in command of a northern army and delegated to him responsibility for sending messages and current information to the Mongols upon their arrival. (Another point in the Javanese texts which suggests that Wiraraja was indeed the messenger sent by Wijaya as mentioned in the *Yuan shi*.)

Khubilai orders a punitive expedition

We have now arrived at the point at which we began: "In the second month of the year 1292 the emperor issued an order…"

Since the Javanese sources say nothing of the preparations for war nor the journey to Java, the *Yuan shi* provides the principal narrative for learning of these matters. Yet penury is not our problem, for immediately the *Yuan shi* tells us the purpose of the expedition is to subdue Java, that the soldiers will be collected — 20,000 of them, 30,000 according to the *Yu pi xu zi zhi tong jian gang mu* — from Fujian, Jiangxi and Huguang in southern China, that there will be 1000 ships, provisions for a year and 40,000 bars of silver. It is enough to make one think of a trading expedition, albeit one carried out by soldiers rather than merchants.

The soldiers were collected in the south, and if the Mongols followed the same practices here as elsewhere, it is likely that a good number of subjugated peoples, i.e. Chinese, perhaps former soldiers of the Southern Song, were conscripted into the army for the campaign (see Tan (2009) for a more detailed discussion of this point). The officers themselves were not all Mongols: Shi-bi was a Mongol, but Ike Mese was Uighur and Gao Xing Chinese.

What kind of ships they used for the expedition is not noted in the *Yuan shi*, but they were apparently large since smaller boats had to be constructed for entering the rivers of Java. The *Yuan shi* does note when they stopped at Ko-lan (Billiton).

> Ike Mese and one of his subordinate commanders, taking with them their secretaries and accompanied by three officers of the Office of Pacification, who were charged to treat with Java and the other countries, and by a Commander of Ten Thousand, who led 500 men and 10 ships, went first… (Groeneveldt, 1880, p. 22)

That suggests fifty soldiers per ship, plus officers and others. Lo's essay on the Yuan navy gives some details on naval architecture at the time, but makes no mention of this particular expedition. For trading ships, Odoric, Ibn Batutta and other observers noted between "500 souls" on board to 1000 crew members, and that they were armed against pirates with naptha shooters. If there were 1000 large ships and only 20,000 soldiers, that makes for 20 soldiers per ship. Perhaps the number of soldiers given in the *Yuan shi* is too low — they fought against and defeated 100,000 soldiers in the battle at Daha according to the *Yuan shi* itself — or the number of ships too high. Perhaps the soldiers were fifty each on 400–500 ships with their supplies, and the remainder of the ships held merchants, diplomats, weapons and more supplies? (For more detailed discussions of the ships used in the Javanese expedition, see Niwa (1953, 1954); for the Yuan navy and ships in general, see Lo (1955))

However many the soldiers and ships, the trip to Java was somewhat circuitous and involved diplomatic activity in lands other than Java. The account of Ike Mese in Book 131 of the *Yuan shi* describes the journey prior to landing in Java:

> When the army arrived at Champa, they first sent envoys to call into submission Lambri, Sumatra, Pu-lu-pu-tu, Pa-la-la and other smaller countries. … Another envoy was sent to the different Malay states, who all sent their sons or younger brothers as a token of their allegiance. (Groeneveldt, 1880, p. 30)

The main account in Book 210 notes only that "In the first month of the year 1293 they arrived at the island Ko-lan (Billiton) and there deliberated on their plan of campaign." Another source of information for the journey — Ma Huan's treatise of 1433 — records an incident not found in either the *Yuan shi* or in any of the Javanese sources. Mills translates the passage from the *Ying-yai sheng lan* ("The overall survey of the ocean's shores") as follows:

> On a sandbank in the sea there is a small pool of water which is fresh and potable; it is called 'the Holy Water'. Tradition has it that in the time of the great Yüan dynasty the Emperor ordered the generals Shih Pi and Kao Hsing to attack She-p'o; a moon passed and still they could not land on the shore; the water in the ships was already exhausted; the soldiers of the army were at their wits' end; the two generals worshipped Heaven and prayed, saying 'We received the imperial order to attack the barbarians; if Heaven is with us, let a spring of water rise up; if Heaven is not with us, then let there be no spring'; the prayer ended, they thrust their spears with great force into the sandbank in the sea, and at once a spring of water bubbled up in the place where the spears were thrust; the water was fresh to taste; all drank and were able to save their lives. Such was the help which Heaven granted. This spring has existed right down to the present day. (Ma Huan in Mills' translation, p. 89)

Whether this narrative records a historical incident or only folklore, it was written 140 years after the events mentioned and records an incident repeated in other sources based on Ma Huan's account (e.g. Fei Xin's *Xingcha shenglan*) but not found elsewhere. Whether or not the situation and incidents happened as depicted here, it touches upon matters of interest. The sea mentioned is the Java Sea to the north of Tuban which was the principal port for Majapahit. The difficulty of finding a place to land on shore is consistent with the *Yuan shi* biography of Shi-bi in which it is noted that "the wind was strong and the sea very rough, so that the ships rolled heavily and the soldiers could not eat for many days" (Groeneveldt, 1880, p. 25. For further discussion of Ma Huan's brief note, see Part II.)

Wang Dayuan mentions another incident related to this storm that Ma Huan did not mention, nor is it recorded in either the *Yuan shi* or the *Yu pi xu zi zhi tong jian gang mu*:

> When the dynasty (of the Yuan) was first founded, the forces to attack She-p'o (Java) were driven by the wind to this island and the junks wrecked. One junk fortunately escaped with stores of nails and mortar. Seeing that there was a great deal of timber on this island, they built some tens of junks here, everything from ribs to sails and bamboo poles were supplied (from the island). Over an hundred men who were ill from the long beating about in the storm and were unable to leave (with the rest of the expedition) were left on the island, and today the Chinese live mixed up with the native families. (translation by Rockhill, 1915, p. 261)

Arriving in Java, they split the forces up into one group sent ashore and a second which proceeded by boat, after the officers of the Office of Pacification "who were charged to treat with Java and the other countries" had gone ahead first "to bring the commands of the Emperor to this country." (Groeneveldt, 1880 p. 22) That the officers of the Office of Pacification were charged to deal with not just Java but "the other countries" raises more questions than can be answered. Does "the other countries" refer to the many places where they stopped along the way to Java, asked for submission and took family members? This does seem to have been as much a part of the plan as its terminus in Java. Or were the various kings in Java — Kertanagara, Jayakatwang, Wiraraja (?) — thought to represent different countries? Wijaya did give the Mongols a map of the country of Kalang, Jayakatwang's territory, and this country was apparently considered separate from Java, for the biography of Shi-bi states that "Java carried on an old feud with the neighbouring country Kalang" and Gao Xing is recorded in the same biography as having said that "Though Java has submitted, still if it repents its decision and united with Kalang..." (Groeneveldt, 1880, p. 26) Either way, it seems that the officers mentioned were there with orders to deal with more countries than Java, and that relations with these other countries had been among the reasons and goals of the expedition which were not mentioned along with the mistreatment of Meng Qi.

From this point on, the Chinese and Javanese accounts tell the same story, although they are not always paying attention to the same thing and are writing from different pasts: the *Yuan shi* follows from the command of Khubilai to subdue Java, whereas the Javanese texts follow from Wijaya's desire and Wiraraja's deception. Khubilai's desire to subdue Java is present in the Javanese texts also, but only metaphorically: Khubilai desires the beautiful princesses of Java and is drawn to Java by the promise of receiving them as a reward. The two traditions, born in different pasts and raised apart, did not meet in a common narrative prior to the intervention of foreign students in the 19th century.

In Book 210 of the *Yuan shi* the Office of Pacification reports that Wijaya offered his submission but could not leave his army; the account of Shi-bi in Book 162 states that "when he heard that Shih-pi with his army had arrived, he sent envoys with an account of his rivers and seaports and a map of the country Kalang, offering his submission and asking for assistance." (Groeneveldt, 1880, p. 26) The *Pararaton* makes no mention of submission at this early date; rather Wijaya waits until the arrival of the Mongol messengers before attacking Daha in a three-pronged attack by his own army together with Wiraraja's men from Madura in the east and the Mongol army in the north. The *Panji Wijayakrama* offers a slightly different account in which Wiraraja's army attacks from the north and Wijaya's army from the south.

The Mongols and justice in Java

On the 1st day of the 3rd month, the troops were assembled at the small river Pa-tsieh. (Groeneveldt, 1880, p. 23)

The first engagement of the Mongols against Javanese troops is amusing but no indication of what is to come. The *Yuan shi* records it thus:

[T]he first minister of the Javanese, Hi-ning-kuan, remained in a boat to see how the chances of the fight went; he was summoned repeatedly, but would not surrender.
The commanders of the imperial army made a camp in the form of a crescent on the bank of the river and left the ferry in charge of a Commander of Ten Thousand; the fleet in the river and the

cavalry and infantry on shore then advanced together and Hi-ning-kuan, seeing this, left his boat and fled overnight, whereupon more than a hundred large ships, with devil-heads on the stem, were captured. (ibid.)

The *Pararaton* gives a very brief account of the following war against Jayakatwang:

> Only after the arrival of the emissary from Tatar did he [Wijaya] attack Daha. The army from Tatar came from the north and the Madhuranese and the Majapahit army attacked from the east. King Katon was bewildered. He did not know which one should be faced. Then the Tatar army marched to attack him from the north. Kebo-mundaran, Panlet and Mahisa-rubuh faced the army which came from the east. Panlet was killed by Sora, and Kebo-rubuh by Nambi, while Kebo-mundaran had to run away. He was chased and finally killed by Rangga Lawe at the Trinipanti valley after telling Rangga Lawe "Ki Rangga Lawe, I have a daughter. Please give her to Sora as a reward for his bravery."

> King Jaya-katon took his Dadap shield and went to the north. The Tatar army attacked him furiously. Consequently he was caught and imprisoned by the Tatar army. Raden Vijaya quickly entered the inner part of the Daha royal palace and took away the younger princess to Majapahit. (Phalgunadi, pp. 111–13)

The *Kidung Panji-Wijayakrama* gives more details, but not the same as the *Yuan shi*. Jayakatwang is meeting with his officers quarreling over who is responsible for permitting Wijaya to gather an army and attack, when suddenly he receives a visitor from Tuban who informs him of the presence of the Mongol army:

> The king of Tatar — Tarulaksana — had arrived with a powerful army whereof one part had already landed at Dataran and that the rumour was that he had come at the request of Wijaya and Wiraraja.

> The troops had landed and set up along the coast and had destroyed
> Tuban, whereupon the inhabitants had fled in terror. (*Rangga Lawe*,
> from Berg's summary, p. 21)

This is the only reference in the older Javanese texts in which the Mongols destroy towns and send people fleeing in terror. The above narrative continues with a description of a pitch battle in which both the Tatar and Javanese soldiers are killed, leaving the Tatar king Tarulaksana and Jayakatwang facing each other. In the manuscript published by Raffles, Laksemana (Khubilai) kills Jayakatwang in this combat. In the manuscript edited by Berg, Jayakatwang is captured by Tarulaksana (Khubilai) and turned over to the soldiers of Majapahit. The version which appears in the *Kidung Harsawijaya* is fantastic: the Daha soldiers are defeated all round and Jayakatwang appears on his elephant, prepared to die, an event he had seen coming and refused to prevent because he knew that Wijaya was the great king who was destined to rule the kingdom. The soldiers of Majapahit hesitate to kill royalty and Wijaya also hesitates to kill the king who has become his friend and given him so much. Jayakatwang begins to meditate and suddenly vanishes into the heavens. Everyone is in awe at such greatness and his soldiers then fight for his immaterial majesty till their deaths.

The accounts of the war which appear in Books 210 and 162 of the *Yuan shi* are similar to the Javanese versions but lack any reference to the princesses and the miraculous dissappearing act of Jayakatwang. The main account in Book 210 is brief: messengers arrived from Wijaya explaining that the king of Kalang had forced him all the way back to Majapahit and he requested troops to aid and protect him. The soldiers from Daha came to attack Wijaya on the 7th day of the month, Ike Mese and Gao Xing came on the 8th; some Dahanese were defeated, others ran into the mountains. On the 19th the Mongols and their allies arrived in Daha, fought more than 100,000 soldiers, attacking three times, killing 5000 outright while forcing many thousands into the river where they drowned. Jayakatwang retreated into his palace from whence he was summoned to surrender. After coming out and offering his submission, Khubilai's orders were given to him and he was sent back home alive.

Further details are provided in the biographies of Shi-bi and Gao Xing in Book 162. From the account of Shi-bi:

> Tuhan Pidjaya [Wijaya] had attacked Hadji Katang [Jayakatwang], but could not overcome him; he had therefore retired to Modjopait [Majapahit] and when he heard that Shih-pi with his army had arrived, he sent envoys with an account of his rivers and seaports and a map of the country Kalang, offering his submission and asking for assistance.

> Shih-pi then advanced with all his forces, attacked the army of Kalang and routed it completely, on which Hadji Katang fled back to his dominions.

> Kau Hsing now said: 'Though Java has submitted, still if it repents its decision and unites with Kalang, our army might be in a very difficult position and we do not know what might happen.' Shih-pi therefore divided his army into three parts, himself, Kau Hsing and Ike Mese each leading a division, and marched to Kalang. When they arrived at the fortified town Daha, more than a hundred thousand soldiers of Kalang came forward to withstand them. They fought from morning till noon, when the army of Kalang was routed and retired into the town to save itself. The Chinese army surrounded the town and soon Jayakatwang came forward to offer his submission; his wife, his children and officers were taken by the victors, who then went back. (Groeneveldt, 1880 p. 26)

The account of Gao Xing adds the following note:

> They also awed into submission different smaller states and as Hadji Katang's son Sih-lah-pat-ti Sih-lah-tan-puh-hah had fled to the mountains, Kau Hsing went into the interior with a thousand men and brought him back a prisoner. (Groeneveldt, 1880 p. 28)

Wijaya's request for assistance and offer of submission noted in the account of Shi-bi may refer to the same event which the Javanese sources describe as Wiraraja's request. Identifying Wijaya's request in the *Yuan shi* with Wiraraja's request in the Javanese sources brings the two traditions much closer; the true identity of the one who actually requested Mongol military assistance remains a question, but such an interpretive move is very attractive. According to the *Yuan shi*, Wijaya had already attacked Jayakatwang without success when he heard of the arrival of the Mongols and requested their aid. This version of events could easily be reconciled with the Javanese accounts if the Chinese account was referring to the same battles against Jayakatwang's army described in the Kudadu inscription and the *kidungs*. It may even be that Wiraraja had already submitted to the Mongols, perhaps as one of the smaller states mentioned in the *Yuan shi*, and that is why he claimed that he was the friend of the King of Tatar and could bring him to Wijaya's aid: the Tatar ships are in the harbor when he reveals his plan for Tatar assistance. The Mongols were already there in all accounts: for business according to the *Pararaton*, for war according to the *Yuan shi* (and with the help of Heaven according to Ma Huan).

Wijaya fights, finds the younger princess and flees with her to safety (Again Wijaya makes love, not war)

At this point the chief difference between the *Yuan shi* narratives and the Javanese accounts is that the former nowhere mentions Wijaya's leaving with the younger princess, only that he returns to Majapahit, while in all the Javanese versions he returns to Majapahit only after having sought, found and left the battle together with her. Another difference is the fate of Jayakatwang. The *Yuan shi* gives slightly differing accounts in its various sections: he is captured and released in Book 210 and in the account of Shi-bi in book 162; subdued (and then later killed) in the account of Gao Xing in Book 162; and simply subdued in the account of Ike Mese in Book 131. The *Yu pi xu zi zhi tong jian gang mu* states that "Bi and the others thereupon combined to capture the king of Ge-lang to take back" (Wade's translation; Mailla (v. 9, p. 453) has "The soldiers of Kolang, defeated, sought refuge in the town where they were surrounded by the Chinese and the Javanese together. Jayakatwang asked to surrender and submitted.")

In the *Pararaton* he is captured, released and after his release writes a poem, the *Wukirpolaman*; in Berg's version of the *Kidung Panji Wijayakrama* he is captured and while in prison writes the *Wukirpolaman*; in the *Kidung Harsawijaya* he ascends into heaven; and in Raffles' text he is killed by the King of Tatar. The latter text further departs from the others in stating that Mundarang and the whole army of Kediri surrender with the death of Jayakatwang, whereas in the other accounts more battles and deaths follow.

Wijaya's reunion with the younger princess in the Javanese narratives varies only in its more or less romantic language, and on the issue of whether Wijaya personally or his companions whisk the princess back to Majapahit. In Raffles' text we read "Browijaya [Wijaya] then eagerly went into the kadaton [palace] and was received by his faithful wife. They embraced with tears of joy; and Browijaya was so enraptured at recovering her, that without taking further notice of the kadaton, he returned with his wife to Majapahit." (Raffles, 1830, v. 2, p. 116) The *Pararaton*, briefly and matter-of-factly states "Raden Vijaya quickly entered the inner part of the Daha royal palace and took away the younger princess to Majapahit." (Phalgunadi, p. 113) In the *Kidung Harsawijaya*, all the royal ladies have killed themselves after hearing the news of Jayakatwong's death/ascension except his daughter Pusparasmi (the younger princess of Tumapel and Wijaya's betrothed, called Ratna Sutawan in the *Kidung Panji Wijayakrama*), who is prevented from committing suicide by Jayakatwang's daughter Ratna Kesari and by his widowed queen who had adopted her to keep the king from trying to marry her. In this story, instead of slipping away with her to Majapahit, Wijaya orders his companions to accompany her back to Majapahit, while he himself goes to Bobot Sari. In the *Kidung Panji Wijayakrama*, immediately after the Tatar soldiers had captured Jayakatwang, Wijaya went into the palace, freed the younger princess and himself brought her and her two handmaidens Sodrakara and Madraka to Majapahit.

Although there is no mention of a princess, the *Yuan shi* does note the taking captive of the family members of Jayakatwang, including his children, and even their being taken back to the Mongol court. Thus in Book 210 "On the 24th the army went back, taking with it the children and officers of Hadji Katang, altogether more than a hundred persons" and in the account of Shi-bi in Book 162 "Hadji Katang came forward to offer his submission; his wife, his children and officers were taken by the victors who then went back." and finally in the account of Ike Mese in Book 131 "and they returned with their prisoners and with the envoys of the different smaller states which had submitted." (Groeneveldt, 1880, pp. 25, 26, 30) Although Jayakatwang's children were taken back to the Yuan court, his adopted daughter, the younger princess of Tumapel, was apparently not among those captured. There is also no mention of a mass suicide of the palace ladies in the *Yuan shi, Yu pi xu zi zhi tong jian gang mu* or any Javanese texts other than the *Kidung Harsawijaya*.

The *Yuan shi* offers slightly varying but not incompatible accounts of the return of Wijaya to Majapahit. In Book 210, Wijaya does not go back to Majapahit of his own volition but "On the 2nd day of the 4th month Tuhan Pidjaya was sent back to his dominions in order to make preparations for sending tribute, two officers and 200 soldiers went with him as an escort." In the account of Shi-bi in Book 162 "Tuhan Pidjaya asked permission to return to his country, in order to prepare a new letter of submission to the Emperor and to take the precious articles in his possession for sending them to court; Shih-pi and Ike Mese consented to this and sent two officers with 200 men to go with him." The account of Gao Xing, also in Book 162 states that "Shih-pi and Ike Mese had already allowed Tuhan Pidjaya to go back to his country, with an escort from the imperial army, in order to make preparations for sending tribute." (Groeneveldt, 1880, pp. 26, 28) The difference between Wijaya being sent back, his asking permission to be sent back, and his having already been allowed to go back is perhaps little more than stylistic; the issue of his freedom to go versus being compelled to go on the one hand, or his slipping away versus being allowed to return are not decidable on the basis of the Chinese texts.

Whereas the Chinese texts all present a situation in which Wijaya in submission is sent or permitted to return to Majapahit, the Javanese texts present the return to Majapahit as being due to the initiative, will and intelligence of Wijaya alone, or at the instigation of Wiraraja. There is more divergence among the various Javanese accounts than there is in the Chinese statements noted above. In the *Kidung Harsawijaya*, Wiraraja advises Wijaya to ask the Tatars to go back to their camp while he cremates the heroic Majapahit soldiers. Then he goes to Daha to take care of the royal ladies, but they have all committed suicide except Pusparasmi, the younger princess of Tumapel. He sends Pusparasmi back to Majapahit with some of his men and goes to Bobot Sari. The *Kidung Panji Wijayakrama, Pararaton* and Raffles' version as quoted above note only that Wijaya runs to the palace to free the younger princess and leaves with her, not mentioning Chinese/Mongol knowledge, participation or permission to do so.

Two beautiful princesses for the King of Tatar

After the defeat of Jayakatwang and the return of Wijaya to Majapahit, the Chinese and Javanese accounts — except for the manuscript described by Raffles — are again in close agreement on the military matters, but not on matters of the heart: the Chinese accounts as always lack any reference to princesses. In the Javanese accounts, the king of Tatar comes looking for the princesses, expecting the fulfillment of the promises made to him before he embarked on the campaign. The *Pararaton, Kidung Harsawijaya* and *Kidung Panji Wijayakrama* provide slight variations on the initial confrontation over the fulfillment of Wiraraja's promise of two princesses for the king of Tatar:

> The Tatar army came to Majapahit and demanded the princesses as promised by Wiraraja, who had said that the two princesses would be given to them after the fall of Daha. This issue bewildered all the ministers. Sora said: 'Well I will fiercely attack the Tatar army if they come here!' (Phalgunadi, p. 113)

The *Kidung Harsawijaya* recounts the story of how Wijaya was embarrassed when accused by the khaan's envoy of having taken the princess promised to the King of Tatar, but Wiraraja intervenes, claiming that not only Ratna Kesari, princess of Daha, daughter of Jayakatwang, but *all* the palace women had killed themselves (another deception by Wiraraja). Upon being informed of this explanation the King of Tatar at first believes it and is disappointed that all his efforts have come to nothing, but after being informed by his spies that Wijaya had with him in Majapahit not only the princesses of Tumapel but also the two princesses from Malayu, he became angry and ordered the army to march against Majapahit.

The *Kidung Panji Wijayakrama* version appears in two variants, that published by Berg and the shorter version found in Raffles:

> At Majapahit, Wijaya's attitude towards the Tatars regarding the taking of the princesses is apologetic. Soon the Tatars sent envoys to the Javanese to remind them of their promise: two officers, Sundarsana the son of Janapati, and Suryanasa, the son of Taru-Janaka, accompanied by 200 men. (Berg, summary of *Kidung Panji Wijayakrama*, p. 23)

> He [Browijaya] invited the King of Tatar to visit him. On his arrival Browijaya received him with every attention, and made him a present of a beautiful virgin. (Raffles, 1830, v. 2, p. 116)

Wine, women and war (Two — or four? — beautiful princesses for Wijaya)

The events which follow are related very briefly in the *Yuan shi* and *Yu pi xu zi zhi tong jian gang mu*. Some of the Javanese accounts agree with the *Yuan shi* on the military escort, an ambush, and the victory of the Majapahit warriors, but the deception appears in only two accounts. The *Pararaton* and *Kidung Panji Wijayakrama* recount a plan and a deception which leaves the escort isolated, defenceless and vulnerable; the *Kidung Harsawijaya* jumps directly into a pitched battle; and Raffles' text describes several royal parties, two very happy kings, and life happy ever after. It should also be noted that the Chinese accounts and the *Kidung Panji Wijayakrama* agree exactly on the numbers involved on the Mongol side — two officers and 200 men came — but the Chinese accounts record that this small force was sent for the purpose of affirming Wijaya's submission to Mongol rule and stipulating the conditions of vassalage. The Javanese accounts offer a different explanation of the Tatar march to Majapahit: according to our present day prejudices we may interpret them as telling of a king in a quest for the beautiful princess whose beauty was known to the whole world; the politically motivated union of two royal houses in which the men decided but the women decided otherwise; a metaphor in which the princesses

symbolize Java, which Khubilai wishes to rule and their marriage would
be Java's submission to China; or, if we wish to describe it in the least
favorable manner, a simple tale of women as the spoils of war. However
we choose to characterize the Javanese versions, we should keep in mind
that the thirteenth century Javanese experience — male and female — was
undoubtedly very different from ours in the twenty-first century, and not
necessarily portrayed accurately in these later romances. By refusing to
limit ourselves to any one of the many possible interpretations, we allow
the greatest opening for the Others — the men and women of medieval
Java — to speak to us here and now.

One Chinese version appears in the *Yuan shi*'s principal narrative with
additional material found in the biographies of the commanders of the
campaign. Groeneveldt gives his translation of the account in Book 210 :
"On the 19th Tuhan Pidjaya secretly left our soldiers and attacked them,
by which the whole party came to grief" (Groeneveldt, 1880, p. 25).
Groeneveldt's translation has recently been criticized by Tan Ta Sen who
provides the following translation of the same passage:

> On the 19th day, Raden Vijaya rebelled and escaped. The guard
> refused to fight (Liu-jun-ju-zhan). The two officers, Niezhibuding,
> Ganzhoubuhua and a Chinese secretary Fengxiang were killed. On
> the 24th day, the troops left for home..." (Tan, 2009, p. 186)

In Tan's translation the phrase "The guard refused to fight" leaves us with
a description in conflict with the accounts found in Shi-bi's biography in
Book 162 as well as the account in the *Yu pi xu zi zhi tong jian gang mu* and
all of the Javanese accounts. (Tan, whose discussion will be examined in
more detail in the next section, does not mention the account found in the
Yu pi xu zi zhi tong jian gang mu nor any of the Javanese accounts.)

The account of Shi-bi in Book 162 adds to this that after Wijaya left for
Majapahit with the two officers and two hundred soldiers, he

> killed the two officers on the way and revolted again, after which
> he availed himself of the circumstance that the army was returning,

to attack it from both sides. Shih-pi was behind and was cut off from the rest of the army, he was obliged to fight his way for 300 *li* before he arrived at the ships. (Groeneveldt, 1880, pp. 26–27)

In this account as in the *Yu pi xu zi zhi tong jian gang mu* it is noted that more than three thousand soldiers died during the entire expedition. The account of Gao Xing offers a more positive evaluation — Gao Xing was the one officer who objected to letting Wijaya return to Majapahit. According to his biography

Tuhan Pidjaya killed the men sent with him and revolted again; he collected a large quantity of soldiers to attack the imperial army, but Kau Hsing and the others fought bravely with him and threw him back. After this they killed Hadji Katang and his son and returned to China. (Groeneveldt, 1880, p. 28)

The *Yu pi xu zi zhi tong jian gang mu* as Wade translates it gives this version:

Then Tu-han Bi-she-ye again rebelled and Bi and the others engaged in fierce battle in order to defeat him and take him back. The dead numbered over 3,000 men and the officials estimated that the captured goods and valuables were valued at 500,000 [liang of silver]

Mailla offered the following version which clearly is not that of the *Yu pi xu zi zhi tong jian gang mu* but he does not identify any other source:

Wijaya, who then ruled the kingdom of Java, drew up an letter of submission for the emperor which he gave to Shi-bi as well as the royal seal. He behaved toward the Chinese generals with whom he had come to Kolang as though he were a vassal of China, and, not doubting his good faith, on his return to his capital he was escorted by only 200 men. But when they had come within the territory of

Java, he attacked these 200 men, killing many, and readied himself for repulsing the Chinese should they come to attack him.

The Chinese, indignant at his treason, retraced their steps in order to make him pay, but they fell into an ambush and were beaten. Shi-bi, in charge of the rear, was harassed during his retreat for 300 *li*, all the way to the sea where they boarded their ships and sailed back to China. (Mailla, v. 9, p. 453)

The accounts in the Javanese texts are much longer than the Chinese accounts, and narrate much more than just the battle. As noted above, two of the accounts relate a deception which plays the King of Tatar's desire for the princesses against the news of the suicides of the royal family in Daha. The deception narrated in the *Pararaton* was planned by Wiraraja. He told the Tatar army which came to take the princesses:

Hey all of you in the Tatar army! Do not be in a hurry. The princesses are in a state of shock because they have undergone some shattering experiences at the time when Tumapel was defeated and particularly while Daha was being destroyed. They will really be frightened if they see all your pointed weapons. Tomorrow I will hand them over to you. They will be put in a box decorated with clothes. They will be brought and escorted to your boat. The reason to put them in the box is that they do not like to see the sharpness of the weapons. Moreover, whosoever from the Tatar army comes to take the princesses should be clean and have a comely bearing and he should not have too many companions. The princesses have clearly stated that if they see any weapon, they will jump into the sea as they reach the boat. So, all the risks which you have taken in battle will go in vain if the princesses jump into the sea. Will it not be all futile then? (Phalgunadi, p. 113)

The Tatar soldiers believed him and returned the next day, most of them without weapons. Once inside the palace grounds, the Majapahit guards closed and locked the gates. Sora attacked those inside, while Rangga

Lawe attacked those outside, chasing the defenceless soldiers all the way to their camp at Changu harbour. The *Pararaton* also includes the interesting statement that the two princesses of Tumapel "were involved in deceiving the Tatar troops" (Phalgunadi, p. 115. There is a novel or a film just waiting to be made on this theme!)

In the *Kidung Panji Wijayakrama*, the same deception is advanced, but through the words of Sora. The King of Tatar orders a return to Tatar-land to make wedding gifts for the princesses and sends a procession to Majapahit to receive his new brides. The unarmed members of the wedding procession are brought inside the audience hall and entertained, while the palace women are taken further inside by Wiraraja. Sora and Lawe stay with the Tatar soldiers who eat and drink and then lay about resting, until the two Majapahit warriors attack, killing many and taking captive the rest. Afterwards, the Tatar ships, booty and many other soldiers are taken captive.

In the *Kidung Harsawijaya*, while the Tatar army marches toward Majapahit, the wives of Wijaya are preparing for his marriage to Pusparasmi, the latter still unhappy about the deaths of her friends and family in Daha. After her marriage to Wijaya, the Tatar army arrives to take her away by force and Wijaya, frightened of the Tatar forces, asks her if she wouldn't rather be the wife of the King of Tatar. She declines, and Wijaya decides he will fight to the death for her. A battle follows, the Tatars are defeated and the King of Tatar himself killed in the fighting, dying "according to the dharma in the shadow of a white lotus." (Berg, 1931, p. 22)

Aftermath

> The king receives the sacral name of Krtarajasa... and under Krtarajasa's wise reign the empire prospers and the other islands (*nusantara*) — Bali, Tatar, Tumasik... — recognize him as their suzerain. (Zoetmulder, p. 415)

In the *Kidung Harsawijaya* the outcome is that the "island" of Tatar becomes a vassal of Majapahit, the empire prospers and everyone lives happily ever after. In the account found in Raffles' *History of Java*, the King of Tatar returns to his country with a beautiful virgin after being grandly entertained by Wijaya and everyone lives happily ever. In the *Panji Wijayakrama*, the Majapahit winners get rid of all their enemies and capture prisoners and booty. In the *Pararaton*, the long-absent soldiers on Kertanagara's *Pamalayu* expedition return a few days after the defeat of the Mongols. They are accompanied by two princesses from Malayu who become queens for Wijaya. In the *Desawarnana*, the whole world is made right and peace reigns because of the victory of the Majapahit and Tatar soldiers over the usurper Jayakatwang.

The fate of the surviving Mongol soldiers in all the texts besides the *Desawarnana* and the Raffles manuscript is that they were either killed or captured. The *Kidung Harsawijaya* states that most of the soldiers were killed, and in Robson's description of the text "those left beg for their lives and submit. The people of Majapahit rejoice and compete in taking prisoners" (see Robson's essay in this volume). The *Pararaton* states that "In the end they were all killed." In the *Kidung Panji Wijayakrama* the King of Tatar ordered a return to Tatar-land to prepare wedding gifts and then Sora and Lawe attacked "killing many and taking the rest captive. Likewise the Tatar ships which lay on the beach with all they contained were captured … and a great number of prisoners were brought to Majapahit, where all were distributed among the captains." (Berg, summary of *Rangga Lawe*). If this latter account is true, the 3000 soldiers which the *Yuan shi* states were lost during the campaign were not all deaths, and perhaps there are still babies born in Java with the "Mongolian spot" on their backsides.

The outcome as noted in the Chinese texts views matters from the other side. The *Yu pi xu zi zhi tong jian gang mu* gives the following account:

> However, as so many had died and they had failed to punish Tu-han Bi-she-ye-s crimes, the Emperor ordererd that one-third of the family assets of Shi-bi and Yi-hei-mi-shi be confiscated. Only [Gao] Xing was exempted as he had not been involved. (Wade translation)

Mailla elaborated as follows:

> He [Shi-bi] arrived in Quan-zhou after a journey of 68 days and lost during this expedition more than 3000 of the best soldiers. He had gotten much booty in gold and precious stones which were

estimated at more than 500,000 taels of silver. Upon his arrival at the court he turned over all these riches to be given to the emperor, but the prince would not pardon him for having returned without fulfilling his orders and for allowing Wijaya to escape. He was condemned to receive 70 lashes and all of his possessions were confiscated. (Mailla, v. 9, pp. 453–54)

Gaubil's sources provided him with the following account, stressing that the officers were "good officers" and that in the eyes of the Chinese government elite, the campaign had even been a success:

During that expedition he lost 3000 men, and took much booty in gold and precious stones. The Emperor punished him and confiscated two thirds of his property for not having carried out his orders and having let *Touhanpitouye* escape; the same punishment was meted out to *Yehemiche*. Yet eventually they were pardoned, being good Officers, and the Mandarins had succeeded in doing what they had most wanted, that being to have shown the King of *Kouaoua* and the others that despite the distance they were powerful enough and determined enough to avenge any affronts that might be made to the Chinese.

The main account in Book 210 of the *Yuan shi* says nothing other than listing a few items brought back to the court. The account of Shi-bi in Book 162 gives his fate:

On account of his having lost so many men, the Emperor ordered Shih-pi to receive seventeen lashes and confiscated a third of his property. In the year 1295 he was raised again to office and a memorial was presented to the Emperor, pointing out that Shih-pi and his associates had gone over the sea to a distance of 25.000 li, had led the army to countries which had never been reached in the last reigns, had captivated a king and awed into submission the neighbouring smaller countries, and that, for these reasons, mercy should be shown to him. (Groeneveldt, 1880, p. 27)

(Somewhere in the writing, publishing or translating of these two histories, 10+7 or 10×7 was reversed or misunderstood.)

Tan (2009) criticized the account in the biography of Shi-bi on the matter of the number of casualties, since in the various narratives in the *Yuan shi* the figure "more than 3000" appears in his biography alone. The survival of the Yuan soldiers was of particular interest to Tan who argued that many of those soldiers were Chinese Muslims, and that the main account in Book 210 of the *Yuan shi* "mentions neither the killing of the escort party nor who killed the three Yuan officers" (Tan, 2009, p. 186). He offers a different interpretation of what transpired:

> After Vijaya had escaped, the small escort party realized that they were entering a danger zone right in the home base of the enemy and so they defied the officers' order to pursue Vijaya. Consequently, they eventually killed the officers and deserted the imperial army. (Tan, 2009, p. 187)

Following this line of interpretation, Tan suggested that many of the members of the escort party of 200 settled in Java, since, having refused to fight and then having killed their officers, they could hardly return to the service of the Mongol army. Furthermore, the 3000 dead mentioned in Shi-bi's account "is questionable" because Shi-bi

> had no way to verify the exact casualties in a hostile foreign land but he still had to account for them. So, all the missing men were regarded as dead and reported as such. A portion of the reported dead could have been deserters or prisoners of war. Therefore, it is strongly suggested that there were survivors of the Mongol invading imperial army, many of whom were Hui Muslims. They were the forefathers of the Chinese Muslims in Java whom Cheng Ho had met during his visit.

The existence of remnant Mongol soldiers was also supported by a Yuan traveller, Wang Dayuan who toured Southeast Asia including

Java from 1337 to 1339, forty-four years after the Mongols' invasion of Java. In his book *Daoyi zhilue*, he wrote about the remnants of Mongol fighters living in Gelam where the troops stopped to build small wooden boats, "In the early Yuan period, the troops invaded Java. The fleet met with a storm at the foot of Gelam Hill, and boats were damaged... As the hill is rich in timber, they then constructed more than eleven boats there... and departed. Over 100 men were too sick to leave and they were left behind in the hill. Now the Chinese live in the midst of the natives." (Tan, 2009, p. 187; the quotation from Wang Dayuan Tan gives as: Wang Dayuan 1981, p. 248)

Reid (1996) had earlier argued that there must have been many soldiers who having survived the battles remained in Java (a matter corroborated by the *Kidung Harsawijaya*) and in fact those surviving soldiers had a profound and lasting effect on the Javanese economy and society. In addition he mentions the numerous origin legends of northern Borneo and other island societies that incorporate "a 'Chinese princess' (*puteri Cina*) into the story of its rise to glory" (Reid, p. 25). According to the genealogical legends of the Wolio published in Zahari (1977) and discussed in Yamaguchi (2003), Gao Xing, rather than return to face the Khaan, settled on the island of Buton with his wife, the woman who would become the first queen of the Wolio in 1335.

The fate of the other generals was not so bad as the fate of Shi-bi and the 3000 dead or missing. In contrast to the Wolio legends, the more widely known and accepted account found in the *Yuan shi* states that Gao Xing, on account of his disagreeing with the decisions of Shi-bi and Ike Mese, was not only not punished, but rewarded 50 taels of gold. That a reward was offered to any of the generals is one indication that the campaign was not a total disaster.

Ike Mese, like Shi-bi, was reprimanded and one third of his property taken away, but his property was soon restored. Whether his property was restored before the death of Khubilai or, as in the case of Shi-bi, after his death, is not stated. The account of Ike Mese includes an interesting note on deliberations taken by the three commanders apparently after the battle against Wijaya:

The generals thought of carrying on the war, but Ike Mese wished to do as the emperor had ordered them and first send a messenger to court. The two others could not agree to this, therefore the troops were withdrawn and they returned with their prisoners and with the envoys of the different smaller states which had submitted. (Groeneveldt, 1880, p. 30)

This passage suggests first of all that the Javanese reports of utter defeat of the Tatar army and destruction of both soldiers and ships were inflated, boastful or simply later additions (cf. no such comments occur in the *Desawarnana*). The Mongol army left Java having suffered a loss, and Khubilai certainly evaluated their efforts negatively. But their discussion was not on whether or not they could fight another battle and revenge their losses, but *whether or not they should send a messenger*. Even more interesting is the fact that the officers at this point debate first sending a messenger to court "as the emperor had ordered them." Is this merely a reference to Khubilai's orders quoted at the beginning of the *Yuan shi* account? Or is this an example of Mongol diplomatic protocol during military campaigns? Is this an exceptional meeting which would not have taken place in mainland Asia because of the existence of the overland couriers who could have relayed inquiries and orders? In the end — according to the *Yuan shi* — it was lack of consensus on whether or not they should send a messenger back to the court — not on whether or not they should or could continue the war — which led to the decision to abandon the war and return home. The meaning of this incident leads to numerous questions, and I make no claim to having asked them all; nor can I answer them. But one salient matter will be touched upon in a later section: the rule of law among the Mongols, how the experience of authority moved, guided, formed and informed the Mongols as a people, and as this passage suggests, individually as well.

The biographies contain another interesting matter for consideration: the Mongol commander Shi-bi and the Uigher commander Ike Mese are punished for their role in the failures of the expedition; the Chinese Gao Xing is rewarded. Do we have here a hint of Khubilai's "sinization"? Does this passage record a favoritism or orientation toward "Chinese" rather than "Mongol"? Taken alone, the passage would neither suggest nor provide evidence for such an interpretation, yet when considered together with other events and attitudes, the suspicion arises that there may be more here than can be proven. The passage may indeed be relevant to a detailed study of Khubilai's attitudes towards Mongol and Chinese ways of living and thinking.

And how did the campaign effect the history of eastern Java and the southeast Asian archipelago?

> Kublai Khan's unprecedented series of interventions in Southeast Asia all failed to achieve his object of permanent submission. Nevertheless, they had incalculable side effects. … Wijaya was able to manipulate the Chinese troops to his own advantage and then harry them out of Java, leaving him on the throne. Thousands of Chinese soldiers reportedly died in Java, and many must have been captured by the Javanese or remained voluntarily among them rather than face the rigours of a return journey. This episode not only marked the rise of the new dynasty of Majapahit, but also brought a major injection of Chinese technology to Java, notably in shipbuilding techniques and coinage. (Reid, p. 17)

Reid continued his discussion of the "long-term Chinese interaction" with Java by noting that Wang Dayuan claimed "that the use of Chinese *cash* was one of the demands made by the Mongol expedition", and that "The Chinese or Sino-Indonesian communities left behind by the Mongol invasion may have played a longer term role in stimulating commerce." (Reid, p. 20).

We come now full circle, back to where we began: Why were there no horrific descriptions of lands laid waste and cities leveled, why no lamentation and weeping? Pigeaud notes that the Mongols' penetration "far into the interior of the country probably was of real consequence to Javanese economy in the succeeding period", yet there is no archaeological evidence, and no tales of woe. On the contrary, Wijaya's reign was prosperous and the only references to the Mongols dating from the Majapahit era refer not to destruction but to Mongol cooperation. If the Mongol battles in Java were carried out as joint military ventures with the Mongolian and Javanese armies fighting together against a usurper — as *all* accounts agree — then no attack on the civilian population would have been necessary or desirable. Perhaps archaeologists will some day provide a clearer picture of the economic conditions of Majapahit before and after the Mongols which will lead to a reassessment, but until then, all we know is that Majapahit prospered under Wijaya before the Mongols, after them, and most importantly, because of and thanks to them.

****

> Java is situated at the southwest of Champa. In the time of the emperor Kublai of the Yüan dynasty, Mêng Ch'i was sent there as an envoy and had his face cut, on which Kublai sent a large army which subdued the country and then came back. (*Ming shi*, in Groeneveldt, 1880, p. 34)

The whole Mongol episode in Java is briefly mentioned in Book 324 of the *Ming shi*. Meng Qi was sent and branded, for which reason "Kublai sent a large army which subdued the country and then came back." This falsification through reduction by the Qing historians has been repeated in many subsequent histories, probably due as much to its brevity as to its pallatability: it lacks the taste of defeat. Unfortunately for those who prefer this version of the events — and they are many — it takes an unusual and instructive incident and renders it "typical" — yet another people conquered — and uninteresting. Whenever this version is preferred and accepted, there are no more questions to ask, and one looks no further.

For the historian of the Mongol Empire, the great diversity of sources in many languages, in many kinds of texts, written within many different traditions, is a source of great difficulty for study and research; yet this great diversity of sources itself permits the "other side of the story" to be heard from many directions, and with that multiplicity of viewpoints comes the possibility of a history that is not merely national and self-serving but far-reaching, both humbling and magnanimous, a story both of the world and for the world. The Javanese versions of the Mongolian expedition to Java present a view of the Mongols which both challenges and enlarges the more widely known views found in other Asian and European chronicles and eye-witness accounts, and further study based on both traditions — Javanese and Chinese — promises to enrich our understanding not only of the Javanese campaign, but also of Khubilai, his reign, and the imperial period in general.

PART II

Stories and Histories

Although Chinese writers and historians have had little to say about the Mongols in Java, the peoples of Java have a long tradition of poetic references to the Mongols (always "Tatars" before the 20th century). The spread of Islam throughout most of Java interrupted the transmission and renewal of the early texts and their themes, but after the discovery and publication of the *Desarwarnana*, the *Pararaton* and the *kidung* literature in the late 19th and early 20th centuries, the Mongols once again appeared in new literary works. Whereas in Part I the narrative was drawn from all of the sources to provide a composite account, Part II takes each text separately, not to summarize, but to comment on certain salient features and questions which each one raises. We begin with the Chinese sources, proceed to the Javanese poetical histories ancient and modern, and end with the other histories, those from the world outside Yuan/Ming China and medieval Java.

The Chinese accounts

The principal Chinese account is that found in the *Yuan shi*, the main narrative occuring in Book 210, and supplementary material in the biographies of the generals in charge of the campaign, found in Books 131 and 162. Groeneveldt published an English translation of the relevant sections in 1876. Gaubil's *Histoire de Gentchiscan et de toute la dinastie des mongous, ses successeurs, conquérans de la Chine; tirée de l'histoire chinoise, et traduite par le R.P. Gaubil* (Paris, 1739) was a translation into French of material found in Chinese histories, but he did not identify his sources. Although his account is brief, it does contain material found in the *Yuan shi* and the *Yu pi xu zi zhi tong jian gang mu.* Howorth (p. xvii) wrote that Gaubil relied on the same sources for his translation as Hyacinthe (Iakinf) did in his "history of the first four Mongol Khans" (p. xix), i.e. the *Yuan shi* and the *Yu pi xu zi zhi tong jian gang mu.* Gaubil's and Groeneveldt's translations are both included in the appendices of this book.

A later Chinese version is found in one of the supplements to the *Tong jian gang mu* prepared by Shang Lu and others according to an imperial order of 1476 (Irwin, 1974), about a century after the compilation of the *Yuan shi.* An abridged translation of the *Tong jian gang mu* and its supplements into French (based on the 1708 Kangxi edition and in part on the Manchu version) by Mailla was finished in 1737 but only published in 1777–1785. Since his translation was finished in 1737 and Gaubil's book appeared only in 1739, either Mailla himself added material from the *Yuan shi* (or some other source) to his account, or someone else in the interim did (see Irwin, 1974 for more details). It was this abridged translation that served western scholars for a long time: according to Goodrich in his introduction to Irwin (1974), it was still the longest history of China in a western language even in 1974. On the Mongolian expedition to Java, it contains only a two paragraph narrative and lacks the information found in the biographies of the *Yuan shi.* Mailla's translation of this portion of the text is actually far longer than the original as found in the Kangxi edition. As with the Gaubil and Groeneveldt versions of the *Yuan shi,* an English translation of both the Kangxi edition and Mailla's version of this text are included in the appendices of this book.

Amiot (1776/1789) took his account from the *Da Ming yi tong zhi,* a single paragraph only. Luo Maodeng's 16th or 17th century novel *Xi yang ji* is based on both the Mongols' Javanese campaign and the mission of Zheng He. Of Luo's book, Groeneveldt wrote "It abounds in different details, which however have no other guarantee than the fancy of the writer." (Groeneveldt, 1880, p. x. I have not read this work; whether it contains material found in the *Yuan shi,* the Javanese poems or other sources I do not know: I leave the matter for others to pursue.) Scattered remarks are also found in other works, including Wang Dayuan's *Daoyi zhilue* (1349), the *Ming shi,* Ma Huan's *Yingyai shenglan* (1433), Fei Xin's *Xingcha shenglan* (1436), various encyclopedias, and other works (like that published by Schlegel in 1873) which are based on one or more of these sources. A good description of a wide range of Chinese sources for this period in the Malay Archipelago is Ptak (1998).

While the *Yuan shi* has the most material and is of greater interest than all the other Chinese sources, Wang Dayuan's *Daoyi zhilue*, Ma Huan's *Ying-yai sheng-lan*, the *Yu pi xu zi zhi tong jian gang mu* and the *Ming shi* are each of interest due to questions which arise from their contents and their treatment of the topic. Part I closed with a comment on the brevity of the *Ming shi* account; my comments on the *Yu pi xu zi zhi tong jian gang mu* are few and appear elsewhere; of the other Chinese sources only Wang Dayuan's *Daoyi zhilue*, the *Yuan shi*, Ma Huan's *Yingyai shenglan* and Fei Xin's treatise will be discussed below. In none of the studies which I have read has any significantly different material from sources other than these been mentioned; Groenveldt even claimed that there was nothing else worth translating.

Wang Dayuan's *Daoyi zhilue*

Wang Dayuan's work is interesting for a number of reasons. Ptak (1996) noted that it is "one of the few pre-Ming works on maritime Asia that is based on personal experience" and that "among all Yuan works on maritime Asia which describe more than just one place, it seems to be the one with the highest porportion of original information" (Ptak, 1996, p. 127).

Much of this work has been translated into French and English; according to Ptak (1996) English translations of two thirds of it may be found scattered throughout Rockhill's multipart essay "Notes on the relations and trade of China with the Eastern Archipelago and the coasts of the Indian Ocean during the Fourteenth Century" (Rockhill, 1914–1915). Rockhill himself apparently did not have as high of an opinion of this work as Ptak; he refers to it in a footnote in his discussion of the account of the Mongol expedition of 1292–1293 found in the *Yuan shi*:

> As showing the looseness of the statements made by Wang Ta-yüan (or his editors) in the *Tao-i-chih-lio*, I will quote the following taken from his chapter on Java "During the *ta-té* period (of the Yüan, i. e. 1297–1307) I-hei-mi-shih and the Ping-chang (chêng-shih) Shih Pi and Kao Hsing went together to this island and ordered it to make its submission and send tribute to China. They ordered it to build

yamêns, enact laws, arrange military post-roads for the transmission of despatches, and put in force the laws concerning the saltgabelle and the use of (Chinese) copper cash." (Rockhill, 1914, p. 446)

Wang's remarks on the communities in the archipelago that claimed descent from the soldiers of the expedition of 1292–1293 have been noted and commented upon by a number of historians in recent years (e.g. Reid and Tan). His work was also the subject of a couple of essays by Roderich Ptak, and one of Ptak's comments on Chinese sources for the study of maritime Asia is worth mentioning. He notes with fascination that in spite of the "Sino-centric worldview" of Chinese ethnography [and, we add, historiography], Wang Dayuan (and the authors of the prefaces to his work) "accepted the position that the Mongol court had the same rights and attitudes towards foreigners as the preceding native Chinese dynasties" (Ptak, p. 52) and paid no attention to the fact that the Yuan rulers were non-Chinese. Wang's work, like all the texts discussed below, describes the campaign as a Chinese — not a Mongolian — campaign. In this connection, one of the prefaces to his work boasts that Java suffered an invasion because they dared resist the Yuan (Wang, 1981, p. 5).

Yuan shi

The chief source for the history of the Mongol invasion of Java in most previous histories has been the *Yuan shi* by Song Lian. Modern writers on Indonesian history have also relied in part on the *Pararaton*, but even they have favored the *Yuan shi* version in case of conflict. The *Yuan shi* contains far more material than Wassaf and Rashid al-Din; it is written in documentary style rather than as Hindu-Buddhist romance like the *kidungs*; and it is in a language widely used by mongolists — Chinese — and has also been available in English for 125 years. It is from this book that the 18th century historian Gaubil drew much of his material, and all writers since have based their accounts on the *Yuan shi* directly or from its contents as repeated, condensed or digested in later chronicles and cyclopedias.

The salient differences which separate the Chinese accounts and the *Yuan shi* in particular from the Javanese accounts have been noted above; apart from genre and style, they are: 1) Kertanagara's mistreatment of Meng Qi is offered as the reason for Khubilai's venture; 2) the absence of any comment on the events in Java before or after Meng Qi's return up until the arrival of the Mongol force; 3) lack of interest in the princesses from Tumapel, Daha and Malayu; 4) the nature and extent of the Mongols' defeat.

1. Meng Qi: Meng Qi's mistreatment is the sole reason given in the *Yuan shi* for the Mongol expedition to Java; his absence in the Javanese sources requires an explanation. The easiest explanation for the omission of Meng Qi in the Javanese sources is that the Javanese authors when they wrote either did not know of Meng Qi's mission or else did not realize that the Mongol armies were sent as a result of what happened to Meng Qi. The amount of time that passed before the Mongol armies arrived, the momentous events which took place in Java in the interim — including the death of the offender, Kertanagara — added to the problems of languages and translators (recall the troubles on Taiwan mentioned above) could easily have combined to leave the Javanese with the impression that the arrival of the Mongols had nothing to do with the earlier envoy. If we make the additional assumption that the Javanese did not invent the tale of Wiraraja's invitation (and leave aside the question of whether or not the invitation was from Wiraraja or Wijaya), the campaign to Java was due to not just a single cause, but at least two (and perhaps more, e.g. trade issues). The Chinese historians laid their emphasis on the incident concerning Meng Qi because this is what mattered to the Mongols, while the Javanese felt the invitation by Wiraraja was a necessary and sufficient cause: they had no need to recall Meng Qi. In fact, it may be that the Javanese knew of Meng Qi but did not write about him because he was irrelevant to the matters which engaged their attention. Assuming both versions to be true, they can be reconciled. If either version is rejected, many questions arise, not least of which is why these histories were written as they were.

2. Interim: The lack of comments in the *Yuan shi* on the events in Java between the departure of Meng Qi and the arrival of the Mongol army is probably simply the result of the abscence of any Mongol or Chinese chroniclers in

Java during that time. Even if there had been officials of the Mongol court in Java following the departure of Meng Qi — recall the Tatar ship noted by Wiraraja, and the latter's gift of Chinese spices to Jayakatwang — the events of the succeeding years would not have been known: the histories and stories we have now were written only later. Wijaya's own account found in the inscription of Kudadu was written down only in 1294, after the departure of the Mongols. No officer of the Yuan court would have been in the forest of Trik, though one might have been around a nearby port or perhaps in contact with Wiraraja. Unfortunately, apart from the trading ship mentioned in the *Pararaton*, there is no evidence of such a presence, and Mongol/Chinese ignorance of what happened in Java is a natural and easy assumption to make.

3. Princesses: Why would the Chinese historians fail to mention the princesses even once? Mongol khans did receive brides from other lands, and the *Yuan shi* mentions members of royal families being sent to the Yuan court as part of the business of accepting vassalage from other countries along the way to Java. This is in fact the explanation Kramp (1903) offers for the whole campaign: Kertanagara's refusal to supply a family member of the Singhasari court for Khubilai, even after repeated requests. Could it be that the Mongol request for a member of the court became in the Javanese texts a request for the princesses of Tumapel? Or perhaps the Mongols only asked for a family member, but since Kertanagara only had daughters, this request of Khubilai's was for the Javanese the same as asking for the princesses? Is their abscence due simply to the fact that the promised princess(es) were never acquired?

Another possibility is that the Mongols, the Chinese, their translators or their official record-keepers were unaware of the centrality of the princesses in everything which was happening in Java, or they were uninterested. One possible explanation for ignorance of — or disbelief in — the matter of the princesses may be found in the person of Wiraraja. The Javanese accounts do not hide the lies and deceit practiced by Wiraraja and his various allies in their political machinations. Should the Mongols have inquired about the recent history involving Kertanagara, Wijaya, princesses, etc. there is no reason to expect that they would have been told the truth. And if they had been told about one or more of the five beautiful princesses at one time or another available, the Javanese sources indicate that they never saw any of them, and left Java with no princesses at all — reason enough to discount and ignore the whole issue and concentrate on the battles and betrayals.

Still another possibility is that the *significance* of the princesses in the Javanese accounts is a later elaboration: this is the most important question which the *Yuan shi* raises for the Javanese accounts. The existence of the princesses is not in doubt; their roles and importance in the events of 1292–1293 as they are recorded in the Javanese texts remain in question. Whereas the Chinese officials recording the campaign in fact concentrated on battles, booty and political results, the Javanese writers were all looking back on a critical moment in their history and the drama, tragedy, risks and wars waged among the kings, nobles, princes, queens and princesses from which the great era of Majapahit would arise. Wijaya's struggles, his brides and his progeny mattered to the Javanese of later generations, and mattered greatly. Whether or not they mattered to the Mongols, whether, Khubilai sought to marry the princesses or not, the meaning of the princesses for the Javanese was nothing less than the fate of Java.

The *Yuan shi*'s lack of comment on the romantic elements which make up so large a part of the Javanese stories is obvious, but the absence of the princesses in the *Yuan shi* does not mean they were not on the scene in 1292–1293, only that they were not written about in the *Yuan shi*. The younger princess of Tumapel may have been one of the children taken by the victors after the defeat of Jayakatwang, for according to the Javanese accounts she was adopted by Jayakatwang's queen in order to protect her from the king's intentions. The *Pararaton* agrees with the *Yuan shi* that Jayakatwang was taken prisoner, and the *Kidung Panji-Wijayakrama* adds that he was to be turned over to Wiraraja in exchange for the princesses; these texts also state that Wijaya at that time quickly entered the palace, took the princess and fled with her. And perhaps "the victors" who the *Yuan shi* records as having taken Jayakatwang's wife, children and officers included Javanese soldiers, officers or Wijaya himself — not just Mongols — and at that point Wijaya took the lady and ran. The *Yu pi xu zi zhi tong jian gang mu* does state that the Mongols and Javanese together surrounded the town and accepted Jayakatwang's submission.

Whatever possiblities may lie in what was not stated, the *Yuan shi*, like the inscription of Kudadu, mentions no princesses: the absence of the princesses from all recorded speeches and memorials of Khubilai, his chief generals, and the entire account is sufficient evidence to conclude that Song Lian or those who recorded the "veritable records" which he used for writing the *Yuan shi*, did not consider the princesses in their purposes, military plans, nor life back at the court.

4. Defeat: Does the *Yuan shi* downplay the extent of the disaster or do the later Javanese texts exaggerate it? It is clear that Khubilai was displeased; more 500,000 silver taels worth of booty could not spare Shi-bi from punishment. It is also clear that the commanders of the campaign all returned alive, to punishment or to reward, and that contrary to the *Kidung Harsawijaya*, the "King of Tatar" was definitely not killed in Java. There is also a clear progression from the *Desawarnana's* "half with Tatar men he beat" Jayakatwang, with no mention of the later Mongolian defeat, to the *Kidung Panji Wijayakrama* where the soldiers are killed and chased to the harbor, and there more are killed and their beached ships destroyed, to the *Pararaton* which has the Mongol soldiers being chased all the way to the harbor at Canggu and in the end all killed, all the way to the death of the King of Tatar in the *Kidung Harsawijaya*. On this matter, any reader must come away with the impression that the Javanese tell a taller tale with each retelling. Whether the *Yuan shi* errs in the opposite direction there is no way of knowing.

For all four of these major differences between the Chinese and Javanese texts, the *Yuan shi* can be accepted as a fairly accurate account in what it does state without dismissing the Javanese texts as (mostly) "romantic fictions." (There is no question that some of them *are* romantic fictions; it is their dismissal as having little or no historical value which is unwarranted.) Many of the differences between these two traditions are in fact omissions in one or the other source, not contradictions. They can both be accepted as two different points of view written later and based on documents inaccessible — or uninteresting — to the writers in the other hemisphere. The *Yuan shi* must be read within the tradition of Chinese historiography, and much is known about the qualities, potential, and weaknesses of that tradition.

Yingyai shenglan (Ma Huan) and Xingcha shenglan (Fei Xin)

In his only paragraph on the Mongols in Java, Ma Huan offers a glimpse of a vanished world. The contents of the prayer quoted above suggest a tradition no longer extant apart from his text and Chinese accounts which repeat his narrative. In the prayer the Mongol general claims to have received the order to attack the barbarians. Whether this text presents historical memory or an invention of folklore from the Tuban region, whether it was recorded from one of the many Chinese immigrants living there when Ma Huan visited, from a native Javanese, or even one of Khubilai's soldiers who the *Kidung Panji Wijayakrama* claims were taken captive and distributed among the Javanese nobility, it records local knowledge (or invention) in Java of the Mongol journey by sea not found in any old Javanese text. If this were the local lore of the early 15th century, then there must have been some knowledge of some Mongolian or Chinese version of the story (who else could have related those events?), although not the *Yuan shi*, since this incident is not recorded there. Neither the *Pararaton* nor the *Rangga Lawe*, which may have been composed as early as 1334, give evidence of any such knowledge. Assuming that this tale was recorded by Ma Huan in Java, it represents the sole record of a strain of local knowledge/lore subsequently lost in Java, for, as noted above, the explanation of the Mongol campaign to Java as having its origin in the order to "attack the barbarians" is nowhere to be found in pre-20th century Javanese writings. The reference to the "barbarians" points to a Chinese origin — the Chinese in Java or Ma Huan's viewpoint and language — since it seems unlikely that the Mongols would refer to the Javanese as "barbarians", and certainly the Javanese would not.

Ma Huan's brief note tantalizes with the possibilities it suggests; yet no conclusions can be drawn from this text. Someone told a story and Ma Huan wrote it down, or at least a tiny portion of it. As far as I know, no Javanese ever did.

Fei Xin used Ma Huan's text in writing his treatise *Xingcha shenglan*, and added to this story some elements from the *Yuan shi* as well as a description of the subsequent war in Java which contains material that I have not found in any other source. Mills translated this section of Fei Xin's text as follows:

> The village of Tuban marks another place name. On a sandbank in the nearby sea there is a pool of water; it is fresh, insipid and potable, and is styled "the holy water." During the Yüan period, when the generals Shih Pi and Kao Hsing were sent out to invade this country, the invasion forces passed one moon here and no rain fell, so that on the ships there was a lack of victuals and the soldiers were at their wits' end. The two generals, Shih and Kao, then prayed to Heaven saying: "We received the imperial command to attack the southern barbarians. If Heaven gives us water, we shall live; if not, we shall die." With this they struck their spears into the briny sandbank and at once a spring bubbled up in the place where they had thrust the spears. The water was sweet and all the soldiers drew of it and drank. Then their leaders gave out further instructions saying "Heaven grants his assistance to you!", and the troops, filled with ardor, dashed against the enemy with loud battle shouts. More than a hundred thousand foreign soldiers were routed. Having already landed on the shores, the invaders killed them as they moved inland. They also took foreign soldiers as prisoners, and cooked and ate them. So, to the present day the locals claim that Chinese are able to eat human beings. Thereafter they seized the principal chief to take him to China, but he accepted punishment, was set free, and reinstalled as ruler with the title "King of Java." (Fei Xin, translated by Mills, 1996, p. 50)

If indeed the Javanese locals told Fei Xin (or someone) tales of Chinese cannibalism, then there may be Javanese sources mentioning the practice, but I know of none. On the eating habits of the Mongol/Chinese soldiers, there are oral traditions that have survived to the present: Myra Sidharta reported that current residents of the town of Kediri "claim that tofu came to their city first, brought by the troops of Kublai Khan in 1292" (Sidharta,

2008, p. 197). Tofu, it should be noted, was not a traditional part of the Mongolian diet, but it can safely be assumed that whatever the ethnicity of the soldiers who went to Java, they all ate the food brought on board, whether or not they were accustomed to eating it.

The View from Java

Whatever the reasons may be for the neglect of the Javanese sources by historians of the Mongols, lack of material is not one of them; language probably has been a major obstacle to their appreciation among Mongolists. For early writers like Howorth, the primary sources had not yet been published; Raffles' brief version of (or summary, selections from) the *Kidung Panji Wijayakrama* alone had been published, and only later did anyone realize that it refered to the Mongol invasion (see Walckenaer, 1842). But since the 1894 discovery of the sole manuscript copy of the *Desawarnana (Nagarakertagama)*, several editions and translations of that work have appeared, as well as editions and summaries (in Dutch, Indonesian or English) of the *Pararaton, Kidung Harsawijaya* and *Rangga Lawe*, this latter including as its first part the *Kidung Panji Wijayakrama*.

Apart from the inscriptions which have been found in Java and elsewhere, the reading, copying and study of the early Javanese accounts had all disappeared from Java before the 19th century; the manuscripts have been found only in Bali. Of the four works mentioned in the previous paragraph, all were discovered in Bali, and all of the pre-20th century manuscript copies of these texts found to date were not only found in Bali, but clearly produced there. The retention of Hindu religion and culture in Bali provided a more receptive social environment for their preservation than did the spread of Islam throughout most of Java.

While these works were absent from Javanese cultural life, perhaps for centuries, throughout the 20th century they received considerable attention not only from philologists, but also from historians and even the Indonesian government, which sponsored performances and publication of a variety of modern translations and adaptations of these stories. Today probably most literate Indonesians are familiar with the story of the Mongol expedition to Java as told in these texts. Things are otherwise amongst Mongolists for not even specialists in ancient Mongolian history seem to be aware of the Javanese sources. In fact, these publications have not been noted by Mongolists anywhere: they do not appear in bibliographies, are absent in collections of sources, and receive neither mention nor discussion in accounts of the Mongol empire and Yuan China. Spuler's collection of source material *History of the Mongols Based on Eastern and Western Accounts of the Thirteenth and Fourteenth Centuries* contains no mention of the Javanese sources: in the entire collection Wassaf alone mentions the events in Java. Sh. Bira's volume on sources for the study of early Mongol history contains no mention of Java, much less any Javanese texts. Among histories and biographies of the Mongols, only Rossabi's biography *Khubilai Khan: his life and times* includes material found in the Javanese texts, although without mentioning them. He cites Groeneveldt, Berg, and Cady, referring the reader to Zhang Xing-lang's *Zhong-xi jiao-tong* for a brief account and to Hall's *A History of South-East Asia* (2nd ed., London, 1964) for a fuller account.

Even apart from the difficulties of translation and publication, the Javanese sources present formidable problems as sources for the study and writing of history. How to read the texts, as what kinds of texts, what they were written to be and for what purposes, and what one may hope to get from them: these are the questions which have generated a great deal of commentary by those who have studied them with a view to their historical value. Nearly everyone agrees on their importance for the study of history; yet confronted with the particulars, with variation, with miraculous events, with known inaccuracies and unverifiable details, attention to their characteristics, to genre and to authorial intention are a necessary prelude to any evaluation.

Javanese historical genres: poetical histories and historical fictions

In his 1876 article "The expedition of the Mongols against Java in 1293, A.D." Groeneveldt, one of the earliest commentators on the Javanese accounts (he mentions both the Balinese manuscript quoted in Raffles, and "traditions current in Java"), translates the relevant passages from the *Yuan shi* and then writes "we think it advisable to state in a few words what we know about that epoch from other sources." He follows with a brief selection from the material published by Raffles and then comments:

> In utilising these various accounts, it must be remembered that the Chinese version is a sober narrative of facts, disfigured, it is true, by many errors and inaccuracies, but free from all fiction. The Balinese account has been handed down through many generations, gradually losing in accuracy and becoming mixed with much of the fantastic and marvelous, whilst Javanese tradition has been violently interrupted by the introduction of Islam and, having been raked up from its embers at a later period, hardly seems to deserve any credit at all. (Groeneveldt, 1876, p. 252)

Similarly, Krom in his *Hindoe-Javaansche geschiedenis* states that there is no doubt that the main sequence of events — Wijaya fled from the fighting in a northerly direction and escaped to Madura as a refugee — is historically valid, but that "All the rest is romance." (Krom, p. 351) Earlier than both Groeneveldt and Krom, John Crawfurd in the article on Java in his *Descriptive dictionary of the Indian islands & adjacent countries* (1856; he does not mention the Mongol campaign at all) claims that all Javanese literature is poetry, and "its general character is that of inanity and childishness." (p. 182). Concerning the writing of history in Java, he says "The Javanese cannot, in any rational sense of the word, be said to possess any writing deserving the name of history" (p. 184). We have come a long way since Crawfurd and Raffles, but even now scholars like Creese, Hobart and Nordholt in their efforts to overcome these earlier attitudes at times come very close to saying that the Balinese and Javanese in fact like a beautiful poem and care not at all for what happened if it does not suit their needs and desires.

It should be noted that when both Raffles and Groeneveldt refer to "traditions current in Java" they are referring to Islamic historiography — e.g. the *Babad tanah Jawi* — and not to the old Hindu-Javanese texts which are the object of investigation here. Except for the one manuscript published by Raffles, these earlier texts were all unknown to Raffles (and probably to Crawfurd and Groeneveldt as well, for they mention none of them). The value of the early Javanese-Balinese sources for the study of

Javanese history was the subject of considerable debate among historians of Java and Indonesia after their publication in the late 19th and early 20th centuries, and the debate has continued vigorously up to the present. Since Berg's publication of the *kidungs* in the 1920–30's, some historians have studied those texts as valuable historical documents, while others have regarded them as merely literary and mythical texts with little value for the historian. The debates on the meaning and importance of the Balinese, Javanese and Sundanese *'babads'*, *'geguritans'*, *'kidungs'*, and other indigenous historical literatures have focused on the meaning of historiography for the Balinese and its political uses.

The issues and theories involved have been at the forefront of the wider world of historical and literary scholarship for decades now, and it is not my intention to review and criticise the various positions which have achieved prominence. My own approach will be made clear, and for the Mongolist reader unfamiliar with the particular nature of the Javanese material and the controversies surrounding the specific texts in question as well as the larger issue of the genres to which they do (or do not) belong, a brief review of such matters is necessary.

Fact and Fiction

Because the traditions in question were maintained in Bali — wherever they may have originated — both Balinese and Javanese historiographical traditions must be considered. Though they have much in common, they differ in certain important ways.

> [I]f we are to reflect critically on foreign commentators' or Balinese representations of the past, should we not begin by considering how far, and in what way, problems of history resolve themselves into issues of cultural differences of narrative style? In short, to what degree are debates about Indonesian and Malay ideas about the past ... actually about different conventions of writing and telling stories? (Hobart, pp. 131–32)

Whatever genre one wishes to assign to the Balinese *babad*, Hobart insists that they are written, read, heard, understood and stated to be representations of the past. Writing about Javanese historiography of the colonial era, Ann Kumar claimed that "Of the total surviving literatures of the Indianized kingdoms, only one or two works can at all be described as histories." The two works which satisfy Kumar's historian are both works which are considered here: the *Pararaton* and the *Desawarnana*. For Pigeaud, only the *Pararaton* counts as history, while for Krom, even the *Pararaton* is history only in its basic chronology. Thus we can see the range of opinion, but there are still more possibilities. Helen Creese contrasts the "Javanese classics" (our texts) with the Balinese *babad*:

> Balinese *babad* differ in content, form and function from their Javanese counterparts. Javanese *babad* are generally written in verse form, deal with a single event or series of events of limited duration, and are concerned with reporting a particular view of these events. ... [M]ost Balinese *babads* are written in prose. ... It is largely a spurious undertaking to seek to separate 'fact' from 'fiction' or 'history' from 'literature' in Balinese *babad*. (Creese, 1991, pp. 238–39)

Echoing Creese, Nordholt remarks that "There are in Balinese literature no separate genres called "history" and "fiction". Consequently the distinction between true stories and (false) fantasies makes little sense." (Nordholt, p. 27) He proposes that one must leave behind the "unproductive fact-fiction dichotomy" and view the *babad* as political documents which "construct — and re-phrase — that past in order to make the present meaningful" and thus "may offer important historical information." The Balinese *babad* — and he is not referring to the Javanese texts preserved in Bali — were written according to two "complementary criteria": summarizing complex processes through a literary device, and the making of an ordered past as a means of controlling present threats of disorder (ibid., pp. 32–33; 38).

Nordholt proceeds to contrast the genre *babad* with the genre *uwug*, "songs of destruction," investigating one text in particular, the *Kidung Nderet*. We can compare his comments on the Balinese *uwug* with the two Javanese *kidungs* we have taken as sources, *Kidung Panji Wijayakrama* and *Kidung Harsawijaya*:

The story focuses on a specific sequence of events which is narrated in chronological order. It presents the precise minutes of a process of decline, forgetting, loss of confidence, confusion, misunderstanding, treason, chaos, and defeat...

Whereas the characters of the *babad* lack any personality, since they represent basically ideal types, the leading figures in the *kidung* are, in the first place, individual human beings who try, refuse, or simply fail to live up to their (political) responsiblities. ...

Whereas the *babad* creates a story about origin and descent in order to make it real, the *kidung* uses reality in order to discuss the moral problems which have to do with leadership and loyalty. The realistic nature of the story makes the moral issues raised virtually inescapable: this is not just a story in which ideal models are enacted; it is real and imminent, and so are the issues.

...[T]he leading characters of the *kidung* are, as far as I know, based upon historical persons. There are no indications that certain figures, or even scenes, were invented for the sake of the story. (Nordholt, p. 46)

Like the Balinese *uwug*, the Javanese *kidung* is a story about revolt, war, and "above all, about the nature of leadership." (Nordholt, p. 43) In contrast to the *uwug*, the Javanese *kidungs* all tell a tale of Majapahit. Decline, treason, defeat, "individual human beings who try, refuse" or fail: we recognize our texts here. History as a source of knowledge of the "moral problems which have to do with leadership and loyalty", moral and religious tales in which right and wrong, *karma* and *dharma* are seen in action. As has often been noted, the peoples of South-East Asia were preoccupied with the religious meanings of their lives, not with historical fact as this has been theorized, sought and presumably written down in Western historiography.

Acknowledging that moral problems and religious meanings are the real 'stuff' of the *kidungs* leads directly to the real difficulty of dealing with the Javanese sources: the Javanese certainly have a past — no one will deny that — but their histories as they themselves have written them are formed of different materials, according to different rules and for different purposes than those which are found in the West. If one wants to write history according to the standards, rules of evidence, methodologies, and a desire for objectivity (in so far as that is possible), Western style, how can one use as sources texts which are clearly written without regard for any of those requirements, for avowedly partisan purposes? Nordholt claims that Balinese *babad* were written to serve as weapons:

> Since the authors ... were not able to use violence to seize power, they used the power of words to achieve their political goals. Their 'literary' texts became, in other words, an important weapon. (Nordholt, p. 57)

If history is to be written as a weapon — for whatever purposes — entirely at the discretion of the author-historian-poet, the past vanishes: we are left with nothing but texts called *babad* or "histories" or some other designation when they are in fact nothing but propaganda for nationalist, racist, sexist, dynastic or personal futures. Must we accept whatever past its "owners" (or descendents) write for us?

Nordholt describes a "very interesting" *babad* which while "perhaps containing more 'reliable facts' for a Western historian" was found worthless by his Balinese friends. A Balinese writer who provides a different history, one which might be more highly valued by a Western historian is dismissed by the other Balinese on the grounds that "This is not our babad. It is a false one with many mistakes. Moreover, it is an ugly text; it is poorly composed." The Balinese are not interested in 'facts'; any history written by the 'other' will not be read, it will be wrong and of no interest because it was written by an 'other'. Is this approach not as disparaging of the Balinese as Krom's dismissal? Nordholt claims that this *is* the Balinese approach to history.

The early Javanese texts which tell of the Mongols in Java were not written according to the expectations of modern Western historical writing. Such conventions and practices as the Western tradition has developed were obviously non-existent in the time and place of their composition. When the voice of the past as Other speaks, it does not speak in our language, nor of our world. The Javanese authors of the past wrote and lived in another world and it is to that world that our ears must be attuned. The past as Other does not always say what we want to hear, nor did minds of the past think and live according to the dictates of microeconomics, psychoanalysis, materialism or deconstruction. We must read these texts for what they offer, not for what they do not offer. We enter a world where all of life is experienced as moral and religious, where the meaning of the story is paramount. Whether the people, places and events are the same as those appearing in other texts may not have mattered at all to the authors and their contemporaries. We do not know: the amount of variation on these details is astonishing, we know only that something happened, and that what happened we can know only through reading what those authors have left for us to read.

Devin DeWeese has adopted an approach which I regard as a particularly fruitful manner of reading the *kidungs*, although not the only one. In his "Aims, assumptions, approaches" he remarks:

> [O]ur only access to the meaning of conversion for these peoples lies in such narrative responses. "Conversion" is inevitably a process of such considerable psychological and social complexity that even a thorough reconstruction of the historical setting and events that occurred, and even a precise description of "what happened" could not convey the *significance* of the conversion understood and felt, religiously, by the adherents of the new faith and their communal heirs. The "conversion" happened, and had historical antecedents and consequences, but in and of itself was at the same time beyond the ken of historical reconstructions, and yet important and central enough for those who felt themselves intimately connected with it that it had to be talked about and recounted and related... (DeWeese, 1994, p. 10)

Dewees is concerned, he writes, with

> what people say happened... the religious meaning revealed by the relationships between successive narrative developments, *not* the

relationship between 'historical reality' and the narrative tradition in part inspired by it. (ibid., p. 12)

In a footnote to the paragraph from which the preceding quotation was taken, he adds the following comment:

> While it may be possible to reconstruct with some degree of accuracy the historical context and the actual "events" that accompanied the conversion of Ozbek Khan to Islam, the limited value of such an approach must be acknowledged. (ibid., p. 12)

While our texts do not deal with the topic of conversion, the authors of the *kidungs* very clearly wrote about what the past meant to them as they wrote: it was not the author's intention to study the past to represent it with the greatest accuracy in numbers, names, dates and places. The meanings of the *kidungs*, like all poetry, are far more matters of religious truths for the author's world — political and otherwise — than treatises on the past as past. Reading the *kidungs* together with works like the *Pararaton*, the *Desawarnana* and the *Yuan shi*, we can hope to acquire not just a knowledge of names, dates, numbers and facts but also the inner history of how that past continued to live and change the world which came after. We have, after all, as many paths into the past as we have views of that past. And unlike DeWeese, we may find that these multiple paths into the past will allow us to better understand "the relationship between 'historical reality' and the narrative tradition in part inspired by it," the events which took place as well as the meanings attached to them in different traditions. A search for the "historical context and actual 'events' that accompanied" the spiritual experiences will never lead to "what really happened" but may be just that other perspective from which we can order, judge and better understand the narrative traditions which followed.

Variation and distortion

The problem of variation in Javanese texts differs from similar problems in European codicology chiefly in the more extensive degree of variation. In describing variation among manuscript versions of related Javanese texts Kumar mentions the great variation in the recording of names and numbers:

> There are differences of detail — nearly always in names and numbers, with minor variations in plot occurring only rarely... (Kumar, 1984, p. 229)

> The tendency for proper names to become distorted directs our attention to two important and related characteristics of *Babad* writers: that they appear to have little recourse to independent records or archives (the basic resource which a historian requires of his environment) where there is something which is unclear in the text(s); and that they do not find it necessary, as copyists in other manuscript traditions do, to reproduce the antecedent version exactly even when it is unclear. (Kumar, 1984, pp. 236–37)

After suggesting that the *babad* writers regarded their works more as literary works than historical records, Kumar then discusses variation in unrelated texts which treat the same subjects as a way of trying to understand the "distinctly cavalier treatment of the specific, "factual" information passed down from antecedent manuscripts." The variation in unrelated texts being far greater than that found in related texts, she suggests that the *babad* writers based their narratives on genealogies or court diaries, "that Babad were intended to be "read" either within the *kraton* itself" or among a select few connected with the palace.

As an example of how crucial such variation is for understanding the past to which these texts refer, we can look at the narratives of the death of Kertanagara. In the *Desawarnana* this occurs prior to Jayakatwang's actions, i.e. the latter makes his move not against Kertanagara but in the absence of a king, after Kertanagara's death but prior to the accession of Wijaya. In the *Pararaton, Kidung Panji Wijayakrama* and the *Kidung Harsawijaya* Jayakatwang's soldiers attack and kill Kertanagara. This is a major point, not just a matter of chronology but of the greatest importance for understanding the character of Jayakatwang, the letters and character of Wiraraja, the legitimacy of Wijaya's reign, and so on. It is, of course, a problem of chronology, of how the Javanese texts and the *Yuan shi* account will fit together, but the chronology only matters because of the meanings which have been attached to what happened.

There is also the related problem of condensation and summarization. Ricklefs describes the textual history of the *Babad tanah Djawi*, which originally appeared in 688 pages in 1874. The text was based on a manuscript which was later partially published in 31 volumes totalling about 2,500 pages. A similar consendation must have taken place in the text published by Raffles, for his version occupies not quite four pages, while Berg's edition of the *Kidung Panji Wijayakrama* covers 70 similarly sized pages. (Whether Raffles found such a short manuscript or condensed it himself for publication, I was unable to ascertain.)

Religion and the supernatural

> In the end, of course, the problem is a religious one. A question of meaning always is. (Vining p. 160)

Another matter which perplexes the modern historian is the presence of the religious and the supernatural, the making and narrating of meanings rather than facts observable by an outsider. When the author of the *Kidung Harsawijaya* states that Jayakatwang vanished into the heavens while seated on his elephant meditating, was he using inaccurate sources or indulging in poetic licence? In this case, the matter may perhaps be explained in the same manner as Ricklefs suggests for the ascension of Brawijaya in the *Babad tanah Djawa*: it is "a refined restatement of some older tradition that the king was killed." But the Javanese texts are full of such observations and interpretations of events which a modern observer could not see, much less credit: he would simply refuse to believe his eyes and search for the source of the illusion. Even if we could seek for metaphorical meanings and treat all of these incidents as 'refined restatements' of the ordinary events of everyday life, should we? Would such an approach increase our understanding of the Javanese past or the Javanese views of their past? Far from a simple problem, there are in fact multiple issues, each requiring a different way of reading and interpretation.

If we desire to understand what happened — or what people say happened — in Java in 1293 or any other date, we may not ignore entirely the causal explanations couched in religious language, the miraculous events recorded, the meanings which the authors saw so clearly but which unsettle us. We would do so at our peril, just as much as if we were to accept them literally, i.e. as though the author were writing to us today about events now in such language. To understand how the authors of these texts from another world and time used their words, what they meant their readers to understand, and how these events were perceived and acquired such meanings: that requires an effort of empathy and imagination greater than most of us can lay claim to, a task which can be neither avoided nor replaced by modern superstitions unless we entirely forsake our interest in that past world.

Understanding the religious elements in a text must be based on what is written. The "methodological presupposition of mind", so important in Vining's analysis of law and the courts, must underlay the inquiry, an author, a real presence assumed at the start. The texts with which we are concerned do not speak with one voice. They do not speak our language. And their authors are both unknown and dead. Only through their texts as they have come down to us can we try to understand what they intended to say, and they knew this when they wrote: we should presuppose neither an 'evil demon' dedicated to deceiving us nor a mere weapon aimed at some long vanished enemy.

While the religious elements are frequent in the Javanese texts, these do not present the only problems, and we would do well to keep in mind that "people may write about and understand their past in ways far more radically different" (Hobart, p. 139) than we have ever dreamed. The early texts were written for diverse purposes and date from the year after the Mongol campaign on into the 16th century. Whereas sections of each of these texts were interspersed in the narrative above, in the following section each one will be considered separately.

Early Javanese Accounts

In addition to a preliminary note on epigraphy, there are four early texts which will be described and discussed briefly below; the relevant sections of the texts themselves, or summaries of them, appear in the Appendices. The texts are presented in roughly chronological order as far as can be determined: *Desawarnana (Nagarakertagama), Pararaton, Kidung Panji Wijayakrama, Kidung Harsawijaya*. There are perhaps other texts in the various languages of the Indonesian archipelago which contain interesting material, but the above mentioned texts are the only texts that I have been able to examine so far, and all are well known and have been discussed at length by historians of Java.

Epigraphy

Like so much of our evidence for ancient Indonesian history, the dramatic story of the founding of the great kingdom of Majapahit was preserved by accident. In 1780 an anonymous digger discovered a set of 6 sheets of copper about 30 cm long and 20 cm wide on Mt. Butak, a few kilometers west of Malang, East Java. The plates were taken to Surakarta in 1782, where they were transcribed into modern Javanese characters. The original plates then disappeared and have never been rediscovered.

The transcription was found in a chest of papers willed to the library of the Royal University in Leiden in 1888. In this way the historic events of Saturday, September 11, 1294, have been preserved. (John N. Miksic, "Introduction" in *The Legacy of Majapahit*. Singapore, 1995, p. 13)

While there are no known inscriptions making reference to the Mongols, the Kudadu (or Gunung Butak) inscription found in 1780 records the story of Wijaya's escape from Jayakatwang and the aid he received from the people of Kudadu while in exile. Engraved the year after the departure of the Mongols the importance of this inscription lies in 1) its being the only contemporary account, 2) its composition having been ordered by the major Javanese figure in the Mongol campaign (Wijaya), and 3) the events recounted confirm much of the narrative found in the later Javanese texts. It has been published in facsimile, in transliteration and in Dutch and English translations. A partial English translation and discussion may be found in

Slametmuljana's *Story of Majapahit*, a complete Dutch translation is included in Brandes' edition of the *Pararaton*. Robson's previously unpublished 1962 complete translation into English appears in the revised version of his thesis published in an appendix in this volume.

Other inscriptions from the reigns of Kertanagara, Wijaya and later rulers offer corroboration of a number of names, dates and events which appear in the later Javanese accounts. Kertanagara's relations with southern Sumatra, his religious practices, and his death are all indicated in such inscriptions as those of Amoghapasa and Candi Singasari. The texts of all the relevant inscriptions are reprinted and discussed in Yamin's *Tatanegara Madjapahit*.

Desawarnana, or Nagarakertagama (1365)

In 1894, a Dutch expedition to the island of Lombok sacked the palace of the Balinese ruler and set it aflame. A young Dutch official attached to the expedition in order to recover important antiquities and historical materials managed to save from the fire a number of manuscripts, one of which was found to be a copy of a poem written in 1365. The poem, popularly known as the *Nagarakertagama* although its real title is *Desawarnana* ("Description of the country"), gives the most complete description of any ancient Indonesian court. (John N. Miksic, "Introduction" in *The Legacy of Majapahit*, 1995. p. 14)

The *Desawarnana* was written in 1365 but unknown to western scholars until its discovery in 1894. It treats of both the Singhasari period and the founding of the kingdom of Majapahit and contains one of the earliest Javanese references to the Mongol army in Java. The Mongols — called "Tatars" — are mentioned only once, in canto 44, stanza 4, line 4:

Half with Tatar men he beat *haji* (lord) Jaya Katwang; exterminated altogether; (Pigeaud's translation, 1960)

Jointly with the Tatars he attacked King Jayakatwang and wiped him out completely. (Robson's translation, 1995, p. 57)

Slight though the mention is, it is consistent with both the Chinese sources and later Javanese accounts in stating that the Mongol army fought with Wijaya against Jaya Katwang.

The most important element in this text is the name 'Tatar' itself, which appears here for the first time in the Javanese language as an ethnonym or toponym. It appears as an ethno- or toponym in only four other texts: the *Kidung Harsawijaya, Rangga Lawe* (in the first part, *Panji Wijayakrama*), the *Pararaton* and the *Kidung Sunda*. In all cases where 'tatar' is used as an ethno- or toponym it refers only to this particular episode: the Mongols in Java. In the *Kidung Sunda*, a text composed about 1550 which tells not of the Mongols but of later episodes in the history of Majapahit, the word 'tatar-nagari' [=Tatar-country] appears in a description of a ship "which was a junk, like the ones made in the land of Tatar [or: land of the Tatars] since His Majesty Wijaya's war and the fall of Kediri". (In modern Sundanese *tatar* means "land" or "country", e.g. *Tatar Sunda* means the country or region of Sunda in Jawa Barat.) There is another word for 'China' used not only in earlier and later texts but even used later on in the *Desawarnana*, in Canto 83: 'Cina'.

From the restricted usage of the term 'tatar' in old and medieval Javanese it is necessary to conclude that, contrary to Zoetmulder in his dictionary of Old Javanese, 'tatar' means Mongol(ia) and not China, and is used as both ethnonym and toponym. The fact that in texts later than the *Desawarnana* such as the *Kidung Harsawijaya* the 'island' of Tatar is referred to as a vassal of Majapahit suggests that perhaps from the time of the composition of the *Desawarnana* in 1365 until the mid- or late19th century the Javanese may not have known where the land of Tatar was nor that the King of Tatar was Khubilai, Great Khaan of the Mongols, Emperor of the Yuan Dynasty, ruler of China. This is not as surprising as it appears to be, for it was not until the mid-19th century that Chinese and European scholars could locate the "Koua-wa" — Java — of the *Yuan shi*. The Arab and Chinese traders of the time certainly knew where Java was, where China was and who Khubilai was, but both the court historians and the poets in Majapahit and China alike were writing about matters which happened "long ago and far away."

Whether the name 'tatar' came to Java via the Arab traders, was used by the interpreters accompanying the Mongol army — the interpreters probably were Arab merchants themselves — or had its origin in China (the Chinese ethnonym 'tata'er' 塔塔兒 and variants) has not been discussed in any of the literature I have read. Zoetmulder offers no etymology in his dictionary. Where the name 'tatar' came from and how it came to be used in Java to refer to "Mongol" is a problem for the philologists that I shall not pursue.

Against those historians who deny the value of the *Desawarnana* as historical writing, Pigeaud noted that the absence of any more detailed references to the Mongol invasion and its economic consequences may be explained by its character rather than as a "desire to turn over a black page of Javanese dynastic history." In Pigeaud's judgement "it is not a book of history like the *Pararaton*. Its primary interest is in contemporary Court matters and religion in connection with the Court." (Pigeaud, v. 4, p. 135) In so stating his judgement, Pigeaud also gave his judgement on the *Pararaton*: it *is* a book of history.

Although the arrival and branding of Khubilai's envoy Meng Qi is not mentioned, the entire Canto 44 describes the situation in Java after the death of Kertanagara. Since the section is short, Robson's translation is quoted here in full rather than relegated to an appendix:

Canto 44.
1. When King Krtanagara returned to the abode of the Buddha,
The world was fearful, sad and tumultuous, as if it would revert
    to its condition in the Age of Kali.
There was a vassal king, a villain known by the name of
    Jayakatwang,
Who there in the land of Kadiri desired to replace him and was
    outstandingly clever at laying schemes.

2. When formerly Sri Krtajaya went forth in Saka "oceans-Manus-
    One" (1144, AD 1222),
The Son of the Lord of the Mountain ordered that Jayasabha should
    be the one to replace him as ruler.

In Saka 'eight-one-one', (1180, AD 1258) Sastrajaya in turn took his place in the land of Kadiri,

And in Saka "three-nine-Sangkaras" (1193, AD 1271) King Jayakatwang finally became king.

3. Each of the kings had been devoted to the descendants of the Son of the Lord of the Mountains

Especially to King Krtanagara — even the other islands obeyed him.

Now, however, when the King passed away, King Jayakatwang became blind and strayed from the path;

Due to the difficulty of protecting the world in the Age of Kali it was evident that its welfare could not be long-lasting.

4. Through the influence of his knowledge of the scriptures and the force of the King's efforts before,

It came about that there was a son of His Majesty's who defeated the enemy and restored the world.

His relationship was son-in-law, and Dyah Wijaya was the title by which people praised him —

Jointly with the Tatars he attacked King Jayakatwang and wiped him out completely.

The poem does not mention that Jayakatwang had Kertanagara murdered — stating instead that Kertanagara had died prior to Jayakatwang's bid for power — but does describe him as a villain (Robson's translation; Pigeaud has "rascal" and "greedy, false"). In contrast, Wijaya is (in Pigeaud's translation) "son of the Illustrious Prince, defeating the enemies, setting right the world." The recognition –or opinion — that the Mongols were united with "the son of the Illustrious Prince" to fight the "rascal" Jaya Katwang and set right the world — accomplices, not hell-bent invaders — characterizes all subsequent Javanese accounts. The *Desarwanana* presents one of the earliest instances of this salient difference between the Javanese view of the Mongols, and those more widely known negative views of the European and Asian chroniclers of the Mongol campaigns elsewhere.

According to Mpu Prapanca, the author of the *Desarwanana*, before the arrival of the Tatars "The world was fearful, sad and tumultous" (Robson; Pigeaud has "the world was terrified, in disaster and tumult"); after their departure (which Mpu Prapanca does not mention) Canto 45 states that "the whole of Yawa-land (Java) turned mindful (of its duty), most humbly they entered into the Presence" (Pigeaud's translation). For Prapañca and later writers it is Wijaya's wisdom and righteousness which set the world aright, not the Mongol army, but the participation of the Mongols is noted, and noted specifically as cooperation with the forces of good against the forces of wickedness. There is perhaps additional significance in the fact that no derogatory mention is made of the Mongols: if the dishonorable treatment of Meng Qi by the "Illustrious Prince" Kertanagara had been mentioned, this would have both disgraced Kertanagara himself and justified an invasion by Khubilai. Any mention of an invasion as opposed to a cooperative military venture to punish a "villain" would have required a wholly different — and negative — treatment of the Mongol appearance. By omitting both the original infraction and the intended punitive nature of the Mongol army's presence, the author was able to present a wholly laudable view of Kertanagara and explain the presence of the Mongols as a righteous army. By further omitting the fate of the Mongol armies at the hands of Wijaya, Prapanca gives an account in which the good are always good and the good prince triumphs over the "villain" Jayakatwang. The Javanese desire for propriety, ethics and etiquette rules over the narrative and the Mongols come out smelling like roses.

Perhaps the absence (or forgetting) of the Meng Qi episode in Prapanca's account was the crucial historiographical "error" which forced later Javanese accounts to emphasize or invent — if indeed it is an invention — the explanation for the invasion which appears in the *Pararaton* and all subsequent accounts: Wiraraja's invitation. By leaving out the reason(s) for the Mongol involvement in Javanese affairs, a huge hole appears in the narrative, a hole which must be filled for a religious consciousness keenly interested in karma, the law of spiritual history. By another reading, following Pigeaud, the absence of Meng Qi and all other references to the Mongols is due simply to the fact that the story of the Mongols in Java was not the story which Mpu Prapanca wanted to tell. In the absence of any evidence, this latter interpretation will be followed. There are in fact excellent reasons to follow Pigeaud in this matter. They will be discussed in Part III.

Pararaton

Several manuscripts are extant, the earliest of which contains a colophon date of 1535 Shaka (AD 1613) according to Damais (1958, p. 59). It is a prose work rather than a poem like the *Desawarnana* and the *kidungs*. The text as it is known today has been established on the basis of much later manuscripts found in Bali. A number of editions and translations have appeared; the first English translation appeared in 1996.

The story as found in the *Pararaton*, with additional and different material, is found in both the *Kidung Rangga Lawe* and the *Kidung Harsawijaya* but the relation between the *Pararaton* and the *Kidung Rangga Lawe* is not clear. The former, probably written between 1478 and 1486 (a volcanic eruption of 1486 is mentioned, but the rise of Girindrawardhana Dyah Ranawijaya in 1486 is not), has been considered to be the source for the latter, yet if, as Damais (1958) argued, the *Rangga Lawe* were originally written in 1334, the reverse would seem to be true. Gonda (1976, p. 236) felt that Berg's view that the *Pararaton* was "the 'mother' of all works dealing with the same historical personages" was incorrect, and "the *Pararaton* draws on the same tradition as the other works" (ibid.). Gonda further argued that "There is no reason to reject the supposition that not all parts of this compilation originate in the same years and milieu. Since the manuscripts are Balinese in origin the assumption seems legitimate that at least part of the work was composed in Java and after 1481 brought to the smaller island where the compilation may have been amplified... and obtained its present form" (Gonda, 1976, p. 237). For my interests and for the purposes noted in the preface, the dates and relationships between the *Pararaton* and the other texts does not matter, and I have made no effort to pursue the issue.

Originally ignored by historians as romance, it is now widely regarded as history (except its "romantic" elements!). Along with certain other works, it is absent from Zoetmulder's survey of Old Javanese literature, for, he says, "however interesting they may be in other respects, [they] are not discussed here because they do not fall within the concept of literature used in this survey." (Zoetmulder, 1974, p. 437) On the other hand Gonda thought "It is not beyond possibility that the facts contained in the chronicles originally were reliable and that the evident mistakes are due partly to carelessness of the copyists, partly to deliberate modifications" (Gonda, 1976, p. 237).

Panji Wijayakrama

Brandes in his edition of the *Pararaton* remarks that the manuscript discovered by Raffles and published in his *History of Java* is a version of the *Rangga Lawe* and is the same version as the one mentioned in Friederich's 1850 article. From Damais' discussion of the existing manuscripts it appears that only the version published by Berg was written early enough to have been read by Raffles. (The other three manuscripts Damais dated as having been produced in 1846, 1853 and 1871; one of the manuscripts used by Berg for his edition of the the *Rangga Lawe* was identified as being in Friederich's handwriting.) Brandes also assumes that the *Rangga Lawe* itself is based on the *Pararaton*. Damais (1958, pp. 55–57) argued that the *Rangga Lawe* was originally written in AD 1334, interpreting the chronogram as 1256 Shaka rather than 1465 Shaka (AD 1543) and that it was the first *kidung* written after Jayakatwang's *Wukir polaman*. Written in Middle Javanese and known only from manuscripts both made and discovered in Bali, it is one of the most important sources for the Singhasari-Majapahit era of Javanese history but the nature of its value for historical research has been much debated.

The work itself has two parts, the first part *Panji Wijayakrama* being the story of Wijaya from the events leading up to the fall of Kertanagara until his own death, while the second part *Rangga Lawe* is the story of Rangga Lawe and his rebellion, the first great crisis for the Majapahit dynasty after the departure of the Mongols. It is from the second part that the whole gets its name, and in fact Rangga Lawe plays an important role not only in the second part but in the first as well.

Slametmuljana uses this text freely for certain parts of his narrative, and offers his evaluation of it in a passage which occurs immediately before his description of the events which take place after Wijaya's stay in Kudadu:

The following story is mainly based on the *Panji Wijayakrama*, which is classified as a historical romance. In general the story is reasonable and contains several historical facts which bear out checking in the inscriptions. (Slametmuljana, 1976, p. 37)

Zoetmulder does not summarize the *Rangga Lawe* but includes his comments on the chief differences between this work and the *Kidung Harsawijaya*:

...*Rangga Lawe*, contains in its first part the story of prince Wijaya. It accords with that in the *Kidung Harsawijaya* as far as its main outline is concerned, but there are many differences of detail. Nothing is said about Narasingha's reign or Wijaya's youth — there is not even an indication as to whose son he is. The story opens when Krtanagara (he is always called Siwa-Buddha) is already king, and the period prior to Jayakatwang's attack is treated briefly. From this point onward the story runs parallel to the KHW [*Kidung Harsa-Wijaya*].

... In the KHW [*Kidung Harsa-Wijaya*] the Wijaya-story has been embroidered upon in a free and leisurely way. It is more than three times longer than its counterpart in the *Rangga Lawe*. Apart from the romantic episode of Ratna Sutawan, the latter has few additions and embellishments. It is more matter-of-fact and more prosaic. (Zoetmulder, 1974, p. 415)

The version of the *Panji Wijayakrama* which Raffles' gives in his History of Java differs from Berg's edition and from the accounts found in the *Pararaton* and the *Kidung Harsawijaya* in several places, and these differences are especially interesting when considering Javanese views of the Mongols. Unlike the Javanese traditions which Raffles discusses first (i.e. the *Babad Tanah Jawi*, in which there is no mention of Mongols), this Balinese manuscript contains a few paragraphs on the Mongols. This unnamed manuscript has similarities to the *Kidung Panji Wijayakrama* but the differences are great: Kertanagara is portrayed in a very unflattering light; Wijaya is Kertanagara's younger brother, not nephew, and has only one wife who is captured by Jayakatwang;

Wiraraja, rather than being a devious traitor, has been falsely accused of a crime, and only because he feels himself in danger of Kertanagara's injustice does he contact Jayakatwang; the King of Tatar Sri Laksemana is a guest of Jayakatwang and the latter — not Wiraraja — promises to give him Wijaya's wife whom he has adopted as a daughter; after repeatedly asking for the princess, the King of Tatar sends a letter to Wijaya saying he will join him in his fight against Jayakatwang so long as Wijaya promises to be friends, and in the end the Tatar king himself kills Jayakatwang in single combat. Wijaya, reunited with his wife, forgets everything and returns to Majapahit overjoyed; then remembering his friend the Tatar Khan who wants the beautiful princess, not submission, he invites him to Majapahit and throws a round of parties. Sri Laksemana parties with Wijaya who then gives him a gift of a beautiful virgin (but not his wife), and the Tatar Khan finally returns home in his ship with the woman of his dreams. A happy ending which appears in no other source, and a truly extraordinary refashioning of the entire story in a few pages.

The account as Raffles presents it is so different from all the other accounts, Chinese and Javanese, that it has been rightly rejected as a source for names, dates, places, chronology and description of events, but it is a concise and exact depiction of what those events meant to the Javanese: the proper union of king and queen brought about the reign of peace and justice, and everyone lived happily ever after. Whether Raffles was translating, mistranslating, summarizing or retelling is not stated in his book; in the text as it is most of the main elements of the other accounts appear, but in such a manner that the resulting narrative is far from the other accounts, and, most importantly, from the other versions of the *Panji Wijayakrama*. Yet even though it cannot be used for narrating the events to which it ostensibly refers, it is nonetheless fascinating to see the direction in which the story progressed over time. Is there a brighter, more splendid or more convivial account of the Mongols of the empire period anywhere in the world's literature?

Kidung Harsa-Wijaya

In 1931 Berg edited and published a transliteration and Dutch summary of what was at that time the only known manuscript of the *Kidung Harsa-*

Wijaya which he found in a private library in Singaraja in 1928. Robson (2000) mentions a second, more complete manuscript that was subsequently located and transliterated in the Bali Project. Whether the transliteration of that second manuscript is the one published in 1989 as *Alih aksara lontar Kidung Harsa Wijaya*, I have not been able to confirm, but the latter narrates the events occuring in only the first two of the six sections of Berg's version, and the Mongols do not appear at all (they are introduced in the 4th section of Berg's version).

The manuscript that Berg edited contained the date '65 which Berg (1931, p. 3) interpreted as 1765 Shaka (AD 1843), but Damais (1958, p. 73) argued must be interpreted as 1665 Shaka (AD 1743). On the authorship and date of the text Robson remarked:

> The text does not state who the author was or where he lived (as is usual in this kind of literature). However, Hooykaas did offer information from a Balinese source, the Babad sang Brahmana catur, which states that Nirartha's grandson Manuhaba had a wife from Tianyar, and their son Padanda Kekeran composed the lambang (poem) Harsa-Wijaya, suggesting as time around 1600, and as place Bali (Hooykaas, 1961: 388). Unless further data come to light, we must adhere to this.
>
> There is a colophon, stating that Berg's text was copied at a place called Ratnarasa (perhaps Panarukan according to van der Tuuk, 1897: 737), in Bali, on a date equivalent to 20 September 1743 (Damais, 1958: 73). It is possible that another date is embedded in the end of the text itself (6, 120a) in the words katigas srutirasa, which might yield 1326 Saka or A.D. 1404, but this is rather doubtful. (Robson 2000, pp. 243–44)

Although of little aid in determining the date of the text of the *Kidung Harsa-Wijaya*, there is a series of reliefs at Penanggungan site LXV illustrating a romantic scene from the story as found in the text. Although undated, A. de Vries Robbé (1987: 203) noted that they appear among many others from the 15th century and probably may be similarly dated, thus providing some support for the possible date of 1404 A.D. mentioned by Robson. Those reliefs have been discussed in detail and some of them reproduced in an essay by J. Terwen-de Loos (1971).

In the introduction to his edition of the kidung, Berg wrote "It is no surprise that legend has later taken possession of this perhaps most dramatic period in the early history of Java. It contains much that is unacceptable for the historian, although it does present the advantage that it shows the above events in their mutual relation, even though the Old Javanese poet often saw this relation differently from us. And with the exception of some stories that are somewhat strange for the Western reader, it provides quite a lot of valuable comparative material. (Berg, 1931, p. 1; English translation quoted from Robson, 2000, p. 245). We noted above Zoetmulder's characterization of the *Kidung Harsa-Wijaya* as being a freely "embroidered" version of the *Rangga Lawe*; the crucial issue for understanding the poem is whether the "embroidery" was really "free and easy" as Zoetmulder claims, or whether there is actually a definite meaning (or moral) being developed and made clear through historical illustration. Robson (1962 and 2000) pursued this question at length and his remarks will be discussed in more detail later on.

The work is far more a work about true kingship and karma than about history and chronology, and many of the variations which distinguish it from the other Javanese versions are easily accounted for as alterations to make the character of each king more in line with how a Javanese king should be and act. In these texts the religious motivations and foreknowledge of Kertanagara and Jayakatwang work consciously with the divinely foreordained future rule of Wijaya.

According to Schrieke (1957, v. 2, p. 11) "The *Kidung Harsa-Wijaya* contains the Kadiri version of the history of the fall of Krtanagara" while the *Kidung Panji Wijayakrama* presents the Madurese version of those events. With the inscription of Kudadu and the *Pararaton* offering the Majapahit version of these events, we have a wonderful chorus of complementary narratives describing the same actors and events. The Kediri origin of the *Kidung Harsa-Wijaya* would explain, at least in part, the different treatment accorded to Jayakatwang: he ascended into heaven rather than being killed.

This may also explain the presence of descriptions of Mongol slaughter and terror upon their arrival in Tuban, matters not mentioned in any other Javanese sources.

The *Kidung Harsa-Wijaya* and the *Kidung Panji Wijayakrama* contain the lengthiest descriptions of the Mongolian episode in Javanese history in any language. In Berg's edition of the *Kidung Harsa-Wijaya* the Mongols are mentioned after 80 pages recounting the reigns of Kertanagara and Jayakatwang (the text totals 130 pages) and the *Kidung Panji Wijayakrama* introduces the Mongols on the twenty second page of seventy.

Twentieth (and twenty first) century texts from Java

The modern Indonesian, Javanese and Sundanese texts which mention the Mongols in Java exist in a variety of genres: folklore, poetry and drama, popular histories and scholary treatises. Folklore related to the Mongol invasion constitutes an area of research that remains virtually unexplored. Myra Sidharta (2008) noted the connection in Javanese folklore between the Mongol soldiers and the introduction of tofu to Kediri, and Wilson mentioned references to Khubilai Khan's forces in discussions of the history of martial arts in Indonesia (Wilson, 2002, p. 32), but these are little more than isolated remarks. Zahari (1977) first published the genealogical legends of the origin of the Wolio people on the island of Buton, an ethnic group who trace their origins to Khubilai's general Gao Xing, and Yamaguchi (2003) contains not only a study of those texts but accounts elicited from residents of Buton in the late 1990s. The Wolio genealogy was apparently first written down by a ruler in the mid twentieth century and several versions are currently circulating. One narrative is that Dungu Ciangia (Gao Xing) with some of his soldiers settled on Buton with his local wife (or princess of Majapahit) rather than return to the Mongol court, and that his daughter Wa Kaa Kaa (frequently refered to as the grand-daughter of Khubilai Khaan) was appointed queen in 1335, becoming the first ruler of the Wolio. One may find numerous references to this Wolio genealogy on the Internet, including exhortations to see a (supposedly) original Mongolian soldier's outfit from the 1293 expedition on display in the Buton Museum. (See e.g., http://www.kaskus.us/showthread.php?t=1118554&page=2)

In contrast to the lack of research on current folklore, there has been a great deal of scholarly interest in the inscriptions and the early texts, and Indonesian scholarship offers a wide range of materials on 12th–13th century Southeast Asia (e.g. Yamin's seven volume *Tatanegara Madjapahit*) as well as a few specific discussions of the Mongolian campaign. The interest of the literary texts lies in the present: how they draw on both the indigenous and Chinese sources, and how they perpetuate much the same view of the Mongols as the old and middle Javanese writings, but have been written for very different purposes. It is still possible to find popular scholarly accounts of the founding of Majapahit and the Mongol invasion in which the Chinese version of the story is never mentioned and only the old Javanese sources utilized (e.g. the brief account on pp. 16–22 in Purwadi (2004)). The image of the Mongols in Javanese literature has always been and remains even now very different from the images presented in other national historiographies and literatures.

The three twentieth century literary texts discussed here are Kadir Tisna Sujana's *Babad Majapait*, the *Banjaran Singhasari*, and *Banjaran Majapahit*. The first text was the work of a Sundanese poet; the latter two texts were produced and published under government sponsorship. There are other texts which focus on Majapahit and mention the Mongol campaigns in passing or in detail (e.g. Wirawangsa's *Serat Ranggalawe*) but in the matters with which I am concerned, they differ little from the works discussed below. Komandoko's historical novel *Sanggrama Wijaya* is the most recent literary treatment of the period and it does not depart from the expected: Komandoko combines Meng Qi's conflict with Kertenagara to set the stage and Wiraraja's offer of some princesses of Singhasari to Khubilai; Wijaya's wives are not mentioned until after Wiraraja discusses the matter with the Mongol generals following the overthrow of Jayakatwang. That combination of the two traditions is the main tendency in 20th century interpretations of a rediscovered story.

Babad Majapait

This long Sundanese historical poem was first published in 1935. The first and second Sundanese editions (or printings) appeared in Batavia in 1935 and 1940, both issued by Bale Poestaka. The Sundanese text was reprinted in

1979 and an Indonesian translation was published in 1987. The first edition of 1935 I have been unable to obtain. The 1940 and 1979 Sundanese editions have no introductory matter. The Indonesian translation identifies the work as a *tembang* or recited style of poem, but says little else about it.

Information on the author Kadir Tisna Sujana (1912–1987) has been hard to find. The most reliable information concerning the author came from a Sundanese scholar who wrote the following:

> Kadir Tisna Sudjana — who was usually known as K.T.S. — was one of the well known postwar Sundanese poets. According to the *Kandjutkundang* (1963), a literary anthology edited by Ajip Rosidi and Rusman Sutiasumarga, K.T.S. was born in Subang, West Java, on 1 December 1912. He is the first Sundanese writer that wrote Sundanese poetry in the form of sajak bebas 'free verse' after World War II.
>
> When he was a teacher in West Java he wrote short stories, journalistic essays, guguyon 'anecdotes', and guguritan (a kind of old poem that is different from free verse) published in *Parahiangan*, a Sundanese periodical. He was also a correspondent of the Jakarta-based newspapers: *Pemandangan* and *Indonesia*. From 1946 to 1948 he was the chief editor of RRI Priangan Timur (the Radio of the Republic of Indonesia in Eastern Priangan). In 1960s he worked as an government official at Inspeksi Djawatan Kebudayaan Bandung (Bandung Inspectorate of Culture Bureau).
>
> The *Babad Madjapait*, which was written in the form of *dangding*, is one of the books that he published. The other one is *Raden Patah*. After World War II many of his works were issued in Sundanese periodicals, e.g. *Warga*, *Sunda*, *Panghegar*, and *Sipatahoenan*. (Hawe Setiawan, email to the author, 15 November 2010)

As a source for understanding Indonesian historiography in the 20th century and the processes of historification, his poem *Babad Majapait* offers much of interest.

K.T.S's choice of topic was probably due to the recent publication of the *kidungs*, as well as the great enthusiasm for Majapahit in the years leading up to Indonesian independence. It is also a good example of Nordholt's description of the *babad* as "history as weapon". Perhaps originally directed at the Dutch colonizers, it was reprinted in 1940, two years before the Japanese occupation of Indonesia. The parallel between Wiraraja bringing the Tatars to vanquish the usurper Jayakatwang, and the Japanese driving out the Dutch is easy to see, as is the necessity of defeating the Tatars/Japanese once the job has been done. Yet however effective it may have been as a weapon (and as poetry), it fails as a history from which other people in other places and other times might learn — at least in the judgement of a mongolist relying on the Indonesian translation.

The narrative of the events from Kertanagara's follies to the departure of the Mongols follows loosely that found in the *Pararaton* and the *Kidung Rangga Lawe*, but after beginning with a description of Kertanagara, Meng Qi appears, and his appearance is attributed to a trade war. For those interested in attitudes toward and perceptions of the Mongols, the work is interesting because of its descriptions of Khubilai and the Mongol soldiers: there are no "hordes", no "barbarians." Instead of Khubilai as king of the barbarians, he is the friend of the Regent of Madura, "One who knows the details, the necessities of soldiers and war," while Khubilai in his speech describes the king of Java — Kertanagara — as being ill-bred, audacious, arrogant and with barbaric speech. The Mongol soldiers are introduced as "rejoicing all the way through the Eastern Sea, neither afraid nor worried, of such character those soldiers!"; they arrived "not haphazardly, but following their military arts"; they battle "completely undaunted, straight forward" and their Javanese enemy soon "could not endure the enemy's never ending assault." Not the kind of description one finds in European tales of the Mongols! But all does not end well, and the Javanese route the Mongols after Wiraraja's deception, chasing them to the sea and killing so many that the sea turned red.

The *Babad Majapait* was the first retelling of the story of the Mongols in Java based on both the Javanese/Balinese and the Chinese versions. Previous discussions that drew on both traditions had made no attempt to reconcile the two versions in a single narrative. In his poem the incident concerning Meng Qi leaves Khubilai with a grudge, but it is not that incident that he uses as a reason for setting sail for Java, but Wiraraja's invitation which offered him a way to get revenge in the act of providing military assistance. The princesses retain their centrality in his narrative and his is the only narrative in either popular or scholarly treatments of the subject that presents the reader with the whole range of conflicting ideas about the events from Meng Qi to the departure of the Mongols and the meanings attached to the actors. It is a text to which I have returned with increased interest in light of Harris's (2004) discussion of the role of poets in historification and how later generations understand the past. KTS's poem contrasts sharply with many of the literary treatments written later, such as the *Banjaran Singhasari* and *Banjaran Majapahit*.

Banjaran Singhasari and Banjaran Majapahit

These two works, published in trilingual Javanese, Indonesian and English editions, were produced and performed in Indonesia to commemorate the 700th anniversary of the foundation of the Majapahit Empire, the first in 1992 and the second in 1993. They are interesting primarily for their combination of the *Yuan shi* account, the early Javanese accounts and modern scholarship, all of which are welded into an openly nationalist artistic program designed to foster unity through pride in a glorious and common but distant past. The language of the published text, the narrated sections and the section headings all point in the same direction. For example, in the *Banjaran Singhasari* the Mongols make their appearance in the performance on the eighth day which is entitled "Kertanegara's effort towards uniting the Indonesian Archipelago."

In the *Banjaran Singhasari* the Chinese merchants are flaunting the sovereignty and tax regulations established by Kertenagara and he for that reason closes the Malacca Strait; this displeases the king of China and the Tatar envoy Meng Qi (Meng Khi in the text) is sent to Java. Meng Qi is branded and sent back whereupon Khubilai launches a punitive expedition. Yet the authors of the *Banjaran Singhasari* offer an additional explanation for the events that follow, namely that "One of the noble families who disagreed with King Kertanegara for torturing the envoy was Banyak Wide, the Minister of Foreign Affairs." So in this modern interpretation, Wiraraja's request for Mongol assistance arises not only from his sense of having been personally wronged, but also his sense of injustice committed by his own sovereign against a representative of a foreign sovereign.

Wiraraja sends his message to Jayakatwang, but then his message to the King of Tatar (found in the ancient texts) is not mentioned. Instead, Wijaya himself learns that the Tatar soldiers are on the way and invites them to join him against Jayakatwang, Wiraraja having dropped out of the picture entirely. Together with the Tatar soldiers Wijaya defeats his enemy Jayakatwang, and the "glorious happy soldiers who won the battle, they are Tartar soldiers who drink palm wine until drunk, off their guard, not paying attention to the danger which will come." The Mongol soldiers (always called Tartars) are then attacked and defeated after which the victorious Javanese soldiers pay their respects to the Creator, while the wounded soldiers "are nursed in religious teachings to become the country's heroes." Economic rivalry, defiant merchants and Meng Qi all play their roles here, even though they were absent in the traditional Javanese accounts, while Wiraraja's role is reduced, and the princesses are nowhere to be found. The Mongols are also given a justifiable reason for their campaign, even though the Chinese merchants were the cause of Kertenagara's closing of the straits and the later branding of Meng Qi.

The published version of the *Banjaran Majapahit* begins with the story told in the Kudadu inscriptions, with references to the latest archaeological work in Trawulan. Wiraraja the brilliant spokesman manages to talk the Tatar soldiers from China into attacking Kediri instead of Singhasari and to do so with a combined Majapahit-Tatar force. After winning the battle together and celebrating, the Tatar soldiers are suddenly depicted as arrogant and indifferent. Whereas the Majapahit soldiers take care of the victims and the wounded, friend and enemy alike, the Tatar soldiers

Cheer happily
And ignore the wounded.
The arrogant Tartar soldiers
Laugh and cheer

While drinking palm wine
Until drunk.
Completely off their guard
They fight for beautiful ladies
Forcing them to make love.
(*Banjaran Majapahit*, p. 8)

Wijaya is astonished at the Tartar soldiers' behaviour and orders his troops to attack and scatter them, all of this being an invention nowhere found in any of the ancient texts, Chinese or Javanese. Wijaya's soldiers win their fight against the Tartars, the surviving soldiers return to China, and Wijaya the king is

Supported by his officers,
loved by the people.
Glowing brightly,
The Majapahit Kingdom,
Rises like the sun in the morning,
Shines over the world.
The cocks crow,
Singing beautifully.

All people,
And their leaders,
Make a firm decision:
To unite Nusantara,
Unity in Diversity.
(*Banjaran Majapahit*, p. 10)

The final phrase quoted above from the *Banjaran Majapahit* is taken from the 14th century poet of Majapahit, Mpu Tantalar and is the national motto; the early architects of Indonesian independence drew heavily on this period of Javanese history for their ideas and aspirations for the modern state. The fact that this native dynasty was brought into power in large measure due to Mongolian military might and that these victorious soldiers were subsequently beaten and driven out was and remains a source of pride because of the extent and renown of the Mongol empire: "A frequently cited example of the sophistication of pencak silat techniques was the defeat of Kublai Khan's forces by the army of the Singosari kingdom in 1291" (Wilson, 2002, p. 32).

There is a curious mixture of "Chinese" and "Tartar" in both these works: the country is always China, the merchants Chinese but the soldiers are Tartar, neither Chinese nor Mongol. The presence of a large Chinese population in Indonesia may have had some role in the choice of ethno- and toponyms here, but the adoption of the term "Tartar" rather than "Tatar" (as in the old Javanese texts) or Mongol must have been due to other factors unknown to the present author.

When reading the ancient texts the princesses are present from beginning to end and their importance is clear. In neither of these two works are the princesses mentioned; the only female presence is the warrior-sister of Wijaya, *dyah* Pamasi who in the last battle fights against the Mongols. The erasure of the traditional account of female participation in the succession of reigns is replaced by Wijaya's fighting sister *dyah* Pamasi, who appears in only one of the earlier texts discussed in the present work: the inscription of Kudadu.

These two texts radically alter the Javanese tradition by deriving the story from the offence against Meng Qi rather than the princesses. Whereas in the ancient state, the palace women were the bearers of royal authority, the necessary foundation of political life, in these texts the only woman receives orders, and instead of the men fighting for her freedom and her wishes it is she who fights for them.

Unlike the *Babad Majapait*, these texts present a striking confirmation of a past tendency: if the narrative begins with Meng Qi the princesses are irrelevant. The battle against the Mongols is no longer over Mongolian demands for the princesses because the princesses no longer have any connection to political life and the well being of the nation. A justification for turning against the Mongols is invented; it is a negative, prejudiced and racist development which is necessarily so because no positive portrayal could justify the betrayal: when the writing of history must serve as a weapon for political ends it inevitably becomes false and unjust. There is a difference between 'true stories' and 'false fantasies' and that difference is all too evident in the juxtaposition of these two *banjaran* with any of the ancient Javanese texts or the *Yuan shi*.

In the end the Mongols come out looking bad, but at least they are still there; the princesses have vanished, along with their importance to the land, the people and the government. The state is no longer founded on the presence, participation and love of women, but has become entirely a matter of power struggles, war, commerce and taxation. With these works of 1992–1993 we have entered the 20th century where women matter only when they do society's dirty work. What this may indicate about political life in Indonesia in the early 1990's I shall leave for more knowledgable persons to discuss.

Views from afar: western and modern Indonesian historiography

When Rashid al-Din wrote his *History of the world* he twice mentioned the Mongol campaign to Java. The first mention is brief: "As for the province of Java, one of the countries of India, he sent an army to take it by war." (Rashid al-Din, 1971, p. 272). When he returns to this event a few pages later, he does not realize that he is telling again the story of the Java campaign; his account is indecipherable to anyone unfamiliar with the event:

> Toward the end of the Qa'an's reign there was a rebellion in a province called Lukin on the sea-coast below the province of Sayan-Fu in Manzi. To quell the rebellion he sent, of the Mongol emirs, Yighmish and Tarkhan, of the Khitayan emirs, Suching, and of the Taziks, Ghulam Sam-Jing and 'Umar Yu-ching, the brother of Saiyid Ajall, at the head of an army. They defeated the rebels and plundered. (ibid., p. 299)

Why he gives two accounts, and what were the sources of each is unknown. His accounts were the first to be written but they are brief: there is little to be learned from either account as they include nothing not found in the Chinese and Javanese sources, and what he does offer is incorrect.

Marco Polo mentions Java but does not mention the events of 1292–1293: "It [i.e. Java] is under the dominion of one king only, nor do the inhabitants pay tribute to any other power. … That the great Khan has not brought the island under subjection to him, must be attributed to the length of the voyage and the dangers of the navigation." (Bk 3, ch. 6. translation of Komroff, 1930, p. 272). A few years later Friar Odoric visited both Java and the Yuan capitol between 1318 and 1330. He wrote "With this king of Java the great Khan of Cathay had many conflicts in war; whom the said king of Java has always overcome." ("Journal of Friar Odoric" in *Contemporaries of Marco Polo* edited by Manuel Komroff, 1989, p. 223) What conflicts Odoric was referring to is unclear: perhaps the one war of 1293 had 'multiplied' in one place or both.

Another traveller from the Middle East — Ibn Battuta — arrived a few years later and recorded a few tantalyzing notes which may relate to the Mongol campaign and perhaps even to the princesses, but his descriptions are too garbled: the names he gives of both people and places have still not been identified with certainty. For example, in his description of "Sumutra", there is an anecdote about a sultan whose daughter was loved by his nephew but given to another, after which the sultan went on a military campaign. While away on campaign, the "nephew rebelled against him and entered Sumutra which at the time was without walls. He laid claim to the kingdom. Some people swore allegiance to him; others refused. His uncle learnt of this and returned. His nephew took what possessions and treasure he could, and the girl he loved, and made for the country of the infidels in Mul Jawa [Java]." (Ibn Battuta, 1958–2000, v. 4, p. 880) This story, tantalyzingly as much like as unlike the tale of Kertanagara, Jayakatwang and Wijaya, begins in the wrong place but does end up in Java. In other comments, Ibn Battuta describes Java:

> Then we reached Mul Jawa, which is the country of infidels. It extends for two months' travel. It has aromatics, and good aloes of Qaqula and Qamara, both places being in the country. In the country of Sultan Al-Zahir, in al-Jawa, there are only incense, camphor, some cloves and some Indian aloes. The greatest quantity of these occur in Mul Jawa. (ibid., p. 880)

> We arrived at the port of Qaqula and found there an assemblage of
> junks prepared for piracy and to fight any junk which might oppose
> them, for a tax is imposed on each junk. (ibid., p. 882)

After leaving "Mul Jawa", which Ibn Battuta's editor, following Tibbetts,
identifies as the island of Java, he travels to a country called Tawalisi, a
country which has yet to be identified. Of Tawalisi he says "It is a spacious
country and its king is like the king of China. He has numerous junks with
which he fights the king of China until they sue for peace on conditions."
This statement, so similar to the comments of Marco Polo, could only refer
to Japan or Java; yet if Ibn Battuta was indeed writing of Majapahit, he fails
to elucidate any of the events which took place during the Mongol campaign
in Java: all the Mongol battles in Java were fought on land, not at sea.

After the compilation of the *Yuan shi* and the writers of the 14th century
— Marco Polo and Odoric, Rashid al-Din and Wassaf — centuries passed
before any of their remarks on Khubilai's Javanese expedition were noted
and commented upon in Europe. Gaubil's *Histoire de Gentchiscan et de
toute la dinastie des Mongous ses successeurs, conquérans de la Chine* (1739)
and Mailla's *Histoire générale de la Chine* (1777–1785) include translations
of the main Chinese accounts of the campaign, and these two publications
served as the basis of d'Ohsson and Howorth's works in the following
century. Gaubil does not say exactly what texts he translated, only "tirée de
l'histoire chinoise, et traduite par le R.P. Gaubil" on the title page. Gaubil's
text suggests that he used both the *Yuan shi* and the *Yu pi xu zi zhi tong jian
gang mu*, combining material from each in a single sentence.

> In the twelfth month of the year 1292 the flotilla was ready; it
> consisted of 1000 ships, including both attack vessels and others.
> There were 30,000 soldiers not counting the sailors, and provisions
> for a year. (Gaubil, p. 218)

Michaud and Michaud in their *Biographie universelle* (v. 16, p. 560) noted that
had Gaubil only utilized all the Chinese sources available in Paris at that
time, he could have written a book ten times as large, but nevertheless it
was a book of immense value as it was the only book which the scholar who

did not know Chinese could use to compare the Chinese accounts with the Persian and European sources. Michaud and Michaud also refer to Amiot's remark that Gaubil himself was displeased with the book, and had in his possession a copy covered with Gaubil's manuscript corrections.

Gaubil's selections, interpretations and translation errors influenced much of what was written for the next two centuries. Gaubil's account of Meng Qi offers an interesting interpretation that sets it apart from both Mailla and Groeneveldt's translations:

> The Chinese were indignant at seeing a great mandarin of their nation dishonored by a prince whom they considered a barbarian, and they urged Khubilai to take vengence. Khubilai raised a big uproar on account of the insult done to one of his envoys, and ordered the mobilization of a great number of warships and others in Chungchou in Fukien. ... The mandarins being interested, they were resolved to make those in foreign lands see that they felt the dishonor done to a minister of the Son of Heaven. (Gaubil, p. 218)

Gaubil also reinforced this interpretation of the reasons for the expedition to Java in his account of Khubilai's treatment of Shi-bi, Gao Xing and Ike Mese:

> However he eventually pardoned them, they being good officers, and the Chinese had accomplished what they set out to do, which was to make the King of Kouaoua and other nations see that despite being far away they were nevertheless powerful enough and resolved to avenge any offences committed against the Chinese. (Gaubil, pp. 219–20)

Gaubil identified the island of *Kouaoua* with Borneo on the basis of a map made "par ordre de l'Empereur *Cambi*" which he had seen in the palace, an error repeated in Joseph de Guignes' short description of the expedition in volume 3 of his *Histoire générale des Huns, des Turcs, des Mogols, et des autres Tartares occidentaux, &c avant et depuis Jésus-Christ jusqu'à présent...*(1756–1758).

In 1789 the fourteenth volume of the *Mémoires concernant l'histoire, les sciences, les arts, les moers, les usages, &c des Chinois par les missionaires de Pékin* appeared containing notes on the island of *Koua-oua* and an account of Khubilai's punitive expedition sent there. Amiot considered the events in *Koua-oua* (whereever that may have been) to have happened in 1287. A list of works published after Amiot's notes in which the Mongol campaign to Java is mentioned can be found in Brandes (1920, pp. 81–82). Of that literature, from Crawfurd in 1820 to Ferrand in 1919, I will mention a few significant moments.

D'Ohsson was the first — in 1834 — to argue that *Koua-oua* was the island of Java. Whereas Raffles apparently lacked familiarity with the *Yuan shi* or other Chinese accounts and did not recognize *Tatar* as referring to the Mongols, d'Ohsson infers from the description given in the *Yuan shi* that the island is Java, and buttresses his opinion with the remarks found in Rashid al-Din's history. D'Ohsson was himself apparently unaware of Raffles' publication: he bases his account entirely on the narratives in Mailla and Gaubil, and makes no reference to the Balinese version discussed by Raffles. In 1842 Walckenaer independently published an argument identifying Java as the island *Koua-oua* in the Chinese histories, and was the first to link the two traditions — Raffles' version of the Javanese account and the Chinese account — by drawing on information from Raffles, Mailla and Stanislas Julien. Howorth's *History of the Mongols* appeared the same year as Groeneveldt's initial article, in 1876. His account varies but little from D'Ohsson's and is based on the same sources, Mailla and Gaubil.

Groenveldt published four sections from the *Yuan shi* in 1876 with a note about Raffles' manuscript and comments on the events recorded. His longer article published in Batavia (now Jakarta) in 1880 includes a list of Chinese materials which include information on the Malay archipelago, among which there is a novelization of Khubilai's campaign to Java, but within his article the expedition is mentioned only in the chapters taken from the *Yuan shi* and very brief notes from Book 324 of the *Ming shi* and Ma Huan. Subsequent discussions of Khubilai's naval expedition to Java do exist, but from Groeneveldt's article of 1880 until Rossabi's *Khubilai Khan* of 1988, the amount of discussion among mongolists must be measured in sentences rather than pages, and general histories of China (e.g. the

Cambridge History of China) offer little more. The following paragraphs offer a quick review of some works on the empire period of Mongolian history published during the last few decades; the quotations show clearly the lack of interest in this particular episode.

In his *L'empire mongol (1re phase)* (Paris, 1941) Grousset mentions "ses tentatives en Indochine et dans les "îles" — Japon ou Insulinde" (p. 334) and nothing more. Otto Franke's *Geschichte des chinesischen Reiches* (1930–1952) has two pages in volume 4 and a few notes in volume 5, all of this based on the *Yuan shi*. E.D. Phillips' book '*The Mongols*" (New York, 1969) has six sentences: "...Kubilay sent an envoy to demand tribute from Java. He returned branded in the face. In 1293 an army of twenty thousand was sent from southern China in a thousand ships. One Javanese prince, Tuan Vijaya, submitted, but his rival in the west, Hajji Katang, had to be defeated. Then Vijaya ambushed the Mongols as they retired. They escaped with difficulty and there was no success in Java." (p. 108). J.J. Saunders' "*History of the Mongol Conquests*" (London, 1971) mentions the Java campaign in one sentence: "...an army under the command of Chinese generals was landed in 1292 in Java, but after taking the capital, the intruder's were expelled by the valour of Raden Vijaya, the hero and founder of the Hindu kingdom of Majapahit." (p. 123). In his essay on Yuan China "Die Yüan Dynastie" (p. 227 in Weiers, *Die Mongolen*, Darmstadt, 1986) Trauzettel writes only "Sogar bis nach Java entsandten die Mongolen Flottenexpeditionen, ebenfalls zweimal, 1281 und 1292/93." Laszlo Lorincz, relying on the *Yu pi xu zi zhi tong jian gang mu* , Gaubil or Mailla in his *Histoire de la Mongolie des origines à nos jours* (Budapest, 1984) states: "In order to complete the conquest of the continent, an expedition consisting of 30,000 men left for the island of Java in 1293. In the initial battles the Mongols were victorious, but did not accomplish their objective because the islanders' increasingly strong resistance forced them to leave." David Nicolle in *The Mongol Warlords: Genghis Khan, Kublai Khan, Hülegü, Tamerlane* (Poole, 1990) suggested that the expedition to Java was only "ostensibly" in response to the branding of Meng Qi; "in reality it probably had more to do with control of the rich spice trade of the Molucca islands, which both states coveted." Spuler's *The Mongols in History*, Benson's 1991 monograph *Mongol Campaigns in Asia* and the 1999 collection *The Mongol Empire & its Legacy* (edited by Amitai-Preiss and D.O. Morgan) make no mention of the Java campaign. Morgan's *The Mongols*, Kaluzynski's *Imperium mongolskie*, Bazylow, Roux, Percheron, Brent and Prawdin contain very little, nothing new and mostly nothing at all.

Military and naval historians of China have also passed over this incident with little or no comment. In *El poder naval chino desde sus orígenes hasta la caída de la Dinastía Ming* (Barcelona, 1965) authors José Din Ta-san and Francisco F. Olesa Muñido end their paragraph on the campaign with the comment: "After having conquered the kingdoms there, the Yuan forces began their return on the 24th of April and arrived in Chuan-chou sixty eight days later." No mention of any of the engagements there, neither the initial battles won, nor the final battle lost. More surprisingly, Hsiao's *The military establishment of the Yuan Dynasty* (Harvard, 1978) mentions the Java campaign only in a list of battle sites in Southeast Asia, and Jung-Pang Lo's "The emergence of China as a sea power during the late Sung and early Yüan periods" (1955) mentions the campaign only in passing remarks. Another brief discussion, again based on the *Yuan shi* with no mention of Javanese sources, appears on pp. 135–37 of the 1993 monograph *Zhongguo gu dai hai jun shi* by Zhang Tieniu and Gao Xiaoxing.

James Delgado's *Khubilai Khan's Lost Fleet* contains the most recent treatment of the topic by a naval historian, but it adds nothing to what may be found in Groeneveldt's article of 1875 and Delgado's other sources, listed in two footnotes: *The Cambridge History of Southeast Asia*, Stuart-Fox's *A Short History of China and Southeast Asia*, and Shaffer's *Maritime Southeast Asia to 1500*. He offers the same explanation for the campaign as we have seen before:

> Historians tend to see Khubilai's attacks on Japan, Champa, Dai Viet and Java as either attempts to assert his authority as the ruler of a new Mongol dynasty of the Chinese empire — the region's dominant cultural and economic and military power for over a millennium — or to show that he, like his grandfather, was capable of carrying the family banner into distant lands, spurred by his contested ascension as Grand Khan and murmurs of his unworthiness to

sit on that throne. While there may be elements of truth in both assertions, there is another, underlying motive, and that is control of trade routes and their revenues. (Delgado, 2008, p. 164)

The following three pages of Delgado's account largely repeats the story found in the *Yuan shi*, adapted to his viewpoint as a story-teller, accompanied by several familiar explanations. He writes of the economic riches of Java and of Zhao Rugua's complaint that the Javanese trade was draining the treasury and then states "So it comes as no surprise that following his conquest of the Song, Khubilai Khan would turn his attention to Java and send his navy there." (p. 165). Leaving the *Yuan shi* he offers a paragraph on the military exploits of Kertenagara and then claims "Kertanagara's success was too much for the Khan" (ibid.). Unlike his discussion of the invasions of Japan his narrative of the Java campaign is a dead narrative copied from what others have said: he asks no questions.

Of the relevant Chinese historiography, pre-20th century publications have been collected and translated by Groeneveldt, and he found very little. He comments on the sources used and published by Amiot and Schlegel, and remarks on the "cyclopedia" literature of China in the following passage:

> The texts translated by Amiot and Schlegel were both compositions of a Chinese official and seem to have been copied from some Chinese cyclopedia, with such abbreviations and embellishments of style, as were thought desirable by a man who knew very little or nothing about the subject.

> Now these cyclopedias, in their turn, have been composed in nearly the same way. Professing to embrace a certain range of subjects ... as a rule the author does not seem to have bestowed much research upon them. He just takes the Dynastic Histories and composes his account from the notices he finds there, abbreviating more or less, and frequently committing serious errors by fanciful corrections of what he does not understand; he throws together and mixes up the information of different times, which thereby loses its fixed dates

and with them much of its value. We have consulted the principal of these cyclopedias, without finding material for a single extract. (Groeneveldt, 1880, pp. iii–iv)

Numerous publications on the Yuan era have appeared in the last few decades and many are cited and discussed in Fang Jun's bibliographical essay "Yuan studies in China: 1980–1991". I have not undertaken a thorough survey of the Chinese language materials — ancient or modern — due to my linguistic limitations. The few recent titles which I have investigated were exactly like their European-American counterparts: a complete reliance on the *Yuan shi*, no mention of the Javanese materials, and very little commentary. Both the three volume *Menggu zu tong shi* (1991) and the *Menggu zu gu dai zhan zheng shi* (1992) each devote only two pages to the expedition. The two biographies of Khubilai which I checked (Zhou Liangxiao's *Hublie* (1986) and Li Penggui's *Hubilie* (1992)) have even less to say, and what is written is again based on the *Yuan shi*.

I have been able to locate only two brief discussions of these events by Mongolian historians. In his discussion of Mongolian relations with Southeast Asia in the 13th and 14th centuries, Ishzhamts (1993) discussed the embassies sent by Khubilai to Java and devoted a few lines to the campaign of 1292–1293, basing his account on Marco Polo and the *Yuan shi*. Earlier Chuluuny Dalai (1973, p. 27) had noted that important studies of Mongolian relations with and campaigns in Indonesia are scarce and among Mongolian historians there are none specializing in this area. He mentioned the embassies sent to Java (p. 82-83) and the military campaigns in Japan and Vietnam, but does not mention the expedition of 1292–1293. In the Russian edition of his book (Dalai, 1983) he mentions the expedition in a footnote: "In 1293 Java and other islands of Indonesia were subordinated to the Yuan Dynasty." The large history of Mongolia compiled jointly by the Soviet and Mongolian academies of sciences *История Монгольской Народной Республики* (Moscow, 3rd ed, 1983) contains no reference to the Java campaign, not even in the nine page long chronological table.

In all of the above, no use is made of any sources other than the *Yuan shi* and later literature based upon that work. The Java campaign was mentioned briefly in Bokshchanin's essay on the Mongols in Southeast Asia and in Shaub's study of the *Desawarnana*, both of which make use of the Javanese sources. There have also been a few Japanese publications in the 1950–1960's including the only book devoted entirely to Mongol-Javanese relations during the Yuan period: Niwa Tomosaburo's *Chugoku-Jaba koshoshi*. Both in this book and in a separate article devoted to the number of ships involved, Niwa based his account primarily on the *Yuan shi* and Fruin-Mees's *Geschiednis van Java* (1922), a work that appeared before either of the *kidungs* had been published. He also comments on the passage — the only passage — appearing in the *Desawarnana*. A 1969 essay by Nakata Kozo — "Gen no Jawa shinto" [The military expedition of the Mongols against Java] — discussed the historical value of the *Pararaton*; arguing for certain of Berg's hypotheses, he rejected its value as a historical source on most of the points he investigated. Yamaguchi (2003) offers a very brief account as background for his analysis of the Wolio genealogy, basing his discussion on Niwa's publications and Zahari (1977).

A number of relevant works on Indonesian history in several languages have appeared, but Rossabi's 1988 biography of Khubilai Khan contained the first reference to the Javanese-Indonesian historiographical traditions in a work devoted to Mongolian history. Subsequent publications on Mongolian history which discuss the Java campaign have not referred to this body of work at all. Since the early Jesuit writers in Beijing and the 19th century historians Howorth and d'Ohsson, interest in and contribution to the study of the Mongol expedition to Java exists almost entirely in the writings of philologists and historians interested in the literature and history of Java and the Malay Archipelago.

Raffles was the first to bring to the attention of western scholars the Javanese historical literature. During the British administration of the Malay Archipelago in the early 19th century, a number of manuscripts were taken from Balinese temples. Raffles visited Bali in 1815, and his *History of Java* contains a discussion of various Javanese historical traditions in chapter ten — "The history of Java from the earliest Traditions till the Establishment of Mahomedanism" — followed by "A different account of the first establishment of the *Majapáhit* empire". This version is found "in a manuscript recently obtained from *Báli*, which may deserve attention, in as far as it differs from the usually received opinion in Java." This account contains several paragraphs on the Mongols and is unique in ways discussed above; to my knowledge the original manuscript has never been published either in facsimile or transcription, unless he was summarizing in a very loose fashion the text published by Berg, since it appears to have been the only manuscript now extant that was produced prior to Raffles' sojourn in Java.

Curiously, Raffles failed to understand which country or people "Tatar" refered to, nor who the "King of Tátar, whose name and title was Sri Laksemána" was. He includes the following footnote: "The Javan traditions furnish no information respecting the locality of this state." In fact there is no indication that Raffles was aware that there had ever been a Mongol navy in Javanese waters for neither Khubilai Khan nor the Mongols appear in the text.

Groeneveldt combed through Chinese historical and literary records in search of information on the Malay Archipelago and published his translations in two articles in 1876 and 1880, the first of which was devoted exclusively to the Mongol expedition to Java. In the first article he notes that "no details about this important enterprise have ever been published; beyond the bare fact, little seems to be known about it." Apparently he was unaware of the accounts to be found in Gaubil and Mailla.

After Groeneveldt and the publication of the *Pararaton*, the historiography of the Mongolian campaign to Java ought to have taken a turn for the better, but Scheltema's early version of 1912 offers interpretation of the Chinese and Javanese version(s) that combine and confuse and interpolate in such a bold manner as to provide us with a wholly misleading account:

> The foundation of Mojopahit has been attributed to scions of several
> royal families, among them to Raden Tanduran, a prince of Pajajaran
> in West Java which, it will be remembered, owed its origin to princes
> of Tumapel. The most widely accepted reading is, however, that a
> certain Raden Wijaya, commander of the army of King Kertanegara,
> great-grandson of Ken Angrok, profiting from his master's quarrels

with Jaya Katong, ruler of Daha in those days, carved out a kingdom
for himself, reclaiming, always with that end in view, a large area
of wild land, Mojo Lengko or Mojo Lengu, near Tarik in Wirosobo,
the present Mojokerto. (Scheltema, 1912)

Scheltema's note about several versions of the origin of Majapahit suggests
that further study of Javanese texts (Balinese and Sundanese as well) may
turn up yet more variations on the Mongol campaign. Unfortunately,
Scheltema does not provide any further clues, and his account of the invasion
itself is not faithful to any of the known accounts. For example, the leader
of Khubilai's troops is said to have "indemnified his martial ardour by
entering the service of Raden Wijaya" (p. 112) after learning of the death of
Kertanagara. This interpretation is at odds with all of the known sources, as
are his statements later on that the price of Mongol military aid had been
stipulated by the Chinese and that the Emperor of China was "wroth that
the beautiful princesses of Tumapel, daughters of the late King Kertanegara,
whom he had deigned to accept as concubines, were not forthcoming"
(p. 112) and for that reason flogged the expedition leader. The *Yuan shi* says
nothing about either the request for princesses in exchange for military aid,
nor about Khubilai being interested in the princesses and punishing Shi-bi
for not bringing them back with him. On the contrary, the Javanese sources
say that the princesses were offered by Wiraraja to Khubilai in order to get
him to commit to sending an army to Java and they make no mention of
Shi-bi's punishment, while the Chinese sources state that Khubilai punished
Shi-bi for losing so many soldiers.

While there may be much other material of interest and value in
Scheltema's *Monumental Java*, his account of the Mongol campaign to
Java should be left unread. Why mention him at all if he should be left
unread? Unfortunately Scheltema's careless and superficial treatment of
the available narratives of the campaign is typical of many accounts; the
extensive writings by Berg are even further from the sources. Of less value
as history than literary treatments such as the *Kidung Ranga Lawe*, Berg's
writing, like Scheltema's account, lacks even the literary value that justifies
Kadir Tisna Sujana's *Babad Majapait*.

Berg and spiritual warfare

Berg was not interested in Khubilai; he was greatly interested in Kertanagara's response to Khubilai's military campaigns. His theories were discussed briefly above, and have had considerable impact on the study of Balinese and Javanese history and literature. The most unfortunate legacy of Berg is that many who encountered his theories ended up believing them rather than testing them. Creese comments:

> Even where Berg himself expressed caution, his tentative conclusions,
> and particularly his chronology, have passed into the realm of 'fact'
> in most discussions of the Balinese past. (Creese, p. 236)

While Creese does not feel that one may separate fact from fiction when dealing with Balinese *babad*, the facts in this case trouble her precisely because they are 'really' fictions — hypotheses — which have been taken for facts. Other recent writers (e.g. Nordholt) have been of the opinion that Berg's theories are not widely accepted; whether they are accepted by few or many, I find no justification for them in those aspects which touch upon the topic of this book.

In Bosch's 1956 article on Berg's theories, he undercut both of the principal supports of Berg's entire interpretation: the *Proto-Pararaton* thesis, and the notion of Kertanagara's consecration to Bhairawa-Buddha which supposedly is the basis and necessary condition for the political-military program Berg describes. The first thesis is remote from the Kertanagara-Khubilai feud and is of no concern here; the second thesis is dealt with by Bosch in philological fashion: the word *kadewamurttin* which Berg understands as "deification" and from which deification all else follows, Bosch renders as "status of deified ruler" on the grounds that the author of the *Desawarnana* commonly uses the word *dewamurtti* in reference to several rulers:

> In these cases it always means "incarnate form of the divinity". This
> is quite in agreement with the prevalent view which considered
> the ruler to be an incarnation or a partial incarnation of the god.

Kadewamurttin therefore means "the status of deified ruler". Once any reason has lapsed to give this word the special meaning which Berg wants to put in it, all traces of a consecration to Bhairawa-Buddha and of the proclamation of a political programme disappear from *Nagarakrtagama* 41:51. (Bosch, 1956, p. 20)

Another problem with Berg's interpretations is that he disregards the dates given in the ancient texts — histories and charters — whenever he needs to in order to suit his theory. His attitude toward all the charters in particular is revealed in the statement quoted by Bosch "Official documents have often been written in order to make the subjects believe what those in authority would like them to believe" (ibid., p. 21). While that may be true, that does not give the historian license to disregard all official dates and make up dates to fit his preferred chronology. As to the reliability of the dating of ancient Javanese texts in general, Bosch argued that the work of Damais has proven that the dates recorded not only in the charters but in the literary texts as well are "beyond all suspicion".

While his fast and loose play with words, etymologies, dates and spiritual powers seem to me to be unworthy of a historian and a philologist, his emphasis on the religious consciousness of both the kings and the peoples deserves more and different attention than it has received. Certainly canto 44 of the *Desawarnana* is wholly infused with a religious appreciation of the reign and demise of Kertanagara, as are cantos 42 and 43, and not a few scholars have concluded that Kertenagara's politics were infused with religious elements after reading such descriptions as the following from canto 43:

Of all the kings of olden times there was none as famous as this king:

He had mastered completely the sixfold strategy against enemies, was learned in the scriptures and expert in the works containing teaching on reality;

He was very virtuous, firm in his Buddhist observances and very energetic in the rites for application of magic;

Hence his descendants have one by one been supreme rulers and
god-kings (Robson's translation, p. 56)

This description suggested to Robson (1995, p. 121) that

> The strong position of Krtanagara's descendants, the rulers of
> Majapahit, is thus attributed to the spiritual power built up by him
> by means of his studies and observances. He must indeed have
> been a remarkable king (line 1); it is possible that he felt a need to
> establish Java's defences against approaching danger.

Robson's remarks, more careful than Berg's, demonstrate the kind of attention
that the religious dimensions of Mongolian-Javanese relations requires.

The larger issue at stake is the role of religious consciousness in
thought and action, an issue which 20th century scholars often have
difficulty comprehending because they regard all religion as an illusion, a
psychopathology, a disease of language, a reflection of social structures, a lie
invented by the ruling class and forced upon "the people", or any number
of other interpretations, all of which assume that religious life and religious
phenomena are to be explained in non-religious terms. If, on the contrary,
religious consciousness is assumed to have real and effective presence, if
religion is assumed to be as much a shaper of economic, political and social
realities as these latter are in turn shapers of religious life and belief, then
a great deal of our histories and our philosophies of history will have to
be rethought and rewritten.

Berg was not the first to look for political-religious connections during
Khubilai's reign, nor was he the last. In a 1997 paper Dabringhaus observed
that Tibetan Buddhist monks sought the favour of the Mongol khans, and
that "Tibet submitted without resistance and was spared destruction"
unlike many of her neighbors. This view suggests a much more likely
interpretation of Khubilai's acceptance of Tantric Buddhism and his relations
with Tibet than Berg's "deification" as prelude to expansionist efforts. For
the Tibetans, both the religion and the people are spared by becoming a
vassal of the Mongols; for Khubilai, there is no evidence that his interest in
religion was rooted in a need to justify his military exploits. Religious life
in the Yuan court was varied, open, and keenly observed by the Mongols,

but for their military campaigns the Mongolian rulers had neither needed nor sought justification beyond unity, security and just punishment of insubordination. In fact I shall argue in the next section that the religious ground was not produced after the fact as justification, and the campaigns arose from traditional Mongolian beliefs, not Buddhism. The relationship between Tibetan Buddhism and the Mongols which followed the submission of Tibet deepened and led to the establishment of Phagspa Lama as State Teacher under Khubilai. Dabringhaus regards Phagspa's theory of religion and state with himself representing religion and the Mongol khan as the representative of the state as being Phagspa's greatest accomplishment. "[I]n this way, Phagspa and the Mongolian ruler were symbolically placed on an equal footing." Thus far we have Tibet's political response to Mongol might — submission — and a religious response which reestablishes equality between the two powers, although on different "levels". But her next comments seem reductive: Tibetan Buddhism becomes a useful tool for "historical legitimation" (and nothing but?):

> For the Yuan emperors, Tibetan Buddhism was very useful as a highly developed religious system. As the state religion of the Yuan empire, it provided them with a historical legitimation, incorporating them into the genealogy of Buddhist universal rulers. (Dabringhaus, p. 121)

Religion may indeed be useful, but if this is taken to be an explanation of conversion, this removes "religion" from the picture entirely. We are left with propaganda, "useful" ideas, mystification, false consciousness, a purely political subterfuge, or self-serving alliances masquerading as "religion." If one begins with a theory of religion which sees it as always and only such masquerading, there can be no other outcome than to find just that. And in the end, Berg's theory must come to the same conclusion, for he also sees the religious interests and practices of both Khubilai and Kertanagara as thinly veiled grabs for power: religion becomes a weapon, like the writing of history does for Nordholt's Balinese. Whether Khubilai's and Kertanagara's religions were subordinated to political uses or were in fact attempts to obtain power or legitimacy is for Berg irrelevant: religion in essence is conceived by him as a political manoeuvre and can never be anything more.

If these two kings' religious actions were at bottom political actions, there remains the difficulty of explaining why they would imagine that religious ritual, tantric sex and drunken orgies would lead to political and military success. It is more likely that any king who sought to gain and wield political power in this fashion would never gain, much less wield, any power at all. If they indeed believed that the road to power was along the religious path, then that belief remains to be explained: personal political goals cannot explain such beliefs, for such beliefs necessarily precede any conscious goals. But to try to understand why they believed in magical-tantric-buddhist-religious rites and committed themselves to them, is to try to understand religion, not politics, and in that case we are back at the beginning: neither Berg nor Dabringhaus have been any help at all.

Underwriting Berg's interpretations of religion and history is his attitude towards 'texts'. A. Teeuw calls him "the first deconstructionist *avant la lettre*" and continues with a description of how he himself and many others respond to Berg's theories:

> Berg perplexes his colleagues, the present speaker included, by his form of textual criticism; we tend not to believe him with his emendations, we hardly dare to take him seriously; we are at our wits' end with his recent publications, as he, although nowhere giving evidence that he keeps up with the developments of literary theory, draws the most extreme consequences from Derrida's adage 'the reader writes the text'. (Teeuw, p. 219)

However one evaluates Berg's contribution to understanding the military and religious situation in 13th century east Asia, his greatest contribution will probably remain the transcription and publication of the kidungs *Rangga Lawe* and *Harsa Wijaya*.

Louis-Charles Damais and chronology

Damais wrote extensively on Javanese chronology and his principal contribution to the study of the Mongol invasion of Java was to settle many issues surrounding the early texts and inscriptions, especially the dates found in them and the nature of the calendrical system in general. A small part of his effort included the establishment of a chronology of the Mongol expedition to Java based on all the materials which have been discovered to date; no new material has appeared since his 1957 paper to alter his conclusions. Unfortunately, the complete report of his research on this particular problem appears never to have been published. (In a footnote to the published summary, Damais states that the complete text would appear in the *Bulletin de l'Ecole Française d'Extrême-Orient*; to my knowledge no article of similar title or content was ever published therein.)

I offer here a translation of the brief statement of the main lines of Damais' reconstruction of the chronology of the events surrounding the Mongol campaign in Jawa which he published as a two page abstract in the *Proceedings of the Twenty-Second Congress of Orientalists*:

> Kertanagara dies between the 18th of May and the 15 of June 1292;
>
> the 15th of October of the same year, Raden Wijaya submits to Jayakatwang;
>
> the Sino-Mongolian troops called Tatar in the Javanese texts land in Java a little before
>
> the 30th of March 1293 and find Raden Wijaya already in open rebellion against Jayakatwang;
>
> after various battles in which Raden Wijaya fights alongside the Chinese, Jayakatwang is forced to surrender on the 26th of April;
>
> the 26th of May, Raden Wijaya gets rid of his Chinese escort which he had separated from the main body of Khubilai's troops under false pretexts;
>
> the 31st of May, Khubilai's troops, in fear of the possibility of even greater disasters set sail for China where they arrive around the 8th of August, 1293.

It is evident that the foundation of Majapahit must be dated between the 15th of October 1292, the day Raden Wijaya came to the court of Jayakatwang and the 30th of March when the Chinese generals, having made contact with Raden Wijaya found him residing in Majapahit, which the Chinese texts mention by name. (Damais, 1957, volume II, *Communications*, pp. 322–23)

The brief chronological sketch presented in the abstract translated above does not cover the events surrounding Meng Qi, the decisions of Khubilai or the journey of the Mongol army by sea; the Chinese texts are the only sources for that chronology.

Stuart Robson on Legend and History

In Stuart Robson's 1962 BA honors thesis I discovered the most balanced and the most interesting discussion of the Mongol campaign to Java that has been written to date. Robson was primarily concerned with understanding the *Pararaton*, the *Kidung Panji-Wijayakrama* and the *Kidung Harsa-Wijaya* "in order to determine the part played in them by history and by other elements" and to "consider their possible historicity by comparison with" the inscription of Kudadu (1294) and the *Yuan shi*. He offered the following general conclusions:

> Whereas the inscription of Kudadu (Butak) and the *Yuan shih* represent something approaching the Western idea of historiography, the Javanese traditions are different. While they contain a historical framework and historical information these sources contain much material not classified as objective historical fact. (Robson, 1962, pp. 37–38)

Robson went on to suggest that the narrative concerning the struggles of Wijaya as they appear in the *Pararaton* "shows an interest in the dramatic which might be attributed to a story teller belonging to the people, noting Pigeaud's claim that "The author of the historical part of the *Pararaton* was a Shiwaite ... Javanese who was not in close contact with Royalty. He was interested not so much in dates and names as in events that could be dramatized" (Robson, 1962, p. 38, quoting Pigeaud). Of Prapanca, the Buddhist author of the *Desawarnana*, little is known other than that he was probably a member of the court and belonged to the literati, and that suggests an interest in "religion, good government, classical poetry" (ibid., p. 39). In contrast, the storyteller of the *Pararaton* was narrating the exploits and challenges of a hero, and for the Javanese folk poet this meant "fitting him into the stereotyped figure and role of a hero, that is to say, supplying him with the trappings of Panji" (ibid., p. 41). In that context, Wijaya's throwing mud in the face of Kebo Mundarang takes on a significance beyond mere mud slinging, and like the story of the coconut that had cooked rice in it when Wijaya opened it up, it is "a significant symbolisation of the fact that Wijaya was no ordinary man drinking ordinary coconut-milk but a hero on his way to triumphant victory. As a symbol... it is not objective fact, ... but a significant sign" (ibid., p. 43).

It is not necessary to pursue his arguments further here, since the reader will find in an appendix of this volume a revised version prepared after its author had spent fifty years studying the texts he first approached as an undergraduate.

Tan Ta Sen and the descendants of the Mongol army in Java

Another interesting discussion of the Mongol expedition to Java is also one of the most recent. It appears in Tan Ta Sen's 2009 monograph *Cheng Ho and Islam in Southeast Asia*. Tan is interested in the Muslim community in Java, in particular the Chinese Muslims, and it is this interest that leads him to look at the Mongol expedition to Java. Tan argues that the Chinese Muslims living in Java whom Ma Huan mentioned "would have been Muslims by birth through their Muslim fathers, many of whom were very likely the descendants of the Hui deserters of the Mongol imperial army" (Tan, p. 184). The argument that he develops is based on "the planning and implementation of the Mongols' military campaign in light of the composition of the invading Mongol army, the military plan and the outcome of the invasion" (ibid.). Tan assumes that the troops sent to Java consisted mainly of Han Chinese and Hui Muslims since "The elite Mongolian troops, being nomadic fighters, were not suitable to be sent to fight Java as they had to travel across the South China Sea. Any Mongolian soldiers among the invading army would likely be few and symbolic" (p. 185). Tan notes that Groeneveldt identified both Shi-bi and Ike Mese as Mongols and argues instead that they were both Muslims, the first Hui and the second Uighur. He further notes that Shi-bi mentions the killing of the two officers but says nothing of the 200 soldiers, while Gao Xing "reported that Vijaya had killed all the soldiers to support his correct assessment of Vijaya" (p. 186). He turns then to the Chinese text of the *Yuan shi*, notes the discrepancy between what it states and how Groeneveldt translated it, and then uses the account in Book 210 of the *Yuan shi* to "re-examine and re-interpret the outcome of the Vijaya case" (p. 186):

> Confronted with impending imperial punishment, the two commanders with vested interest, Shih-pi and Kau Hsing chose to tell an evasive and untruthful story on the outcome of the Vijaya case to their advantage for their own defence. (Tan, pp. 186–87)

Further support for his account of "the existence of remnant Mongol solders" (although Tan claims they were Chinese Muslims, not Mongols) he finds in a passage from Wang Dayuan:

> In the early Yuan period, the troops invaded Java. The fleet met with a storm at the foot of Gelam Hill, and boats were damaged…. As the hill is rich in timber, they then constructed more than eleven boats there… and departed. Over 100 men were too sick to leave and they were left behind in the hill. Now the Chinese live in the midst of the natives. (Wang Dayuan 1981, p. 248, translated by Tan on p. 187)

Looking at these texts with a question in mind that no one had previously asked of them allowed Tan to see problems that readers of Groeneveldt had been blind to for over a century, to see previously unconsidered possibilities, and to suggest new explanations. Different questions arise from different perspectives: that is the main axis round which my analysis has turned. Tan's book came as a complete surprise and a welcome addition to the literature on this episode in Mongolian, Chinese, Javanese and Muslim history. However, Tan relied on Chinese sources only, and as we have seen above, that leaves half the story untold. In the Javanese texts it is indeed Wijaya and his men who kill the officers, and who kill and capture the soldiers as described in the narrative of Part One above. The trouble with some questions, and perhaps with Tan's, is that they are asked in the hope of getting rid of counterevidence to the theory being proposed. Tan's question, and his critique of Groeneveldts' translation I welcome, but his answers and proposals are not as convincing as his question and critique. The fate of the Yuan soldiers — Mongol, Uighur, Han Chinese, Hui Muslim or whatever — who did not return from Java remains a matter to be investigated — and argued — further.

Morris Rossabi and the decline of an emperor

Rossabi's account of the Java campaign is the first detailed account to look at the expedition with a focus on and knowledge of the Mongol side of the story. Set in his biography of Khubilai he suggests more approaches and asks more questions than any previous account. Perhaps because the subject of his book is Khubilai, he does not pursue the story of the Javanese campaign in the Javanese sources themselves but relies on some general histories of South-East Asia and an essay by Berg. From these materials he takes the notions of Kertanagara's conversion to Tantric Buddhism, marital alliances and his reputed desire to control the spice trade. In his 1994 essay in the *Cambridge history of China*, volume 6, he notes his own difficulty in understanding the Javanese campaign ("It is even more difficult to justify the more renowned and spectacular campaigns against Java.") and Kertanagara's fear of having the spice trade taken over by the Mongols. With regard to Meng Qi, Rossabi simply claims that Khubilai had sent him in 1289 "to seek the submission of Java" and used the incident of his mistreatment as a "pretext to initiate a military expedition." If indeed Khubilai sent Meng Qi expressly for the purpose of getting the submission of Java, why refer to the incident of his mistreatment as a "pretext"? The response seems perfectly straightforward and in keeping with usual Mongol practice. There is no "pretext" here.

Rossabi also claimed that "He appears not to have learned his lesson from the failure of his naval expedition against Japan." The lesson is apparently "no naval campaigns"; Rossabi's assumption is that Khubilai should be "Once bitten, twice shy." Why not "Third time's a charm"?

The history that Rossabi describes differs markedly from that offered in Part I above and can be directly ascribed to his use of secondary sources (Hall, Berg, etc.) rather than the Javanese texts:

> Kertanagara, who had been apprised of this impending attack, had already dispatched a sizable military force to Champa and to the Malay Peninsula, where he assumed that the enemy would land first before heading toward Java. With the bulk of his army far distant from Java, he was peculiarly vulnerable to fellow Javanese whom he had not been able to pacify and bring under his flag. One of these leaders, Jayakatwang of the unpacified state of Kediri, did, in fact rebel against him, defeating his troops and killing Kertanagara himself. (Rossabi, 1988, p. 220)

Kertanagara's *Pamalayu* as a preemptory strike against Khubilai goes against the epigraphical evidence and rests upon the speculations of Berg; referring to Kediri as an unpacified state is reading too much into the texts, a reading Rossabi apparently did not make but borrowed from elsewhere. Rossabi's remarks on other matters are suggestive and fascinating for one familiar with the Javanese sources, yet he does not himself make any connections (and of course, there may be none). For example, we have noted the crucial issue of the princesses in the Javanese accounts and their absence in the *Yuan shi*. In his biography of Khubilai Rossabi begins his chapter "Decline of an Emperor" by noting how greatly he was affected by the death of Chabi in 1281 and his favorite son in 1286. Later on he continues:

> The death of Chabi, whom the emperor had prized more than any of his other wives, in 1281 left Khubilai wretched and alone. Her son Chen-chin had been named Crown Prince. She was the only one of Khubilai's wives to be accorded a memorial tablet in his temple. She had been an indispensable helpmate in the early years of his reign. It may be pure coincidence, but there is no doubt that after her

death Khubilai personally, and China as a whole, suffered a series
of drastic reversals. Perhaps Chabi could not have prevented these
calamities, but she might have served as a restraining influence on
some of the more outlandish decisions made during that period.
… Undoubtedly a partial explanation for the capricious decision-
making at the end of his reign lies in his despondency after her
death. (Rossabi, 1988, pp. 224–26)

Rossabi notices this personal matter but like the writer of the *Yuan shi*
connects it in no direct way to the Java campaign. Those who have read
the *Pararaton* or the *Kidung Panji Wijayakrama* must immediately sit up
and take notice. From the Javanese perspective, Khubilai might not have
bothered with Java at all had Chabi been still living in 1292 (for more on
Chabi, see Cleaves, 1979).

   Rossabi's discussion of the Java campaign in his biography of Khubilai
appears in the last chapter, in his portrait of Khubilai in decline. His
particular description of the Javanese campaign as an unmitigated disaster,
an inexplicable mistake by an emperor who has failed to learn his lessons,
his court floundering "from one reckless policy to another" with "Ill-
considered decision…the rule rather than the exception" may be more a
product of his understanding of Khubilai than an understanding of this
particular campaign. In one point of fact, he claims that Shi-bi lost 3000
men in his final battle with Wijaya, whereas the *Yuan shi* actually finishes
the account of the disaster and how many days they journeyed before
returning to China, and only then states that he had lost 3000 men, had
brought back goods, silver, etc. The number must refer to the soldiers who
died during the entire campaign, not just in the final battle with Wijaya.
Lombard, whose chronology differs from Rossabi's (Lombard follows the
chronology given in Damais' work), also provides a different evaluation of
the success of the Java campaign. Compare the following comments from
Rossabi's and Lombard's evaluations:

Thus, yet another costly expedition had resulted in failure.Though
the expenses incurred in the Java expedition were not as great as

the ones for the naval campaigns against Japan, the loss in prestige and the lack of any material gains were just as devastating. The Yüan forces did bring back with them incense ... and a letter in gold characters from Bali. But the value of these goods hardly compensated for the planning and expenses, both in supplies and manpower, of the expedition. (Rossabi, 1988, p. 220)

From this point of view [i.e. the amount of goods brought back, the needs of the treasury], it does not appear therefore that the expedition was a complete failure as historians have repeated ever since. (Lombard, p. 39)

Elsewhere Rossabi notes that Khubilai "sought to govern, not simply exploit" and that "his dream of unifying and administering the known world" was not a part of the vision or ambition of either his predecessors or successors. An approach to the Java campaign which seeks evidence of Khubilai's sense of responsibility, justice, the need for unity and the legitimacy of his rule not based on the circumstances of his accession to the throne but on his abilities as a ruler will produce a very different account of that expedition, in fact an account as different from the *Yuan shi*, the *kidungs* and Berg's as from Rossabi's. Rossabi glimpsed the most important element of Khubilai's reign, but chose to develop his portrait in the opposite direction. Sketches for an account based on "his dream of unifying and administering the known world" will be offered in the next section.

PART III

Meaning and Truth in Histories

No history of the Mongol Empire, no matter how erudite,
which dwells only on Mongol destruction can be satisfactory.
(Halperin, *Russia and the Golden Horde*, p. 25)

The most well-known accounts of the Mongols in central and western
Asia, Russia and Europe are laments and descriptions of terror on one
side, slaughter on the other; the Javanese accounts differ from this pattern,
but they are not the only ones to do so. Wassaf tells of a Shi'i group in a
southern Iraqi town (Hillah) who greeted the Mongols as those who would
destroy injustice, sending an embassy to Hülegü with a letter telling of an
old prophecy which they believed referred to the Mongols:

> When comes the group of horsemen which has no share, by God,
> you will surely be laid in ruins, oh mother of tyrants and abode of
> oppressors, oh source of tribulations — woe unto you, oh Baghdad,
> and unto your splendid palaces with their wings resembling the
> wings of peacocks, disintegrating like salt dissolves in water! There
> will come the Banu Qantura, preceded by a loud, neighing noise;
> they have faces like shields covered with leather, and trunks like
> the trunks of elephants, and there is no country they reach which
> they will not conquer, and no creature which they will not unsettle!
> (Wassaf, quoted in Pfeiffer, 2003)

Hülegü thought that this is how people ought to respond, and like the
Tibetans and others who submitted, the community of Hillah suffered no
harm under Mongol rule.

The Mongol invasions of Japan in 1274 and 1281 and the perceived threat of such an invasion both before and after the actual invasions gave rise to a unique response in Japan: a long-term concerted effort to withstand a future attack. As in Java, the Mongols did not succeed in making Japan a vassal; nor was there a great slaughter of Japanese soldiers and citizens. The Mongols lost their battles and lost badly. But the Japanese continued to fear and plan for future attacks, and this fear even after being twice victorious is the most noticeable feature of the Japanese texts referring to the Mongols. In this, they are strikingly different from the Javanese narratives.

Between history and literature in Java

The events in Java following the Mongol expedition may be the primary reason for the great differences between the accounts of the Java campaign and accounts of the other Mongol campaigns. The result of the campaign was that a great Javanese empire arose which was neither subject to Mongol domination nor to subsequent military threats, the beginning of a golden age which many subsequent chroniclers and poets have celebrated. That empire was established with the aid of the Mongol soldiers who, according to the various Javanese versions of the invasion, were invited to Java to destroy injustice and set the true king on the throne.

Not only do all the accounts of the Java campaign differ from those of other campaigns, but they present very different accounts of the same campaign. The army and state which the Mongol armies defeated in Java were subsequently incorporated into the kingdom of Majapahit, and — with the possible exception of the *Kidung Harsa-Wijaya* — the only extant Javanese accounts of the end of Singhasari were written by the court poets of Majapahit — the sons of the Golden Age — and Madura, not the poets of vanquished Kadiri: Jayakatwang's *Wukir polaman* has not survived. The Chinese and Persian accounts of the Javanese episode are written in apparent ignorance of all that was happening and later happened in Java; the war in Java could not have the same meaning in China and the Ilkhanate because the subsequent history of Java was both unknown and not their own.

Not all of the differences can be so easily explained, however, and there remain two different kinds of difficulties which an understanding of

Khubilai's Javanese campaign must face. The first kind of difficulty lies in judging and combining the different sources into a single account, while recognizing that this account is *another* account rather than *the* account. The second kind of difficulty arises when attempting to understand what the campaign meant for the Javanese, Chinese, and Mongols, how it revealed the mind, policies, internal and external goals, difficulties and assumptions of the Mongols in the last years of Khubilai on the one hand, and on the other hand how the same campaign apparently had other meanings in Java and thus produced histories different from those written in China.

The Chinese and Javanese accounts of the Mongol invasion of Java have enough in common to make it clear that they refer to the same events (unlike Rashid al-Din's and Ibn Battuta's accounts) yet they differ at so many points that one cannot "cut-and-paste" together a composite narrative. What unites these narratives is a common past — that elusive and oft despised matter of what really happened — and what separates them is the viewpoint from which that past was written, i.e. the uncommon (unshared) past. In her article "Majapahit: fakta atau fiksi" [Majapahit: fact or fiction] Edy Sedyawati commented on the difficulty of understanding these viewpoints, referring particularly to the texts which are discussed in this book:

> Our past writers were basically aware of whether they were documenting history or composing a fictional story. The aim of their fiction is usually clear: religious explication, moral education, demonstration of exemplary heroism, reflections on the contemporary situation of their lives. Besides that, it appears that it was always clear for them when the fiction they composed contained elements of history and when not. When there are historical elements, then it is also certain that they are colored or distorted by points of view, political, social and life perspectives. (Sedyawati, p. 35)

To refuse to relate these texts to the past and discuss them simply as texts will not do, since it matters whether the Mongols came to Java to punish Kertanagara for his crime against a Yuan official, or whether they came to assist Wijaya. Those two textually possible worlds are very different worlds indeed, in fact, as far apart as China and Java, where those separate histories held sway for centuries.

If these accounts are read together, using each version to question and inform the others, the reader must consider the view that the Mongols came to Java as a result of both Kertanagara's insult and Wiraraja's machinations. The presupposition that each account may complement and enrich the other by adding one particular side of the story makes it possible to construct a new narrative in which the two traditions do complement and enrich rather than contradict each other, this having become the most common manner of presenting this history since Berg's publication of the kidungs. There is no going back now to what really happened between 1289 and 1293 except through these two traditions and the various versions they present. We cannot always (or even often) choose a version of some particular episode and confidently say "That is what happened."

The Chinese account is sober and factual, as Groeneveldt noted; it is a chronology of names, dates and events. The expedition to Java happened but it meant nothing: it is described almost behavioristically by observers distant in space and time who made no evaluations, no judgments, and offered no interpretation. The events simply happened and for that reason they were recorded. The fate of this account in the subsequent historical and literary traditions of China is not surprising: as is glaringly evident in the *Ming shi* and later histories of China, the story is condensed, garbled or passed over. Neither Mongolian nor Chinese historians have pondered the story searching for its meanings. The story, when noted at all, is presented as a regrettable and forgettable incident of no interest and no consequence. The story died with its first writing: why repeat a meaningless tale of folly and defeat? But to know the meaning of the war a knowledge of what it led to, i.e. subsequent history, is necessary: the future determines the past when we set out to understand not just what happened — the Chinese version — but what it meant: only later generations could know that. And in China, later generations were not interested: they could grasp neither what it meant for the Javanese nor for the Mongols.

The Javanese traditions are vitally different from the Chinese. The arrival of the Mongols is always told in the midst of a narrative about one of the most momentous periods in Javanese history. Victory and defeat, fraternity in battle, alliance, courage, trust and betrayal: all these appear in both accounts, but in the Chinese account they appear out of nowhere and the Mongols leave a strange land never to return. The Javanese accounts present every event in the context of the trials and triumph of Wijaya, the perils of the princesses, and through these, all Java. What happened in Java meant nothing to the Chinese chroniclers; it meant the world to the Javanese writers, poets and even the kings themselves who also wrote of these events: Jayakatwang in his *Wukir polaman*, and Wijaya in the inscription of Kudadu. It is because the events in Java had such different meanings for the Chinese and the Javanese that the historiographical traditions differ.

We do not ask "Which tradition is true?" nor even "When is the Javanese tradition true and when is the Chinese true?" One can assume — as many have — that the *Yuan shi* records a fairly accurate account of those events about which the Mongol, Uighur, and Chinese officers were informed and aware. What the compilers of the *Yuan shi* failed to do — and could not have done — was to understand how these observed actions and events related to what was happening and would happen in Java. The Javanese poets on the other hand, were obviously unaware of much of what is recorded in the *Yuan shi*. Unlike the Chinese historians, the Javanese could not leave the narrative as nothing more than a succession of dates, names, battles, and numbers of the dead. The story they wished to tell could not be observed from the outside, by an outsider. The Javanese story is the story of ideals and attitudes, loyalties and loves, betrayals, rights and wrongs. That kind of history cannot be written by a positivist, cannot be written like an annual report from the Office of External Affairs.

The vitality of the story in Java, its survival in several versions through many centuries and resurgence in the last century, is due to the importance of what happened: "what really happened" (what Harris (2004) called the *res gestae*) and "what people said happened" (Harris's *historiae* and *opinio*), as well as what happened later; the relation between "what really happened" and "what people said happened" remaining forever uncertain. The reason that the story disappeared for centuries was undoubtedly because the story it told was incompatible with the religious world view adopted by most Javanese later, a conversion to Islam which began during the lifetime of Kertanagara. New histories were written and the Mongols were not in it. With the struggle for independence in the early 20th century, the Javanese victory over the Mongols during the period of the latter's greatest power and furthest extent reappeared in histories and literature and was immediately and thereafter understood as an important story for understanding the possibilities and desirability of Indonesian unity and independence from foreign domination: as in the time of Kertanagara and Wijaya, so in the 20th century. Another dimension, previously unknowable, was added to the tale by Kadir Tisna Sujana, and it was his poem that offered the first historical narrative drawing on both traditions. His story, not the historians' tales, became the dominant version in most of the popular and scholarly narratives produced ever since.

Because the story of Wijaya and the Mongols mattered — and Meng Qi did not — the Javanese tale was told and retold through the centuries in varying forms; prior to Groeneveldt always without the unfortunate envoy. The necessity of telling a story which would be both meaningful and understandable in the absence of the kinds of records, resources and methods which underwrite modern historiography offers a partial explanation for why the Javanese versions do not agree among themselves; the unavailability of the Chinese version meant that half of the story was necessarily left out of account. The story was fashioned each time from what was known in order to tell what was deemed important. It is this latter factor — what was deemed important — which is far more important for understanding the differences between the Javanese and Chinese versions.

The amount of comment on the founding of Majapahit — including the Mongol military involvement — is evidence of the fact that the meaning of this period in the Javanese past mattered and still matters greatly. The corresponding near total absence of comment in histories of China and the Mongols reflects the meaninglessness of this event for the historians of China and the Mongols. The lack of interest in this episode of Mongol history is due in part to the *Yuan shi*'s lack of any sense of the importance of this campaign *for Javanese history*. Lacking an awareness of the Javanese versions, relying entirely on the *Yuan shi* account, what more is there to say about a naval defeat so far from home when it is seen as ill-conceived and fruitless?

Roy Harris (2004) suggested that the greatest historian of England's history may well be Shakespeare, and that because he made history matter to his readers in ways that few professional historians ever distinguished between *res gestae* — what actually happened — the historians' versions of what happened — and *opinio*, or what people think happened. He argued that the historians' versions (*historiae*) are shaped by *opinio* as much as the reverse, and that both are dependent upon *opinio* — what people said and say happened — because that is all any of us have at our disposal. Once this is acknowledged, *historiae* and *opinio* both matter, both shape our historical orientations, and both are debatable. The kidung literature and Shakespeare's histories, whether the professional historians like it or not, shape our understanding of the past as well as the questions that we ask and how we read and write *historiae*. And as is clearly the case in works such as *Babad Majapait*, *Banjaran Singhasari* and *Banjaran Majapahit*, the future we desire determines the histories we write as much as the historical sources — whether *historiae* or *opinio* — from which we learn of our pasts.

Regardless of what versions of the story we draw upon, what can be learned from this campaign depends upon what questions are asked. If Khublai's expedition to Java should not be regarded as just a senseless disaster better left alone, what can one learn from it? Asking "Why Java?" again, this time with a knowledge of both extant traditions, brings us back to the larger questions which have been asked of the "eruption" of the Mongols in the 13th century: What set the Mongols in motion? How did they come to see themselves as world rulers? In what way may one refer to Mongol rule as a 'Pax Mongolica'? Was Meng Qi's mission and the various responses that it drew "all about power" or about the proper relation to authority, and what indeed is the relation between authority and power? For authority, we know, is not always the property of those in positions of power, no matter how much they may desire to have it, and no matter how hard they fight for it (her).

Why Java? Why anywhere at all?

The old Messianic faith of mankind told generation after generation that man was a citizen of one great commonwealth. The national warrior...was always a fighter for universal values as well. This paradox is an old paradox. It has always been creative. It has revolutionized and regenerated the race again and again, though the names of the forces have changed. (Rosenstock-Huessy, 1993 (1938), p. 24)

There are two kinds of explanations for the Mongolian romp across the steppes and mountains and over the seas: those which locate the cause in exterior matters (e.g. climate change, trade wars, threats to territorial integrity, population pressures), and those which locate the 'prime mover' within the mental or spiritual world of the Mongols (e.g. the idea of one world under one ruler, the idea of world domination, the ideal of universal peace and justice, Saunder's contention that "nomad aggression is at its maximum when set in motion partly by a powerful religious impulse"). What fits the Javanese campaign?

Climatic change, like the search for greener pastures, can be ruled out immediately — no climate change would drive the Mongols to Java once, never to return. Economic factors, trade and monetary policy, the interests of a growing commercial class were all a part of Khubilai's world of responsibilities from at least 1260. Promotion of trade and trade with Java both preceded and followed the Javanese expedition without any interruption. For these and other reasons noted above in the discussion of Meng Qi, it seems that the military campaign cannot be rooted solely in economic considerations.

Threatened frontiers? The political and military policies of Kertanagara which are given such weight in Berg's account, also seem unlikely causes for Mongol military response; the apparent failures of the missions of 1279 through 1286 to achieve their desired ends in Java — submission and royal hostages sent to Khanbaliq — did not lead to military action. The whole theory of a Khubilai-Kertanagara military buildup seems based on too much speculation and too little evidence.

Fletcher suggested that the practice of tanistry — rule of the fittest — and the need for the spoils of war to obtain and please followers meant that war was the cohesive element in ancient Turkic and Mongolian society. The Javanese and Mongolian military campaigns were therefore the result of this social imperative. In Fletcher's own words

Once united under a grand khan, the nation proceeded to external wars. Indeed protracted peace was impossible, because, without war, booty distributions would cease, and the tribes would cease to cohere with one another as a unified nation. … War was society's cohesive principle. War united. Peace permitted peoples to disintegrate. (Fletcher, 1979, p. 238)

As soon as he [the khan] had finished his struggle for the succession he immediately began to lead them in external wars so as to be able to continue his distributions of booty. This gave the tribes a reason to continue to follow him. External war increased his power and united his tribes. A wise ruler abhorred peace and was always on the lookout for a pretext for war… (Fletcher, 1979, p. 242)

Fletcher was referring to Turco-Mongolian monarchs in general, not Khubilai in particular, but he concludes his paper describing the end of tanistry in the Ottoman empire as being the result of the grand khan having become an emperor. Khubilai became emperor almost 30 years before Meng Qi's troubles; by Fletcher's reckoning could tanistry have continued while Khubilai was Emperor of China? Whatever may be the answer to that question, of greater importance is Fletcher's reference to booty distribution, unity and peace: Fletcher assumes power achieved through the distribution of war booty was the most important factor, wars to obtain booty required social unity, and peace was abhorred as the way to lose everything. This is exactly the opposite of the Mongol attitude, which from the time of Alan-qo'a on sought security and peace through unity, although, as Franke noted, ethical attitudes such as justice were absent, appearing only during the time of Khubilai.

The *Yuan shi* offers the mistreatment of an envoy as the sole justification for the Javanese expedition, the same reason often given elsewhere for other campaigns. Rossabi, apparently following Fletcher's theory, refers to this incident as the 'pretext' for the expedition. The *Yuan shi* also gives Khubilai's instructions to Ike Mese in his biography: "If you occupy that country, the other smaller states will submit from themselves, you have only to send envoys to receive their allegiance. When those countries are brought to obeyance..." This speech might be taken to support Rossabi's contention that the mistreatment of Meng Qi was merely a 'pretext'. But Khubilai's response to Meng Qi's mistreatment clearly fits into the well known pattern of the Mongol past: those who mistreated envoys were punished with severity. Were all these envoys pretexts? If not, why was the mistreatment or rejection of envoys such a decisive matter for the Mongols?

The envoys brought the decrees and demands of the ruling authority; the refusal to act according to the dictates of that authority was simultaneously the rejection of authority and the rule of law, and evidence of disunity, even civil war. According to Voegelin's interpretation, outlined in his paper "The Mongol orders of submission to European powers, 1245–1255,"

> When the power of the Empire spreads *de facto*, the *de jure* potential membership of foreign powers is transformed into a *de jure* actual membership in the Empire. ... The European powers to whom the orders of submission were addressed (the Pope, the King of France, and other Princes), cannot, according to the Mongol Imperial conception, be legal subjects of the same rank and dignity as the Khans. The position of a World-Emperor is exclusive. When the power of the Khan happens to enter into contact with the power of another Prince at any point, on any occasion, for the first time, there can ensue neither a state of peace *de jure*, including mutual recognition of territories and power, nor a *de jure* state of war. On occasion of its first contact with the Mongol Empire, a foreign power has to enter into a relation of submission to, and dependence from, the Mongols. If it does observe this rule it will later be an actual member of the Empire. If it does not obey, it becomes a rebel. The state of violent action which takes place in the second case is not a war but, speaking legally, a punitive expedition, being an act of enforcement of the Order of God. (Voegelin, pp. 404–05)

For Rosenstock-Huessy (1938), whenever humanity is seen as one, all wars must be seen as civil wars. For the Mongols, Heaven was one under the rule of Tenggri, and earth was one under the rule of the Khaan; all earthly wars were therefore civil wars, and since the Khaan derived his authority from Tenggri (Heaven), the rejection of the Khaan's authority was a war against Heaven as well.

Prior to the offence against Meng Qi, Java's position had always been vassalage to China, and in Khubilai's words "the imperial Government has formerly had intercourse with Java by envoys from both sides and has been in good harmony with it." Only after Kertanagara's assault upon Meng Qi was a punitive expedition necessary; the actual past had been and the desired future remained "good harmony." So long as trade was open, embassies came and went, Java was considered to be still in that relation of vassalage which it had maintained with China prior to the establishment of the Yuan dynasty. When the Mongol army came to Java it was not due to a program of imperialist expansion nor to the need for continual war suggested by Fletcher, but the just response of the rightful rulers against a breakaway province. We can be fairly certain that Kertanagara did not see the matter in those terms, but it is likely that Khubilai and the Mongols did. The actual offence was an external cause; what it meant and the particular response it called forth was determined by the Mongols' ideas and beliefs about authority, justice and the government of the world, the same ideas which governed their movements and actions elsewhere.

The Order of God and the disorders of men

The Mongols' religion, their relations with strangers and neighbors, their political ideals and social practices are well known; their sources, effects, evolution and influence on subsequent generations and neighboring peoples can be described and their meanings investigated. No doubt there is a fair share of psychology, mysticism and ideology to be investigated; the investigation itself need not be of the same nature.

There are several elements of the political beliefs and practices of the Mongols which combine in ways which are not unique to the Mongols but have appeared among other peoples. These beliefs are as much religious as political: unity, universality, law, justice, peace. The connection between the religious and political ideals and their realization in Mongolian relations with foreign states is treated at length by Voegelin in his comments on the "Order of God", which he argues is "the basic rule of all Mongol constitutional law." (Voegelin, p. 403):

> The formulas differ in the translation but the identical original meaning back of them seems to be clear:
>> In Heaven there is God, the One, Eternal, Immortal, Most High,
>> On Earth Genghis Khan is the only and supreme Lord.
> The "Order of God" is a curious combination of a legal principle of far-reaching consequences with an argument as to its metaphysical foundation. One intention of the Order is obviously to draw a parallel between the monarchical constitutions of Heaven and Earth. … The thesis that Genghis Khan is the only supreme Lord of the Earth may be considered as part of a dogmatic system explaining the true nature of government in the cosmos and may, therefore, be qualified as a judgment on an ontological subject. But since the cosmos, or at least the earthly part of it, is a world in the making, the formula proves to be a claim to rulership for Genghis Khan and to submission by all other earthly powers. The true essence of world government is not yet in an actual but only in a potential state, and it is bound to materialize itself in the course of history by turning the real world of political facts into a true picture of the ideal and essential state as visualized by the Order of God. By bringing down revealed essence to earth, incorporating essence into history, is the far-reaching comprehensive intention of the Order. It is brimming with dynamic energy and pregnant with visions of fanatical acts born of the desire to transform the world of man into a likeness of God's rule in Heaven. (Voegelin, p. 403)

This last phrase of Voegelin's unmistakeably connects the Mongols beliefs about their place and purpose on earth with the mission of Christ's Church and its doctrines of catholicity (one universal church) and its eschatology (the spiritual triumph of Christ and His Church's eventual establishment of the Kingdom of God on Earth at the End of Time). This connection was explicitly noted by Rachewiltz:

War against these nations was, therefore, morally and ideologically right and necessary, in exactly the same way as the thirteenth-century crusades against the heretics were right and necessary in the eyes of most contemporary Christians. (Rachewiltz, p. 25)

We know from the religious history of the Middle East that before the Mongols attempted by force of arms to enforce submission to the "Order of God", both the Church of Christ and the followers of Allah had made similar attempts to inaugurate the Kingdom of God on Earth through violence. And closer to our own day the Marxists have insisted that the reign of peace and justice must be forced upon the world through revolution, civil war and the elimination of all those who belong to the wrong social class. When the Mongol envoys came to announce the reign of Heaven's appointed ruler, they came with a conscience as clear as their sense of duty and desire for one world living under Heaven in peace. The peoples who received those envoys were unaware of the Mongols' divine right to rule and this fatal disagreement over who had the right to rule often led to actions by the Mongols which made it difficult for their new subjects to see peace — much less justice — reigning on earth. The description of the Romans which Tacitus recorded could well have been understood by many of those who resisted the Order of God: "They make a desolation and they call it peace." (quoted in Ruotsala, p. 23)

Saunders compared the nomadic conquests of the 7th century Arabs with the 13th century Mongols and concluded that the religious beliefs of these two peoples were the necessary condition for these two periods of conquest. The Muslim conquerors

were led and organized by townsmen like Abu Bakr and Omar, who were sincere believers and honestly thought that God had given their people the dominion of the world. (Saunders, p. 39)

As for the Mongols, he claimed that

The brilliant victories of Chingis convinced him and his people that global mastery was theirs, for Heaven must have decreed. Their task

was clearly to establish the reign of peace and justice throughout
the world: resistance to them was resistance to Heaven itself and
must be punished accordingly. It is impossible to doubt that this
unshakable faith was a source of enormous moral strength to the
Mongols. (Saunders, pp. 42–43)

In support of this interpretation Saunders referred to the story from Grigor
of Akanc' about the angel which appeared to Chinggis, and to the letter
from Guyuk to Pope Innocent IV. Grigor of Akanc' records the angel's visit
to Chinggis thus:

When they unexpectedly came to realize their position, being much
oppressed by their miserable and poor life, they invoked the aid
of God, the Creator of heaven and earth, and they made a great
covenant with him to abide by his commands.

An angel appeared to them by the command of God in the guise
of an eagle with golden feathers, and spoke in their own speech
and tongue to their chief, who was named Chinggis. The latter
went and stood before the angel in the guise of an eagle, at a
distance — the length of a bow shot. Then the eagle told them all
the commandments of God.

These are the precepts of God which he imposed on them, and
which they themselves call yasax. The first is: that ye love one
another; second, do not commit adultery; do not steal; do not bear
false witness; do not betray anyone. Respect the aged and poor. If
a transgressor of such be found among them, the lawbreakers are
to be put to death.

When the angel had imparted this, he named their chief Khayan,
whom they called Chinggis Khayan or Chinggis Khan. The angel
bade them rule over many countries and districts, and to multiply
without limit and in countless numbers, which also came to pass.
(Grigor of Akanc' , Blake and Frye's translation, pp. 289–91)

The 1246 letter from Guyuk to Pope Innocent IV explains why the Mongols
attacked Christian nations:

The Eternal Heaven has slain and annihilated these lands and peoples, because they have neither adhered to Chingis Khan nor to the Khagan, both of whom have been sent to make known Heaven's command. (quoted in Saunders, p. 44)

One need only replace "Chinggis Khan nor to the Khagan" with "the Pope nor to the Church" or "the Party nor to the Proletariat" to see how similar the Mongolian attitude was to those found in the political and religious history of Europe. The conclusion at which Saunders arrives is similar to Voegelin's:

The conviction that the Divine Sky was fighting for them and that they had a mission to unify mankind and bring peace and order to the world was one of the strongest forces urging the Mongols on to global conquest. (Saunders, p. 45)

The combination which Saunders describes as "The *idea* of world dominion and the *ideal* of universal peace and justice under their rule" has been clearly established for the ancient Turkic peoples (Turan, 1955) and the Mongols (Franke, 1978; Rachewiltz, 1973); it is similar to the Chinese "Mandate of Heaven"; it is present among the early Arab followers of Mohammad; and it appears as a constant tension in Christian Church history; one may even find it in the early American belief in "Manifest destiny."

The conflict which Voegelin found in the Mongol letters underlies 2000 years of tension in Church history, eschatological thought and millenial movements. From the apocalyptic visions of the Church triumphant of the first century onward, the perception of the necessity of truth's universality and its unity dramatically forces upon the believer the question of what is to be done. Thus, Solovyev wrote in 1883:

The Church, being universal and encompassing the whole world can be realized only through universal history. (Solovyev, 1953, p. 112)

According to the Apostles, all of humanity has its common task, a single common action — the realization of the Kingdom of God on earth. (ibid., p. 127)

The quest for the realization of the Kingdom of God on earth leads to exactly the same kinds of choices which have faced the Arabs, Turks, Mongols, Marxists and defenders of the Free World: the sources and limits of authority, the relations between different powers, and the use of force. In Church history these matters have given rise to positions of ecclesiastical authority claiming universality, doctrines of the supreme authority of the Church over political authorities, and the doctrine of *compelle intrare*. Solovyev notes how these doctrines led to the Church's defending its authority by force of arms: "The Church militant became the bellicose Church" where "All the traits characteristic of a higher order spiritual service are replaced by that of material domination." (p. 143) And finally, when the Church is understood as God's rule on earth

> the theocratic idea appears as a necessary consequence. ... If there exists on earth a particular power to which are given absolute rights from On High and to whom is promised extraordinary aid for directing and governing Christian humanity, then certainly all the other powers, all the other leaders of the world and all the forces of society must be subordinated to that sacred and divine authority. (ibid., p. 146)

A similar combination of ideas can be found in the literature of Majapahit. Not long after the composition of the *Desawarnana* in 1365, the poet Mpu Tantalar wrote his *Arjunawijaya*, "the story of a virtuous king, Arjunasahasrabahu, whom we might designate the World Maintainer, and his virtueless enemy Rawana, the World Destroyer." (Worsley, p. 168). In his essay on this poem Worsley notes that the macrocosmic setting of the battles depicted reflect the

> universality that was ascribed to the Javanese realm and of the absolutism of kingly power within it. The realm could not be divided nor could kingly power be shared. (Worsley, p. 169)

Later on he adds:

> Legitimate royal authority, in the moralizing view of the poem, is universal and therefore absolute. It is the natural attribute of a

royal couple, for it comes into being in the intimate embrace of a king and a queen. There can be but one centre of such authority in the world. ...royal authority in the view of the poem is indeed singular and therefore absolute. However, in order to prevail, such authority must be virtuous. (ibid., p. 180)

This royal authority must be one, absolute and virtuous, but there is yet another authority, priestly authority, and with the introduction of this religious authority we find the same situations we noted in Church history: priestly authority "seeks to excercise its authority in the world" and "it even threatens to intervene in the world to purge it once and for all of any royal authority which does not conform to this model." (ibid., p. 181)

Patocka, writing about the idea of Europe (as a unity) remarked

You hear about the integration of Europe: but is it possible to integrate something regarding some kind of geographical or purely political concept? This is a concept lying upon *spiritual* foundations. (Patocka, p. 179)

According to Patocka, the spiritual foundation of Europe, of the idea of Europe, was the "care of the soul." And beginning with the ancient Greeks, the proper manner of living, the concern of statecraft and government, the "care of the soul" was located not in the local and traditional but in the Good, universal and abstract. The manner of life and of government were no longer legitimized by tradition but sought in the not-yet-realized, in ideals and ideas existing in the mind of the philosopher and statesman.

Later messianic movements, especially those arising from the Judeo-Christian tradition, have all faced the same dilemma in their enactment and expression. Thus Marxism replaces the will of Tenggri (Heaven) with the equally divine will of History, preaching world revolution, one party rule or dictatorship of the proletariat, and in practice Lenin, Mao or Pol Pot resorted to willful violence exactly like Kertanagara, Khubilai and Louis XIV. One truth and one world order: the two ideas of universality and unity are always drawn together like boys and girls or magnets and metal. And they seek justification almost always in the promise of peace and justice on earth.

Peace and justice

When and with whom the phrase "Pax Mongolica" first appeared I do not know; the issue which that phrase indicates is one of the most interesting aspects of Mongolian history. The philological understanding of what 'tubsidke=peace' meant for the Mongols was the subject of an important essay by Sagaster. He asked

> What did the concept 'peace' (tubsidke) have for [the Mongols]? Was there an ethical component to its meaning, that it was the task of the rulers to bring peace and with that order and joy to mankind? Or was the meaning of 'tubsidke' not simply that a people by recognizing Mongol rule were brought into submission, compliant and thus made "level, smooth"? Did the Mongols understand their task, received from Heaven, as a universal Holy task, feeling themselves chosen as the worldly instrument of the highest God to establish an ideal order of peace and justice in a universal state? Or do we have a primitive conception arising here of a merely normal striving for power, with the conception that Heaven gave to the Mongol Khan the mandate to conquer the whole world…? (Sagaster, 1973, p. 224)

However the Mongols may have understood and combined the notions of peace and submission, whether or not their notions were advanced ethical ideas or some primitive urge towards power, "the fact is that the Mongolian conquests in Asia and Europe led towards world empire and towards a state in which security and order ruled, so that one could rightly speak of a 'pax mongolica'." (Sagaster, 1973, p. 225)

The connection between peace and submission is not a lexical idiosyncracy of the Mongolian language. Franke notes that Il-Khan, from Turkish, means 'peaceful sovereign'; it could also be interpreted as meaning 'subordinate to the Great Khan'. The two meanings are also united in the Arabic 'islam', and for the Christian the Lord's prayer is a prayer of submission to God ("Thy will be done"), and it is that submission alone which brings peace to the believer and establishes the Kingdom of God on earth. If the establishment of unity and universality bring in their wake peace, joy and order — the conclusion so often reached throughout the world — the possibility and desirability of 'submission' would immediately arise when peace and submission are thought and spoken in one and the same word. If we understand that for the Mongols from Chinggis Khan through Khubilai (but perhaps not after the latter), unity, universality, peace, joy, *and* submission were all inseparably fused in the will of Tenggri communicated to Chinggis Khan (by the angel according to Grigor of Akanc) we have the most fruitful means for understanding the mind and action of the Mongol people and their khaans.

Turning again to Patocka, we find that he argues that for the Greeks and Romans the ethical foundations of the state

> should be the ground of justice, this should be the state of philosophers... The Stoics really did educate mankind about the universal human tasks of a universal empire. And this empire again was destroyed. ... In the final analysis, it fell because, just like the Greek polis, it was not capable of convincing its public that it was a state of justice. (Patocka, pp. 88–89)

The Greeks and Romans, Patocka reminds us, "tried to bring the city of justice into reality", a city founded on absolute truth. This project, Europe, the Kingdom of God on earth, was something other than and more than the Greek and Roman empires. And Patocka describes what took place "before our very own eyes: *Europe has disappeared*, probably forever." (p. 89) This Europe, which for Patocka developed out of "the care of the soul", the true goal of statecraft and government, turned into something else, something in which lay the seeds of the destruction of Europe as the Kingdom of God on earth: "something that might be deemed a concern, or care about *dominating the world*." (p. 89) The perennial struggle wherever the idea of One World takes hold, is to distinguish and decide between recognizing the "solidarity of mankind" and "dominating the world." The Mongols either failed to distinguish or made the wrong decision.

The thought of the One and Universality tends toward certain conclusions, and all political action depends upon which conclusions are drawn. The political implications were clear in Mongke's letter: "the entire world, from the sun's rising to its setting, has become one in joy and peace." Yet the world did not "become one in joy and peace": why was that? The political actions which a desire for universality often prompt destroy the peace and justice which that universality is expected to bring about. The Solidarity of Mankind is replaced with the Subjection of Mankind. The problem seems to be in the manner in which universality is achieved: whether through the will and consent of the people, or through force and the exercise of power. "One nation under God" becomes one nation under a tyrant when the ruler is not God but tries to act as though he or she were. Universality may bring peace and justice, but when violently enforced by one man upon another, both peace and justice are replaced by their opposites. Politically, the Mongols chose the use of diplomacy followed by force if necessary; in ecclesiastical matters, the Mongols rejected force, and even adopted the religion of their subjects in later years. The religious responses of the Mongols and to the Mongols have been remembered differently than their political actions.

The Mongols did not pursue a path of religious unification; their rule remains one of the most religiously tolerant reigns in world history. Heavenly matters were left to Heaven, and however great an interest the Khaans took in matters of religion, however deeply their own religious beliefs were held, they limited their rule to political matters. The Mongols' own belief in the will of Tenggri, in their obligation and right to rule over the earth, to unite all peoples in a world of peace, order and joy was itself an expression of the inseparable unity of their religious and political thought and action. The separation of the political rule from religious rule in their relations with individuals was a different matter, an acknowledgement of the necessity and rightness of freedom for the existence of both peace and justice.

Unity and universality of authority bring peace and justice to humankind: this is the belief that appears over and over among the Arabs, the Turks, the Mongols, the Chinese, the Javanese, the Christians, the Marxists, the politicians of European Unity, the believers in Free Trade and the New World Order. That authority must be virtuous, otherwise the highest authority of all (Tenggri, God, History, the Hidden Hand, the Proletariat, the Party) will destroy it. (What is 'virtuous' will depend of course on the nature of the higher authority; the Hidden Hand asks for quite different virtues than the Party.) Whence does this belief arise? Have all these peoples taken such fundamental notions from the Chinese as has been asserted to be the case for the Mongols?

Sagaster demonstrated that the "one ruler in Heaven, one ruler on earth" doctrine can be found in all genres of Mongolian literature, from folk literature to historiography, and not just in religious texts, but Franke and Rachewiltz argue nonetheless that the Mongolian belief in "Heaven as king-maker" is an imported concept. Rachewiltz writes:

> This new function implies a whole conception of political unity and tribal organization which, as Barthold correctly says, under normal circumstances is quite alien to a nomadic people. Heaven-sanctioned kingship is a concept borrowed from a sedentary society. (Rachewiltz, p. 29)

For Rachewiltz, Chinggis Khaan, like the Turks, Jurchens and others before him, was influenced by the Chinese around him. He draws chiefly on the *Secret History* for his understanding of Chinggis Khan's own views, then proceeds to outline Chinggis' relations with and the teaching of two Chinese visitors to his court, Ye-lü Chu-cai and Chang-chun. He concludes that the Chinese at Chinggis' court and these two in particular were the chief architects of his political ideals.

I do not think that such a genesis can be sustained. The Chinese influence I do not question, just as it is clear that later on Khubilai listened to and followed other Chinese scholars, adding to the Mongol world a striving for justice. Even so, the origin of Mongol notions of unity and universality need not have been borrowed: these notions are far too widespread for every instance of their combination in political and social life to have their origin in China or some other sedentary society. Something else is at work in human minds and histories, and I prefer another origin, not only for the Mongols but for all appearances of this spiritual constellation: it follows directly from reflection on Oneness. One need not seek foreign influence to understand the political consequences of reflecting on social, political, ethnic, national or religious unity.

The Statesman as thinker

I begin with Patocka's remarks on ancient philosophers:

> The grand philosophers of the ancient world are first of all thinkers of *human practice*. (p. 195)

Patocka is referring specifically to Plato and Aristotle; may we not view Chinggis Khaan, the leader and lawgiver, in this manner also? He has often been recognized as a military genius and great leader, but his finest achievement seems to be acknowledged only by the Mongols themselves: he brought the Mongolian people into existence as a people, through political action, through the creation of law, through a vision of a people and their future.

In order to imagine Chinggis Khaan as an ancient philosopher, statesman and lawgiver rather than simply a primitive barbarian nomadic warrior, it is necessary to identify his thinking, and that we approach through Patocka's phrase "thinkers of *human practice*." Not an academic, not the professional thinker, but a man who understood well the political conditions with which he was faced, the needs of his people and acted for them as much as or even more than for himself. The *Secret History*, the law code of Chinggis — the *yasa* — and the biographical materials that exist are sufficient to make the case.

Whether the *yasa* of Chinggis Khaan was committed to writing or proclaimed and disseminated orally is irrelevant; the significance of that body of law was that it indicated the rule of decreed law rather than simply custom and tradition. The sources of that law were certainly tradition; what differs is that now the law is proclaimed from a person in an acknowledged institution of authority: the Khaan. Moses and Chinggis Khaan, different as they were, established law and authority in a living person and an office, and by means of that authority, unity was achieved. Even the operation of tanistry among the Mongols in subsequent quarrels over succession operated under the rule of the *yasa* and not in violation of it.

In his essay on the political ideas of Chinggis Khaan Rachewiltz mentions the story of the lesson Alan-qo'a taught her sons, a story that Chinggis must have known. But Rachewiltz mentions only the middle passage and is silent about the beginning and the end of the tale, the parts of the story which are most pertinent. The *Secret History* relates how Alan-qo'a

> sat all five boys down in a row. Then she gave them each an arrow, saying: 'Break it!'
> They all broke the arrows easily and tossed them aside. Then she took five arrows and bound them together. She gave the arrows to each boy in turn, saying: 'Break them!' But however hard they tried, the clutch of arrows would not break. ...
>
> 'Why do you whisper such nonsense?
> Why can you not understand?
> My sons are the children of Heaven
> born to be lords of the land.
> With the ranks of the black-haired, the hatless,
> these boys you try to compare,
> why do you not recognise them —
> my sons, who are lords of the air?'
>
> Then Alan-qo'a went on to instruct her five sons with the following words: 'You boys were all born of my flesh. If you stand alone you can easily be broken, just as those five arrowshafts were broken. But if you stand together, like this bundle of shafts, no one can ever overcome you.' (Onon, 1993, pp. 3–4)

I assume that the young Temujin knew this story and perhaps for that reason alone it has survived as an episode in the *Secret History*. In this story may be found those elements — unity and universality, "lords of the land" and "lords of the air" — which the human mind combines with momentous consequences.

There is another story in the *Secret History* which tells of the plan of Bodonchar, one of the sons of Alan-qo'a, to attack a group of neighboring people. He suggests the escapade with the saying "A body needs a head, and a cape needs a collar," after which he elaborates:

> Those people down by the Tunggelik stream, they have no high or low, good or bad, great or small, head or hoof. Everyone is equal. They are simple people. Why don't we plunder them? (ibid., p. 5)

One can draw at least two lessons from this tale: 1) people need a leader; 2) a people without a leader is easy to conquer. Chinggis Khaan undoubtedly learned both lessons, but the latter was more a warning to him and his people than a goad to foreign policy: Chinggis Khaan did not seek weak peoples without "head or hoof" when he sent his armies throughout the world.

These and other stories from the *Secret History* although telling of the time of Alan-qo'a (whether a historical or mythical person is irrelevant for assessing the influence of the stories) give evidence of the teachings, social values and conditions in Chinggis' youth. Chinggis, raised on the teaching of Alan-qo'a, acted on the possibilities which disclose themselves in reflections on unity, on five become one, on authority and weakness, and in so doing brought into being — made One — that people now called Mongol.

The desire for the Good and the will to become One

The relationships between the perception of wholes and unities and the Good, God, Peace, Truth on the one hand; and the relation between division, multiplicity, separation and evil on the other are the foundation of Buddhism, Marxism, politics and science. One is the only good number for the concept of number itself is simply that of pure separation: in the number 2 all numbers, all division, separation, isolation, strife, and infinite conflict are already present.

> In the highest place, in the mathematical world where there stand points, that is, numbers, there are *first principles*, and the first, most fundamental principle is the One. Everything that is, has to be one. Why? In order that something can *show itself* there has

to be something that can be captured, identified in and of itself (in our modern terms). Everything that is has to be one; that is the first precondition for something to be called existent. (Patocka, pp. 185–86)

The dream of One in unity and universality and its connection with political and religious history and the desire for peace and justice is an important theme in Rosenstock-Huessy's extraordinary book *Out of Revolution*, a history of revolutions in Europe. In an introductory section on the change from wars between nations to revolutions, he makes a series of remarks which cannot fail to strike those interested in the political ideas of the Mongols:

> To a mankind that recognizes the equality of man everywhere, every war becomes a civil war. (Rosenstock-Huessy, 1994, p. 20)

> By abolishing war, or changing it into civil war, the future revolution already presupposes the solidarity of mankind. As long as war was waged against unbelievers, pagans or Huns, civilized men could think of their foes as less than human. This is impossible now. Henceforth men are equals, and all wars are civil wars within one society. ... This mutual permeation and world-wide solidarity has been a long time in the making. (ibid., p. 24)

Chinggis grew up with the stories of Alan-qo'a, experienced separation from the tribe when Hö'elun and her children were abandoned, lived with the disunity and rivalry in a disfunctional family in a society without a Khaan. He would come eventually to dream of one people, one world, one khaan and to act on that vision of a world that could be. Why not stop at the Great Wall or the Tian Shan? Why were the letters of submission taken further and further west, east and south? The imagination of One, of the truth as one, of human unity, political unity and the universality of law and government, is sufficient motivation to pursue empire or the "solidarity of mankind", the two not being identical. The individual campaigns of the Mongols were the result of more immediate matters: envoys, rebellions, meetings, weather, even omens perhaps, but the general will and intention to pursue this kind of activity to the ends of the earth, this was due to the Mongols' ideas and beliefs about the way the world was and their place in it.

There may well be an even deeper movement which sends human beings on fantastic and impossible journeys, although it is not possible to regard it as the direct cause of individual campaigns such as the invasion of Java: the desire for the other, the impossibility of knowing oneself without encountering the world. This is the world the child faces, and perhaps the dying as well: it is the philosophical moment. When the Mongols were born, as a people, strong in their knowledge of the will of Heaven, perhaps they would have had to strike out in all directions, even without divine guarantees of military success. It would not be amiss to contemplate the similarities between the Mongolian movements of the late 12th and 13th centuries and the European era of discovery and exploration. Patocka's comments on Plato may be more relevant than the Song generals and the rulers of Central Asia:

> The soul is the only thing that brings itself into motion. Plato also conceives it as the source of all movement in the world. (Patocka, p. 127)

> [T]he movement of the human being is directed toward obtaining clarity about itself. It cannot obtain clarity in itself other than when it obtains clarity about all other things surrounding it. (ibid., p. 193)

The Mongols were making a cosmos out of chaos, Ruotsala claimed, drawing on the theories of Eliade. That cosmos was in the making under Chinggis, but clarity was not achieved, for clarity, like the Devil, is in the details. It was Chinggis' successor Khubilai perhaps more than any khaan before him, who was forced to obtain such clarity, clarity about himself and about the world around him. Khubilai was the inheritor not only of the teaching about unity and the experience of world conquest, but also of an empire which required administration. The actions of Chinggis which gave rise to the empire would not suffice for Khubilai: he was faced with the administration of justice in ways which Chinggis was not. To be a just ruler, to follow the will of Tenggri, Khubilai had to change the forms of administration to fit the demands of the newly existing empire while at the same time remaining conscious of the demands of universality and unity. His repeated efforts in Japan and Southeast Asia in spite of persistent setbacks and failures must be understood as a continuation of the movement which began with Chinggis' tribal unification of the Mongols. These campaigns were not, as Fletcher argued, constant wars to keep internal aggression directed outward, nor were they caused by climate, economy or any other reason: for Khubilai, they were civil wars. Meng Qi was in Java as an official representative of the ruler of the world by the authority of Heaven (as the soldiers on the ships affirmed when the spring burst forth on the sandbar in Ma Huan's account) and the offence committed against him could not be left unpunished.

These actions — the movement of the Mongols from Chinggis through Khubilai — were human actions, not simply the inexorable grinding of the laws of nature or history; they were meaningful — whether we judge them to be good or bad — because they were the fruit of the will and decisions of men. In fact, we can only judge them — as Grigor of Akanc, Juvaini and many other contemporaries did — if we assume these actions to have been meaningful and willed, whether that will is believed to be the will of the khaan as the Pope must have thought, or the will of God, as Grigor of Akanc believed. The Mongol khaans' decisions and actions were rooted in those beliefs in the value of unity and the universality of their rule. Patocka noted that for the ancient philosophers "the authentic manner of life, is the most proper ground on which moves their philosophy." (Patocka, p. 196) The question of the authentic manner of life was as pressing for Khubilai as it was for Chinggis. Chinggis' world was still the traditional world of the Mongol past, but reaching outward; Khubilai lived in the midst of a radically other world, driven inward as much as outward.

Again, Patocka's comments on action are suggestive:

What then is the principle of action? The principle of action is that which action seeks. What realizes action is what concerns it … [and that is] the good. Man is characterizable in that he goes after the good. Right away there is the paradox, that going after the good, we appear to others and often to ourselves as those who strive for evil. What is good for one is evil for the other. (Patocka, p. 198)

What Patocka is trying to do is "to analyze the very ground upon which human acting unfolds as the acting of a being that understands itself — even if in deficient modes." (Patocka, p. 213) And for Aristotle, Patocka reminds us, the "question about the ultimate goal" belongs to "the art of statecraft, the art of ruling the community." (Patocka, p. 201) The Mongol empire split into several empires, all of which eventually lost their Mongolian character and fell to other empires. As the *Yuan shi* remarks, the Mongols could conquer an empire on horseback but they could not rule it in similar fashion. Masters of the military arts, they were unable to master the art of statecraft on a worldwide scale: they needed smaller nations. Attention to local administration, the need for it, exhausted the Mongols' political skills and institutions; the turn inward spelled the end of universality as a practical ideal. But much was surely learned, since the four khanates survived politically long after the death of Khubilai, the last Great Khaan. Ruotsala and others have noted that the empire could "not have lasted so long without some order, justice, and acceptance of different religions." (Ruotsala, p. 23)

Freedom through submission: authority and the rule of law

While the *yasa* gives evidence of the rule of law among the Mongols themselves, the envoys sent to foreign nations and the texts of the messages which they took abroad, from Java to Rome, offer the strongest evidence of the submission to legal authority which gave to Mongol society its singular characteristics. The envoys were sent everywhere to bring the world under one authority and one law; the Mongols sought not merely conquest and booty but more importantly that all peoples should be united under a single authority and recognize the rule of law established by that authority. Only if that authority was rejected could a war begin. And it would be a civil war, not a war of conquest. There were certainly demands and taxes upon persons and goods, but this was only to support the empire; the empire itself, the earthly authority corresponding to the heavenly, the rule of law and unity of all peoples, this was the purpose of the envoys and wars, not merely booty.

The Javanese campaign demonstrates clearly the importance of authority and obedience to that authority among the Mongols of the 13th century. From the mission of Meng Qi to the punishment of Shi-bi, what mattered at every moment was the recognition of authority — of the Khaan or of Tenggri — and obedience to the will of that authority. Authority is everywhere present in the Mongol Empire: the authority of office, of birth, of the *yasa*, of the official envoys and representatives of the Khaan including his seal, personal and spiritual authority of shamans, lamas, and leaders native and foreign. A man in a position of authority must act, everyone demands that he act, and how he acts in every official act matters; the consequences may be life and death for individuals or whole nations. With the death of his father Temujin was thrust into a position of responsibility and authority. Khubilai, born to authority as a prince, found himself occupying one of the positions of greatest responsibility and authority in the world: Khaan of the Mongols, Emperor of China. Two different worlds, two responsibilities to two peoples historically at odds, two empires each claiming to be center and lord of the whole earth; these he had to unite in his person, in his office as Khaan/Emperor.

Khubilai's military campaigns, however many the reasons for them, are understandable only when regarded as arising from his sense of office, his understanding of who he was as ruler of the world, his efforts to fulfill his office; they were the expression of his desire to be the Khaan that he was supposed to be. Interest and effort in the arts of statecraft are evident in his seeking religious men and scholars for teaching, debates and discussions from his youth. Schlegel remarks on one such meeting with the scholar Hao Jing:

> In 1253 Khubilai, at that time still the crown prince, heard that Hao Ching was visiting Chang Jou and that he was very learned. He asked him to come to see him and speak on the right way to govern.

Ching respectfully answered his questions, while he commented on
the ideals of humanity and lawfulness and clearly set forth the evils
of the age. Khubilai Khan was so impressed by his words that he
asked him to write them down. From that time on Ching remained
at the prince's residence as a guest of honour and his advice was
often sought. (Schlegel, 1968, pp. 60–61)

In his book on the United States Supreme Court, Vining asked how it is
that "the focus that a single center brings may possibly be associated with
freedom" (p. 89). The profound, inextricable, often troubling and scarcely
understood connections between authority and freedom are at the very
heart of the experience of the Mongol Empire, both for the Mongols and
for the peoples of the conquered territories. Although the comments here
focus on political issues, the context is much broader.

However, suppose that there is a social contract: then there is also
a natural one, older and more genuine, and the conditions of the
natural contract must be the basis of the social one. Through it all
natural property becomes conventional again, and man in the state
of nature becomes dependent on its laws, i.e., positively obliged
to act in accordance with the very same laws which all of nature
and especially the nature of man has to thank for the preservation
of existence and the use of all means and goods contributing to it.
Since man bears duties to nature, he accordingly has least of all an
exclusive right to and hateful monopoly over his abilities, neither to
the products thereof, nor to the sterile mule of his industry and the
sadder bastards of his usurping acts of violence over the creature
made subject, against its will, to his vanity. (Hamann, 2007 [1784],
pp. 173–74)

None can use a language freely and powerfully without acknowledging the
forms of past linguistic experience and the present expectations of those
from whom the particular language has been learned and with whom one
is communicating; games are both possible and exciting because the players

accept and submit themselves to the rules; refusal to respect (submit to) the laws of nature or the body leads to disaster, sickness and death: fire burns, what goes up must come down. Such connections are everywhere. No society, no people has ever lived who did not acknowledge the reality, the authority of the world which exists and persists regardless of our wishes.

> Should everyone intend to set up his unphilosophical Me as the royal umpire in cases of collision, neither a state of nature nor a state of society is possible. ... all social contracts derive, according to the law of nature, from the moral capacity to say Yes! or No!, and from the moral necessity to make good the word that has been given. (Hamann, 2007 [1784], p. 175)

We acknowledge the existence of the world into which we are born as an authority, whether a deity, religious order, custom and tradition, personal ruler, father, the Party, "the will of the People", or the law of the land. "All societies," linguist Christopher Hutton argued,

> have rules laid down to guide human behaviour, texts or precepts (both oral and written) that have authority over human conduct and regulate human affairs, and specialised forms of linguistic usage that bind those who fall within its domain, as well as authority figures who interpret rules and precepts and mediate in disputes. (Hutton, 2009, p. 62)

Submission to those authorities and the societies they sustain sometimes lead us to the Land of the Free and sometimes to the Gulag; to whom, when, why and in what manner we consent to existing authority is a critical choice for the individual, the unpredictable meaning of all political action.

A world without authors cannot be read; a world without authority cannot be perpetuated for neither the one nor the other can be taught or learned. The rejection of authority, like the rejection of the author, is equivalent to the rejection of the past, the world which exists whether we want it to or not; rejection of the past is rejection of the necessary condition of learning: experience itself.

> Well, if you didn't know any of the past, you literally wouldn't know anything. You'd have no language, no history, and so the first result would be a kind of personal incompleteness. (Wendell Berry, in an interview Jordan Fisher-Smith)

A world without authority, without authors who mean what they say, without an order of things is in fact unintelligible and unknowable, knowledge itself being nothing other than a putting of the world into an order or an acceptance of some such ordering. A being in a disordered world could not know itself, and an observer could never understand but merely describe events from the outside, somewhat like the Chinese historians of the Mongol expedition to Java. Yet authority exists for us only in our recognition of it as authority, and that is where politics — and war — begins.

> Our society imposes itself on the individuals that constitute it by making its truth the authority. And as always, personal conscience must begin not by refusing the truth but by refusing to submit to the truth instead of loving it. For it is the yes without the no that distinguishes the true from the believed. Every free human acceptance implies the possibility of refusal. (Charbonneau, 1991, p. 263)

The question for human beings and societies is thus not "yes or no" to any and all authority, but how, when and what kind of authority: the nature of the ruler, the nature of the laws, and the nature of one's relationship to the authorities — they are invariably multiple. We submit to the laws of nature while striving to master them in much the same way as we accept the laws of our society while demanding that they change. And one of the eternal difficulties for human beings in the face of authority is acceptance and submission: when ought we to accept something as right and good, or submit to it as simply necessary or unavoidable, and when does freedom demand defiance and rebellion? We are born in submission and raised to rebellion; our children teach us what our pasts never do: that we have failed to live in such a manner that "the entire world, from the sun's rising to its setting, has become one in joy and peace."

For the Javanese, like all peoples who found an envoy of the great Khaan at their gates, the question of which authority and how to respond was a matter with momentous consequences. For Kertanagara, neither Meng Qi nor Khubilai had authority. Authority in Java was understood and embodied differently.

Love's story: the meeting of love and justice

Why were the princesses so important in Java? Why are they absent from both the Chinese accounts and Wijaya's own account of his war with Jayakatwang and subsequent exile?

The nature of authority and kingship in Java centered on the couple — king and queen — not simply on the king. Thus Worsley noted that in the *Arjunawijaya* one finds "the association of political authority with the tender intimacy of king and queen," legitimate royal authority "comes into being in the intimate embrace of a king and a queen" and "the queen embodied the king's royal authority (rajalaksmi) and the king's marriage to the queen ensured him legitimate possession of the authority he required to rule." (Worsley, p. 180-181) Only the king who loved and was loved had authority and could receive the willing submission of the people. The tale of the true king had to be a love story and the story of the false kings had to be tales of rejection: whomever the princesses chose was the true king and whomever they rejected had no authority. Thus the elder princess escaped with Wijaya and the younger princess threatened to kill herself if Jayakatwang tried to touch her. Wiraraja's offer of the princesses would have been treason had it not been presented as a trap for the Mongols. (I suspect it was treason but turned out otherwise than he had expected.)

The false king is without the love of a queen and this absence predicts and explains his grasping, violent ways. The queen calls forth the king's love and strength and diverts both to the care and protection of the country and people. It is not the king's possession of a woman which provides his legitimacy, but rather their mutual love: this is a crucial matter for understanding the beliefs about and therefore the nature of political authority in the time of Majapahit. True authority rested in the lovers and their attention to the needs of the country.

For the lovers, submission to love brings peace, justice, order and joy. When king and queen thus submit, that peace and justice, order and joy become the experience of the people as well. The people submit not so much to king and queen, but to the love they realize and embody on earth. True authority belongs to love, and to that authority — the highest authority — rulers and ruled alike should bow in submission. For the Javanese, the story of the mutual love of Wijaya and the princesses of Tumapel explains the splendor and blessedness of the Majapahit era: it was a reign ruled by love.

Comparing the Javanese and Chinese traditions, we can see that what the envoys were for the Mongols, the princesses were for the Javanese: they embodied royal authority. From these two origins the two traditions proceed. Just as the envoy Meng Qi was necessary for the narrative in the Chinese sources but unnecessary for — and absent from — the Javanese versions, so the princesses were necessary for the Javanese versions and absent from the Chinese histories. The envoys were the bearers of royal authority among the Mongols, but in the Javanese stories the messengers are always the bearers of deception, intrigue and treason. Both versions are about the right to rule Java; for the Mongols that was a matter of their unquestioned right to rule over the world, to expect submission and an appropriate response to Meng Qi. For the Javanese, Meng Qi had no authority at all and everything depended on the loves and fates of the princesses: if Khubilai wished to rule Java then he needed the love of the princesses.

One may understand both "what really happened" and "what people said happened" as being not about love at all but that the 'real' story in all its versions is about nothing but the changing faces of power: the princesses are "loved" because they are necessary for Jayakatwang and Wijaya in their bids for power and authority; Khubilai is in Java for no other reason than to extend his dominance and power over the entire earth; Wiraraja's betrayals and allegiances are simply the shrewd positioning of one who hopes to defeat all of his enemies one at a time. And there is no denying that kings went to war, fought over kingdoms, women, hostages or all of the above, kingdoms rose and fell, and royal marriages were made. But to interpret the Javanese narratives as having as their 'real' meaning the changing relationships of power is equivalent to Krom's "all the rest is romance" — except without the romance.

Helen Creese (2000) presented an extended argument, based in large part on the same kidungs that I have discussed, that the women in these texts are simply pawns in the men's game of politics:

> Thematically, kidung pay a great deal of attention to the intricacies of dynastic politics and the efforts of male rulers to ensure military superiority over rival claimants and neighboring vassals. Within this major theme women play a central role. Women are pivotal to the action played out in the wars and battles, for they are the pawns in the forging and severing of alliances, the underlying motivation of men who go to war and the ultimate prizes for sucessful heroes. (Creese, 2000, p. 129).

Creese assumed that "stark political motives are hidden behind fine sentiment and poetic language" and never approaches the texts as symbolic discourses but only as "idealized characters and situations" that offer the reader "a reflection of important social values". In the texts and in the social values they reflect, love is a mask rather than a revelation or an ideal, for the only reality which lies behind the text is the politics of the male other. We have returned to the world of Crawfurd and Krom, except instead of "All the rest is romance" we have "Nothing is romance, everything its antithesis." As in the writings of Berg and Dabringhaus, real history is anti-romance; everything is nothing but a mask for the politics of power and male domination: no other form of social facts exist. This manner of interpreting the texts yields no difference at all between the Javanese and Chinese accounts: the importance of women in Javanese society is denied in toto, and that alone makes it methodologically unacceptable to this author.

What I am suggesting instead is that the princesses do not just symbolize Java the country or authority or power — which they do — but that the Javanese narratives tell the story of the submission to love rather than to power, and that it was this story which mattered, was remembered and repeated in Java. Wijaya submitted to the princesses, not to the King of Tatar. That he was a king and had power and authority is stated in both the Javanese and Chinese sources, but in Java that is only the background for the story of a king who loved. The deeper meaning of the story is neither "women are political pawns" nor "possession of women equals power" but that the great period of Majapahit was great because the king was a true lover.

Instead of seeing in these texts only "the staunchly patriarchal view of appropriate roles and behavior for women of the period" (Creese, 2000, p. 132) we may see instead a didactic poem about the centrality of love, an admonition to the readers to remake the world as lovers like Wijaya, not as grasping usurpers of power who capture, abduct and try to dominate others, including and especially the female other. And of course, outside the narrative, in the real world of 1292 and 1293, Wijaya may not have been much of a lover: we only know what was written. What is up for debate is whether the authors of the kidungs (whether male or female) were writing about male struggles to dominate, or whether on the other hand they were imagining a world in which the love of king and queen symbolized and, perhaps, once upon a time, realized the good society, the just society, a society oriented towards mutual love rather than domination, a society which could, perhaps, be realized again.

Messengers of war and peace: 13th century history for 21st century readers

Endings are easy for everyone but God who cannot avoid dealing in eternities and infinities — the Last Judgment will be but a beginning. With humans, all that is necessary to make an end is to turn away, to write no more, to close the book. And that is what we expect from books — that they will end. The meanings are all within the book, not in the life to come. Yet I am still alive and these stories from the past keep me awake at night. Their meanings are not exhausted in telling of the past; there is more in them than mere history and philology. Therefore, before closing with conclusions, I shall embark on a trajectory.

The misunderstandings between the Mongols and their enemies or unhappy subjects was not due to a refusal to meet and talk; it was not due to deliberate misreadings or disregard of the Others. Both the Mongols and their neighbours made continual efforts to come to mutual understanding. Grigor of Akanc assumed that God had sent the Mongols because the wicked Armenians had not followed the will of God; Juvaini wrote similarly from the Il-khanate. Before the Mongols reached Europe, many Europeans were wondering who the Mongols were: a nation of Eastern Christians, the armies of Prester John, or the hordes of Hell; the range of opinion reflected not simply ignorance but more interestingly and more importantly a genuine will to understand those Others. In Europe, the Mongols stayed only long enough to do battle and inspire laments, laments which remained the only story told in Europe for many centuries. In China, the Mongols stayed a sufficiently long time to be acknowledged as the legitimate rulers possessing the Mandate of Heaven. In Java it appears that total misunderstanding reigned on both sides, but the result of the expedition, being favourable to the Javanese ruler Wijaya, resulted in a complete absence of hostility, malice, resentment or any negative portrayals in the histories written in Java. In China the story of the Javanese expedition could be discreetly treated as a paradigm case of submission and the unpleasant aspects forgotten.

As Kotwicz (1950) noted, throughout the Mongol empire the persistent need to deal with the subjugated peoples gradually turned the Mongols away from the emphasis on the outside world, on the borders and beyond, on the idea of one world, one ruler and the solidarity of all mankind, turning them instead toward the needs of the local populations. Instead of war as the cohesive principle of society, we find that the local administration of justice and the adoption of the religion of their subjects promoted internal peace and the acceptance of Mongol rule. As the Mongols moved closer to their subjects (and further from the Mongol world) those peoples grew closer to their rulers. In this movement we see how the same attitudes and orientations which led to the move outward under Chinggis eventually led to the turn inward. The Mongols' understanding of the requirements of peace and justice changed as the world changed; their political orientation changed accordingly.

The Mongols opened the era of exploration and travel; the rejection of the Other was characteristic of the 20th century, not the 13th. The erasure of the Other in human affairs is not limited to the political sphere, nor does it originate there: it is a matter of the heart and affects every human action. The truth of Turan's comment that the "actions, thoughts and beliefs of a people are closely related to one another" (Turan, p. 77) was terrifyingly demonstrated throughout the 20th century and into the 21st. A reading and writing of history which ignores or scorns our attention to "what really happened", or which abolishes the author entails the erasure of the Other in thought and belief; the actions which such a consciousness entails are predictable.

We have not progressed a bowshot, not even a stone's throw beyond the Mongols of 1193 or 1293 — but we think we have. The Mongols turned from expanding their empire to the administration of local affairs and attention to the needs of the people; seven centuries later we, the enlightened civilized West, still preach world revolution and kill one or ten hundred million people in one hundred years, all in the name of peace and justice, democracy, God, socialism, capitalism, race, choice and science, the lofty banners under which our inner demons run free. The barbarian is always within; Grigor of Akanc knew that and the Mongols both learned that and sought to learn good government and the way to a world of peace and joy. We 21st century barbarians have not learned that; we are still blaming the Other for all the world's evils while priding ourselves on having more knowledge in first grade than all previous civilizations combined.

It is not by accident that the scientific study of history abolishes human responsibility and the scientific study of literature silences the author. While everyone today writes and raves about the Other, often they are referring only to themselves: they abolish the Other in theory and in practice. When the reader writes the text, the real world has vanished and only the reader is left, talking to him or herself. The denial of the author is the rejection of author-ity, the authority of that which exists, the not-the-reader, the past, the Other. Replacing the past with the present — the reader alone — makes the future impossible. Only One exists: the reader who has eliminated all Others. The conclusion is inescapable: contempt for the Author is contempt for the Other. What wars and capitalist exploitation failed to do, intellectuals have accomplished through the 'scientific' study of history and literature: the extinction of humanity.

The move from World Maintainer to World Destroyer is not simply a matter of ancient history and religious dogma. It is a theoretical choice in every history written, every political decision made today. The contradictions between the Mongols' view of themselves and their mission on the one hand, and the multitude of laments, accusations and negative portrayals of the Mongols by the peoples they conquered on the other, is not just an academic matter for a handful of historians interested in the 13th century. In the 20th and early 21st century we find the same situation: peoples convinced that they have a mission to bring peace and justice to the world who are nonetheless received and regarded as tyrants, barbarians, and the children of Satan. Who are we? Americans, Muslims, Israelis, national socialists, international socialists, geneticists, hackers, activists of all creeds and colors. "Going after the good, we appear to others and often to ourselves as those who strive for evil." (Patocka)

The present and future of the world is at stake for these groups of people and many more. Medical research on baby body parts and their legal and profitable trade are advocated with promises that what science may discover will solve all our problems if only we will abandon our silly superstitions regarding the sacredness of the human body; others see only Auschwitz in the medicalization and industrial decomposition of the human body. "No justice, no peace!" the spoiled children of the American bourgeoisie scream as they rampage across Europe unjustly and violently destroying the lovely cities of ancient civilizations in that far-off land; is their cry a demand for submission like the message delivered by Meng Qi to Kertanagara? Or a description of the world they are in fact creating and living moment by moment, in which others can find neither justice nor peace? "If you are not for us you are against us!" is loudly proclaimed in central and western Asia, not by the ambassadors of Chinggis or Hülegü but by the leaders of the "Free World." "If we do not get our way, we will kill ourselves and you along with us!" Who follows the will of Heaven? Who are the barbarians and who the Scourge of God?

The would-be saviors of our world all act on the belief that their views must triumph, and that their reign must be enforced "by any means necessary." The "care of the soul", the "peace and justice" which are the avowed purposes and meaning of most of these movements are ignored, abolished and destroyed by the actions undertaken for their establishment. This is the very problem which the Mongols faced from the beginning of their movements outward. Their practice of first sending envoys to discuss peace, and an army afterwards only if peace was rejected is one of the most interesting and perplexing aspects of their empire, for the message of peace was understood — or misunderstood — to entail submission as well. The discovery that there could be submission — but not peace — without justice was not made in Seattle but in Khanbaliq and the court of the "Peaceful-Sovereign" Hülegü (and probably in many other places at many times).

The exclusive and absolute positions of the divisions and oppositions in our 21st century are difficult to see clearly for the passions we bring to them and the very fact that our lives now and ever after are determined by our present decisions and the conditions we create with our every act. Perhaps by looking back at the Mongolian empire humbly, attentively and honestly with the desire to learn, the sons and daughters of Alan-qo'a, the princesses of Tumapel and Wijaya can teach us lessons which they learned long ago, the hard way, if not the best way. And if we learn something worth remembering and repeating, it will not matter whether we learn it from history or from literature; in either case we will have a debt to some long dead authors, for it is their wisdom and intelligence — not our reading proficiency — which speaks across the centuries.

Conclusion: misunderstandings and meanings

The historiography of the Mongolian expedition to Java reveals a history of misunderstandings of a historical series of misunderstandings. The original sequence of events, from Meng Qi to the Mongol-Javanese alliance of Wijaya to Wijaya's ambush is as far as can be determined a history of Mongol-Javanese misunderstandings much more than a history of Wiraraja's deliberate deceits. And the histories of that history, are two histories following national lines; each completely misunderstanding and even being completely unaware of the other. Even the name of the Mongols and their country is a misunderstanding in the Javanese versions! The two histories proceed from the facts which had meaning for their writers: Meng Qi and the princesses, the symbols and bearers of authority.

What the campaign reveals of the Mongols and Khubilai at the end of his reign has never been seriously considered. Mongolists and Javanists have discussed the number of ships, the chronology, and the economic or religious background, keeping the discussion focused on details while failing to provide a story in which these details could acquire any meaning. Historians writing on this period of Indonesian history have developed elaborate narratives of spiritual warfare and the clash of worlds without first acquainting themselves with the nature of Mongol religious and political attitudes and practices. Twentieth century commentary on that original sequence of events has followed one or another of those early versions by either relegating the story to a footnote, regarding it as the incomprehensible and misguided folly of an emperor in decline; or by viewing the Mongols as an unimportant detail, a foreign power beaten back shortly after arriving. Neither the extraordinary importance for the Mongols of envoys in general and Meng Qi in particular nor the importance of the princesses for the Javanese has been understood by modern scholars in discussions of these works and the history they describe and interpret.

One of the intentions of the present work was to focus on those elements of the stories which permit us to glimpse however sketchily the one version of the story which was never told: the Mongol version. By that I do not mean the version which would have been found in Shi-bi's report or even Gao Xing's, but the story which narrates what these events can tell us about the Mongols, the story which will have meaning for the Mongolian people and will be worth repeating: the role of the envoys, the sailors' appeal to Heaven on the sand bar, the negotiations with Wijaya and Wiraraja, the trust shared between the allies, the discussion over sending another messenger or directly punishing Wijaya, and as interesting as all that which happened, the history of "what people say happened", how the Javanese remembered the Mongols. Additionally, much can be learned by noting the numerous misunderstandings which are recorded: the failure to realize the importance of the princesses in the *Yuan shi*; the failure to understand the true relationship between the intended object of punishment — Kertanagara — and the two kings which they found at war upon their arrival; the amazing account of the two officers and 200 soldiers going apparently unarmed (or at least greatly outnumbered) to accept submission — all of these failures reveal both an obedience to and trust in the word of authority, an ignorance of all things Javanese, but an open and even innocent engagement with Wijaya which is both the precondition for understanding and the path to peace.

My original interest in the whole episode was the existence of these views of the Mongols which are so different from those views propagated among the Christian and Muslim populations of Eurasia. How is it that the Europeans remembered hordes from Hell but the Javanese remembered the friends of Wiraraja, the jolly good fellows who came to the aid of the great and good king Wijaya in his hour of need? How can the same people be seen in one place and time as demons and in another as polite and orderly friends, even saviors? And for the campaign itself, such completely different accounts written in Java and China and the astonishing divergence of meanings attributed to them. I sought to discover how one sequence of events could give rise to such different histories; to understand that required not just the strictest attention to what the other authors wrote, but to that which they have in common — that which actually happened — yet *that*, their common source, I could know *only* through their divergent stories. And there the difficulty and the fascination begin.

The History and Legend of the Foundation of Majapahit
Stuart Robson

1. Introduction

The present paper is a thoroughly revised and rearranged version of a small honours thesis which was originally submitted in the Department of Indonesian and Malayan Studies, University of Sydney, in 1962. The topic was suggested by the then Head, Dr F.H. van Naerssen, who was an expert in the early history of Java, and managed to inspire some of his young students with the same interest.

The period chosen for discussion is a narrow one, AD 1292–1294, but is appropriate because of the range of sources available and because of the momentous nature of the events described there. The events were an invasion of Java and the foundation of a new capital. These events were also significant in view of the involvement of two different Asian societies, the Chinese (Mongols) and the Javanese, one a major power in continental Asia and the other located in the island world of what is now Indonesia. This juncture in early Javanese history has also been discussed in detail by N.J. Krom, in his *Hindoe-Javaansche Geschiedenis* [Hindu-Javanese History] (1931, pp. 346–68).

The paper aims to review, and quote at some length from, the sources, namely Javanese inscriptions, Javanese literary works and Chinese histories, and then to draw some conclusions regarding the course of events, bearing in mind the different nature of the various sources. In this way it is hoped to contribute to knowledge of a particular moment in the history of Java.

It may be useful first to situate the discussion. Geographically, we are looking at the eastern part of Java. For some centuries, this had been the site of successive centres of royal power and a civilization termed 'Hindu-Javanese'; somewhat earlier, from the mid 8th to the mid 10th century, the same also applied to Central Java. We find ourselves thus in a period before the establishment of Islam in Java in the 16th century.

Up to the year 1222, the court of the kingdom of Java had been at or near Kadiri (a town that still exists) on the Brantas River in the interior of East Java. In that year Kadiri fell and a new centre was established by a new line of kings, further to the east, not far from the present town of Malang, at Singhasari. This was a shift in the hegemony among the various small, competing, Hindu kingdoms of the area, and its consequences would play a part on the events under discussion below.

In this way in 1222 the upstart Ken Angrok defeated the ruling king of Kadiri, Kṛtajaya, and set up his court in Singhasari; his descendant, Kṛtanagara, was on the throne there in 1292. However, the Kadiri line still existed, and was waiting for an opportunity to take revenge. Now read on.

2. The inscriptions

Inscriptions have been preserved from the Hindu-Javanese period. These were mainly issued by kings, and have the nature of a legal document, transferring taxation rights from the king to another institution, such as a temple or local community. In this period the language used is termed Old Javanese and the material is copper (or bronze) plates. For historians the inscriptions are of great value, as they provide the full name of the issuing king (and other officials), a dating system that can be verified, and often an account of what occasioned the grant. Furthermore, the inscriptions (with the exception of copies) are contemporaneous with the events alluded to. The inscription of Kudadu, also known as Gunung Butak after the mountain in the district of Surabaya where it was found, contains a long narrative section relevant to our subject. It was issued by King Kṛtarajasa Jayawardhana and is dated 11 September 1294. The text was published by J.L.A. Brandes in 1896, with a Dutch translation. It begins as follows:

Hail! Śaka-years elapsed 1216...[1] on that day came down the
command of His Majesty, the sovereign to be praised as most heroic
of all, the courageous, sublime king, who brought destruction to his
adversaries, the rulers with great armies, who is highly endowed
with character, strength, virtue, beauty and a sense of duty, the lord
of the whole island of Java, the protector of the rights of all the well-
disposed, sprung from the family of Narasingha the (embodied)
royal rights-quintessence, the son of him born in Narasingha's
image, (the man) who has the privilege to marry the daughter [or
daughters] of Kṛtanagara, and who was anointed as king under the
name Kṛtarājasa Jayawardhana...

Next the officials to whom the order passed are listed. This passage is
followed by one describing the reason for issuing the decree:

His Majesty the king's command which is being published ordains
that a Royal Decree be made for the village of Kudadu which forms
part of the holy estate of Klĕme, furnished with the seal of Kṛtarājasa
Jayawardhana, on stone and on copper, and to be preserved by the
village-headmen of Kudadu, which shall establish the exemption
of the village of Kudadu, for it is created by His Majesty a free
district, with all its high and low fields, its mountains and valleys,
and shall cease to be part of the holy estate of Klĕme, in favour of
the headman of Kudadu, to be enjoyed hereditarily by his children
and children's children, now and ever into perpetuity.
The occasion [Old Javanese *sambandha*] for it is the conduct of the
headman of Kudadu, who once attentively granted His Majesty a
place of concealment, when he was not yet king and was still called
Narārya Sanggramawijaya, on the occasion when he was led into
the village of Kudadu in difficulties and followed by the enemy, in
the following circumstances.
The then king, His Majesty Kṛtanagara, who departed this life in
the Śiwabuddhālaya, was formerly attacked by His Majesty Jaya
Katyĕng of Gĕlanggĕlang, who appeared as an enemy, did things

below his dignity, betrayed his friend, and dealt contrary to his agreement out of a desire to conquer His Majesty Kṛtanagara who resided in the kingdom of Tumapĕl. When it was known that an army of His Majesty Jaya Katyĕng had come to Jasun, His Majesty Kṛtanagara sent His Majesty the (present) king and Ardharāja against them. Ardharāja and His Majesty the king were both sons-in-law of His Majesty Kṛtanagara, but Ardharāja was at the same time, as is known, a son of Jaya Katyĕng. After His Majesty and Ardharāja had set out, and had reached the village of Kĕdung Plut, His Majesty at first held the enemy. His Majesty's troops gave fight, and the enemy came off losers and fled, after having lost very many men. His Majesty's army then marched to Lĕmbah, but no enemy were found there. They then marched forth to the west from Lĕmbah to Batang, and the vanguard of His Majesty's forces met fresh enemies, but the latter withdrew without fighting. Having passed Batang, His Majesty came to Kapulungan. There they fell upon the enemy again, and then His Majesty's troops pressed to the west of Kapulungan anew, and again the enemy suffered a defeat, fleeing in distress after great losses. This was the position when His Majesty's troops marched forth again and came to Rabut Carat. Not long afterwards enemies approached from the west. Thereupon His Majesty fought with all his men and routed the enemy after heavy losses again, and it seemed that they had all fled for good. In these circumstances, however, there appeared to the east of Hañiru red and white enemy banners fluttering, and then Ardharāja withdrew from the conflict, conducting himself shamefully, and fled aimlessly to Kapulungan. This brought His Majesty's army to nothing, yet he remained loyal to His Majesty Kṛtanagara. Therefore he stayed at Rabut Carat, and then went northward to Pamwatan Apajĕg, north of the river. His Majesty still had about 600 men with him. At daybreak the next day the enemy came after His Majesty, whose troops marched to meet them, and they withdrew and were put to flight, but although it was thus, His Majesty's troops had become still fewer, for those who sought to get out of harm's way deserted and left him, and so he was afraid of being caught completely depleted of men. So His Majesty deliberated with those still with him. His intention was to go to Trung in order to take counsel with the *akuwu* there, *rakryan* Wuru Agraja, who had been appointed *kuwu* by Kṛtanagara, so that His Majesty could help collect the people east and north of Trung. All were in agreement with this, and after nightfall His Majesty went across Kulawan, out of fear of being overtaken by the enemy who were very numerous. At Kulawan he encountered the enemy again and was followed by them, but he withdrew from them by going northwards to escape to Kĕmbang Śri if possible. He found enemies there too who pursued him, and then he fled with all those who were with him as quickly as they could, swimming north across the great river. Many perished in it, others were overtaken by the enemy and dispatched with lances, and those who managed to survive were scattered everywhere. There were only twelve left to protect His Majesty.

At daybreak His Majesty, hungry, weary, cross and sad and despairing of his life, came to the people of Kudadu. The disaster which had struck His Majesty was out of the ordinary, but when he came to the headman of Kudadu he was very courteous and sympathetic in his reception, as was shown in his bringing food, drink and rice. He gave His Majesty a place of concealment in which to reach his destination, so that he might not be found if the enemy should seek him, while in the end he showed him the way and took him as far as the district of Rĕmbang[2] so that His Majesty could escape from there to Madura as he wished to.

Thus His Majesty was formerly brought to Kudadu in difficulties, and the headman there conducted himself very politely and sympathetically in his reception of the prince and this has made His Majesty very thankful.

His Majesty after that became king and thus the protector of the world, and so he must necessarily recompense what he experienced, and his pleasure to him who once occasioned him pleasure, and therefore the headman of Kudadu also receives a handsome token of grace from His Majesty.

May Kudadu, extensive as it is, with all its high and low fields, mountains and valleys, because of His Majesty be certified as an independent free estate with a symbol, on behalf of the headman of Kudadu, also to be enjoyed hereditarily by his children and children's children in perpetuity. May it be understood well that the village of Kudadu ceases to be part of the holy estate of Klĕme; henceforth may this concern itself with it no more, for His Majesty has made it an independent estate, with a symbol thereof.

And to the extent that it now concerns the fact that His Majesty makes bold to take away a part from the holy estate of Klĕme, namely the village of Kudadu, in favour of the headman of Kudadu, let it be known that His Majesty Jaya Katyĕng when he had killed His Majesty Kṛtanagara, in putting his trust in his kingdom of Daha, as has become known generally over the whole island of Java...

The text breaks off here. For the Old Javanese text and a Dutch translation, see Brandes 1896, pp. 78–84. The only other inscription known to allude to these matters is the inscription of the Prime Minister Gajah Mada dated 27 April 1351 (Damais 1952, p. 77). The relevant passage runs as follows:

In Śaka 1214 [AD 1292] in the month of Jyesta, His Majesty, who is buried in the sanctuary in which Śiwa and Buddha are worshipped with equal favour, achieved redemption. Hail! Śaka-years passed by 1273 [AD 1351]... the Right Honourable Governor of the realm Mada, acting as intermediary for Their Majesties the seven kings, led by Her Majesty Tribhuwanatunggadewī Mahārāja Wiṣṇuwardhanī, and of the grandsons and granddaughters of His Majesty Kṛtanagara.... at the said moment the Patih, being the restorer of that which had fallen into ruin, founded a *caitya* for the great brahmans (rsis), the Śivaites and Buddhists, who followed the king in death, and also for the *mahāmantri*, who was slain at his feet in the same hour.

The Right Honourable Governor hopes in this way to have attained (his object), namely that the homage (due) (to their souls) will be rendered by the children and children's children of the faithful companions of the king... (Blom 1939, pp. 136–38)

In summary, we have learned from these inscriptions that in 1292 King Kṛtanagara of Tumapĕl was attacked and killed by King Jaya Katyĕng of Daha, and that the son-in-law of King Kṛtanagara, while attempting to defeat the enemy, was driven out and headed for Madura, but by 1294 had become king of Java, with the name Kṛtarājasa Jayawardhana. So how did he manage this remarkable feat?

3. Javanese literary sources

Memories of the turbulent events of 1292–94 were preserved in Javanese society, probably passed down by story-tellers, termed *widu*. These recited tales of the past (*widu amacangah*) or sang songs (*widu mangidung*) (Robson 1971, pp. 18–19). There is a prose work in a variety of Javanese which can be called Middle Javanese with the title *Pararaton* (translatable as 'The Book of Kings'); this probably reflects such an oral tradition, and relates the beginnings of the Singhasari line of kings, later continued in Majapahit. The early part contains legendary material, while the later part is more like a notebook with names and dates. The latest date mentioned is 1481 (for a volcanic eruption), but the oldest manuscript, found in Bali, has the date 1613. Where the contents can be checked against other sources, they do not always correspond, and so we do not need to be too eager to ascribe historicity to all the events described. Regarding the circumstances of the foundation of Majapahit, there are also poetical versions which will be mentioned below, but first the account of the Pararaton should be given, as this probably has priority in terms of literary history.

Here the prince has the name Raden Wijaya. It is told that King Kṛtanagara had two daughters, who were destined to be his wives. During the attack by the people of Daha, Raden Wijaya managed to find the elder of the two and carry her off, while the younger was captured and taken to Daha. Meanwhile Raden Wijaya had decided to cross over to the island of Madura, where he sought refuge with Wiraraja, who had been a minister under King Kṛtanagara and was now a regent of East Madura (Sungeneb or Sumenep). Raden Wijaya promised him he would give him half of Java if he would help him become king. The plan was that Raden Wijaya should return to Java and pretend to make his submission to Aji Jaya Katong (= Jaya Katyĕng, the king in Daha), and as soon as he had won the latter's trust he should then ask for the 'waste land of the people of Trik', and make a new settlement there. Madurese living nearby would come and help with this. He was advised to gather his people from Tumapĕl, as well as any from Daha who wished to take refuge with him.

Having duly arrived in Daha he served the king loyally; in martial combats his men were more than a match for the Daha warriors. This was a signal that it was time for ask for the land and start clearing it. When the Madurese were doing this, one of them did not have enough food and took some *maja*[3] fruits to eat. These turned out to be bitter (*pahit*), so he threw them away. When this became known, the place got the name Majapahit ('bitter *maja* fruit'). Raden Wijaya then asked permission to go and live there, and this was given, as the king had been seduced by his excellent service.

Immediately Raden Wijaya wished to make a move against Daha and invited Wiraraja to join him, but the latter advised him to wait, saying that he was friends with the king of Tatar,[4] and would offer him the beautiful princesses of Tumapĕl as booty if he would help defeat the king of Daha. He wrote a letter to the king of Tatar, as there happened to be a ship there that had come to trade. Wiraraja then moved to Majapahit, taking his whole family and the necessary weapons.

It might be useful to provide a direct translation from the Pararaton for the events that followed.

When the emissaries from Tatar had arrived, they attacked Daha. The soldiers from Tatar approached from the north, and the soldiers from Madura and from Majapahit came from the east. Aji Katong was confused and did not know which one to watch. He was put under pressure from the north by the Tatar. Kĕbo Mundarang, Panglĕt and Mahisa Rubuh were on guard against the forces from the east. Panglĕt was killed by Sora, Kĕbo Rubuh was killed by Nambi, and Kĕbo Mundarang clashed with Rangga Lawe; he fled and was pursued into the area of Trinipanti and killed by Rangga Lawe. Kĕbo Mundarang said to Rangga Lawe, 'Rangga Lawe, I have a daughter. Let her be carried off by Sora, as a reward for his daring.' Aji Katong made a charge to the north armed with his shield, but the Tatars fought him, seized him and locked him up. Raden Wijaya swiftly entered the palace of Daha and carried off the younger princess. He then took her to Majapahit, and when he had reached there the Tatars came to demand the princess, as Wiraraja had promised that when Daha was defeated he would present them with both the princesses from Tumapĕl. All the ministers did not know what to do, and looked for a way out. Sora said, 'Well, just let me attack the Tatars when they come here.' Arya Wiraraja replied, 'Yes indeed, young Sora, but I have another idea.' They kept on looking for something to give them. This is what they discussed together. Sora offered, 'Clearly we will succeed if we attack the Tatars'. In the afternoon toward sunset the Tatars arrived to ask for the princesses. Wiraraja replied, 'All you Tatars, do not be too hasty, as the princesses are upset, because they have watched the soldiers when Tumapĕl was defeated, and especially when Daha was defeated, and are really frightened if they see any kind of sharp weapon. Tomorrow they will be handed over to you, contained in a box (sedan-chair?), carried and provided with garments, and escorted to your ships. The reason for putting them in boxes is that they are not willing to see any weapons, and furthermore the people who receive the princesses should not be any ordinary (common?) Tatars but good men. And they must not bring attendants, for the princesses have vowed that if they see any kind of weapon, even if they have already reached the ships, they will drown themselves, and you will not be able to pay with your lives if the princesses have drowned themselves.' The Tatars believed them and were deceived. The Tatars said, 'What you say is very true.' When the time came to hand the princesses over, the Tatars came in numbers to ask for the princesses, none of them bearing weapons. When they were inside the Bhayangkara Gate,[5] it was closed and locked, inside and out. Sora had bound his kris to his thigh. Then Sora furiously attacked the Tatars and killed them all. Rangga Lawe attacked the ones outside the audience-hall, and pursued them to where they were fleeing, the anchorage at Canggu;[6] they were followed and killed.

About ten days later the expedition from Malayu[7] arrived, bringing two princesses. One of them, named Dara Pĕtak, Raden Wijaya made his *binihaji* (wife of second rank); the elder one was named Dara

Jingga married a *dewa* (god) and had as son the king of Malayu, called Tuhan Janaka, with *kasir-kasir* (name) of Sri Marmadewa and royal name of Aji Mantolot. The expedition to Malayu and the fall of Tumapĕl took place in the same year, Saka *rĕsi-sanga-samadhi*, or 1197. Aji Katong became king in Daha in Saka *naga-muka-dara-tunggal*, or 1198.[8] Having arrived in Jung Galuh, Aji Katong composed the poem Wukir Polaman, and having composed it passed away. (For the text, see Brandes 1896, pp. 23–24.)

In 1927 C.C. Berg devoted his Leiden dissertation to *De Middeljavaansche Historische Traditie* [The Middle Javanese Historical Tradition]. This was a very valuable work, as it opened up a whole group of works for examination, although perhaps more from a historical than a literary angle. Shortly after this, Berg published the text of one of his main sources, what he calls the 'double-kidung' *Panji Wijayakrama-Rangga Lawe* (1930), and then another similar work, the kidung *Harsa-Wijaya* (1931), which had not been used in the dissertation. Neither was translated.

The works called *kidung* here are narratives in verse-form, also linked with oral literature but in written form, and intended to be sung to prescribed melodies. In accordance with the metrical structure, we give references to canto and stanza. Being in verse, we can assume that their nature is different from prose, and that as literary creations they can be subjected to analysis in order to gain insight into the author's aims.

A summary of contents of the *Harsa-Wijaya* and the *Rangga Lawe* can be found in P.J. Zoetmulder's *Kalangwan, A Survey of Old Javanese Literature* (1974, pp. 409–19).[9] While the main line of the story is similar, the details are different. Both contain the story of the foundation of Majapahit, which is our subject here. The language is Middle Javanese, but the style of the two contrasts: the *Harsa-Wijaya* is an elegant literary creation. As Zoetmulder comments, "The style is polished and, as a rule, lucid. There is a well-balanced variety of themes and moods, of narrative and descriptive passages, of romantic scenes (for which the presence of no less than four princesses gives ample opportunity) and heroic fighting" (Zoetmulder 1974, p. 419). More recently, it has been the object of renewed study, with the conclusion that the author was using the concept of Fate (Old Javanese *widhi*) in order to understand the course of events, whereby Raden Wijaya, despite some morally dubious actions, nevertheless became the first king of Majapahit (Robson 2000).

The story follows that of the Pararaton, and in fact the author refers to this work at the end of his composition (HW 6.119b). However, the kidung style is entirely different, with its detailed descriptions of the fine clothes worn by the characters, for example, and the stress on scenes of romance and martial prowess. Some brief paraphrases from the *Kidung Harsa-Wijaya* which may be relevant follow as examples.

In Canto IV stanza 50a we find Raden Wijaya at the court of Kadiri. The king of Kadiri notes that many of Wijaya's followers have arrived there, and wonders where it would be best to put them. He says that if Wijaya goes back to Singhasari he will not be able to see him, as it is far away. The Prime Minister advises that the woods of the people of Trik would be good, as the place is wide and flat, on the bank of a large river, and not far away. The king smiles and says that this is a good idea and asks him to point out the place. Wijaya is pleased, as this is what he wanted. The king tells him that it is his wish for him to move the next day to the forest of Trik, as it is good. Wijaya agrees. The king and his wives leave the audience and enter the palace, where they all take a meal consisting of many foods and drinks, followed by dancing... (63a) The next day it is decided to send word to Madura, so Wirondaya sets out, soon arrives at Canggu and takes a boat to Tĕrung and so arrives in Madura. Meanwhile Wijaya has taken leave of the king and goes to the forest of Trik. His troops bustle about clearing it and set up a rest-house. The Adhipati of Madura has now also arrived with his men, carrying all the tools needed. The sound of people chopping rings out, the trees are cleared and burnt, and the great forest is cleared away (65a). After several days of clearing, houses are set out so that it looks like a village. One man is short of supplies, so knocks down the fruit of the *maja*, but when he eats them they are bitter and he throws them away. So the bitter *maja* gives its name to Majapahit. A palace is laid out, with a square facing north, broad streets and a market alongside fine pavilions....(66a).

In Canto VI stanza 59a we find a description of the final battle at Majapahit. The Tatars have reached the city of Majapahit and with shouts enter the outer courtyard claiming that the people of Majapahit have broken their word, and demanding the princess, otherwise they will wreck the city. The men of Majapahit challenge them to do their worst, the Tatars are furious and then start hacking at the fence. The men of Majapahit meet them from right and left, attacking from the laneways and crossroads. Many die, but Wijaya and his chosen troops are steadfast, and the heroes Nambi, Sora, Gajah-Pagon and Lĕmbu attack and drive the Tatar out [passage on the panic among the women inside the palace]. The Tatars have been defeated, many die and the corpses fill the city (64a). The survivors flee, and the handsome hero says to follow them and wipe them out; at Bubat [the river-port] they are surrounded and including their leader are killed 'to the south of the temple under the shade of a *puskara* (banyan) tree'; those left beg for their lives and submit. The people of Majapahit rejoice and compete in taking prisoners...

There is one final literary source which we should refer to. This is the poem *Deśawarṇana* (formerly, erroneously, known as the *Nāgarakṛtāgama*). This is in the poetical form of the *kakawin*, sometimes said to be equivalent to the Sanskrit *kāvya*, but in this case absolutely unique regarding subject-matter, as it provides a description of the realm of Majapahit, as it was in 1365 when the poem was completed. The author, Mpu Prapañca, who was Head of Buddhist Affairs at court, gives details of the royal family, the layout of the capital, a royal tour through the eastern districts in 1359, extensive historical notes (Cantos 40–49), and much more. The parts relevant to our story are these:

Canto 44.1
When King Kṛtanagara returned to the abode of the Buddha [= died],
The world was fearful, sad and tumultuous, as if it would revert to its condition in the Age of Kali.
There was a vassal king, a villain known by the name of Jayakatwang,
Who there in the land of Kadiri desired to replace him and was outstandingly clever at laying schemes.
44.3
Now, however, when the King [Kṛtanagara] passed away, King Jayakatwang became blind and strayed from the path.

44.4

Through the influence of his knowledge of the scriptures and the force of the King's efforts before,

It came about that there was a son of His Majesty's who defeated the enemy and restored the world.

His relationship was son-in-law, and Dyah Wijaya was the title by which people praised him —

Jointly with the Tatars he attacked Jayakatwang and wiped him out completely. (Robson 1995, pp. 56–57)

This last line is the only allusion to the Tatars in the work, and acknowledges that the defeat of Jayakatwang was a joint (Old Javanese *ardha*) undertaking.

4. The Chinese reports

The official history of the Mongol or Yüan dynasty contains detailed accounts which we can quote here, using the English translation of Groeneveldt (1876), and following his spellings of names.[10] The article on Java found in Book 210 relates the following:

> When the emperor Shih-tsu (Kublai) pacified the barbarians of the four quarters of the world and sent officers to the different countries over the sea, Java was the only place he had to send an army to.[11]

In the second month of the year 1292 the emperor issued an order to the governor of Fukien, directing him to send Shih-pi, Ike Mese and Kau Hsing in command of an army to subdue Java, to collect soldiers from Fukien, Kiangsi and Hukuang ot the number of 20,000, to appoint a commander of the Right Wing and of the Left, as well as four Commanders of Ten Thousand, to send out a thousand ships and to equip them with provisions for a year and with forty thousand bars of silver. The emperor further gave ten tiger badges, forty golden badges and a hundred silver badges, together with a hundred pieces of silk, for the purpose of rewarding merit.

When Ike Mese and his associates had their last audience, the emperor said to them: 'When you arrive at Java you must clearly proclaim to the army and the people of that country, that the Imperial Government has former had intercourse with Java by envoys from both sides and has been in good harmony with it, but that they have lately cut the face of the imperial envoy Mêng Ch'i and that you have come to punish them for that.'

In the ninth month some troops were collected at Ch'ing-yüan (old name of Ningpo); Shih-pi and Ike Mese went with the soldiers overland to Ch'üan-chou, whilst Kau Hsing brought the baggage with the ships. In the course of the 11th month the troops from the three provinces of Fukien, Kiangsi and Hukuang were all assembled at Ch'üan-chou and in the next month the expedition put to sea. In the first month of the year 1293 they arrived at the island of Kö-lan (Billiton) and there deliberated on their plan of campaign.

In the second month Ike Mese and one of his subordinate commanders, taking with them their secretaries and accompanied by three officers of the office of Pacification, who were charged to treat with Java and the other countries, and by a Commander of Ten Thousand, who led 500 men and ten ships, went first in order to bring the commands of the Emperor to this country. The body of the army followed to Karimon (Karimon Java) and from there to a place on Java called Tu-ping-tsuh (Tuban) when Shih-pi and Kau Hsing met Ike Mese again and determined, together with the other leaders, that half the army should be sent ashore and the other half proceed at the same time in the ships. Shih-pi went by sea to the mouth of the small river Sugalu (Sĕdayu) and from there to the small river Pa-tsieh (Kali Mas). On the other hand Kau Hsing and Ike Mese led the rest of the troops, being cavalry and infantry, and marched from Tu-ping-tsuh overland, one of the Commanders of Ten Thousand leading the vanguard. Three superior officers were sent in fact boats from Sugalu, with the order to go first to the floating bridge of Modjopait and then to rejoin the army on its way to the small river Pa-tsieh.

The officers of the Office of Pacification soon reported that the son-in-law of the prince of Java, called Tuhan Pidjaya, wished to make his country submit, but as he could not leave his army, order was given to three officers to go and bring his prime minister Sih-la-nan-da-ch'a-ya and fourteen others, who wanted to come and receive the army of the emperor.

On the first day of the 3rd month, the troops were assembled at the mouth of the small river Pa-tsieh. This river has at its upper course the palace of

the king of Tumapan (Tumapel) and discharges itself into the sea called
Pou-pên (the sea south of Madura); it is the entrance to Java and a place
for which they were determined to fight. Accordingly the first minister of
the Javanese, Hi-ning-kuan, remained in a boat to see how the chances of
the fight went; he was summoned repeatedly, but would not surrender.

The commanders of the imperial army made a camp in the form of a
crescent on the bank of the river and left the ferry in charge of a Commander
of Ten Thousand; the fleet in the river and the cavalry and infantry on shore
then advanced together and Hi-ning-kuan, seeing this, left his boat and fled
overnight, whereupon more than a hundred large ships, with devil-heads
on the stem, were captured.

Order was now given to a strong force to guard the mouth of the river
Pa-tsieh and the body of the army then advanced.

Messengers came from Tuhan Pidjaya, telling that the king of Kalang had
pursued him as far as Modjopait and asking for troops to protect him. Ike
Mese and one of his lieutentants hastened to him, in order to encourage him
and another officer followed with a body of troops to Chang-ku [Canggu],
for the purpose of assisting them. Kau Hsing advanced to Modjopait, but
heard that it was not known whether the soldiers of Kalang were near or
far, so he went back to the river Pa-tsieh; at last he got information from
Ike Mese that the enemy would arrive that night, and was ordered to go
again to Modjopait.

On the 7th day the soldiers of Kalang arrived from three sides to attack
Tuhan Pidjaya, and on the 8th day, early in the morning, Ike Mese led part
of the troops to engage the enemy in the south-west, but he did not meet
them; Kau Hsing fought with the enemy on the south-east and killed several
hundred of them, whilst the remainder fled to the mountains. Towards the
middle of the day the enemy arrived also from the south-west, Kau Hsing
met them again and toward evening they were defeated.

On the 15th day the army was divided into three bodies in order to attack
Kalang; it was agreed that on the 19th they should meet at Taha (Daha) and
commence the battle on hearing the sound of the *p'au*. A part of the troops
ascended the river, Ike Mese proceeded by the eastern road and Kau Hsing
took the western, whilst Tuhan Pidjaya with his army brought up the rear. On
the 19th they arrived at Taha, where the prince of Kalang defended himself
with more than a hundred thousand soldiers. The battle lasted from 6 a.m.

till 2 p.m. and three times the attack was renewed, when the enemy was defeated and fled, several thousand thronged into the river and perished there, whilst more than 5,000 were slain. The king retired into the inner city, which was immediately surrounded by our army and the king summoned to surrender; in the evening the king, whose name was Hadji[12] Katang, came out of the fortress and offered his submission, on this the orders of the emperor were delivered to him and he was told to go back.

On the 2nd day of the 4th month Tuhan Pidjaya was sent back to his dominions in order to make preparations for sending tribute, two officers and 200 soldiers went with him as escort. On the 19th Tuhan Pidjaya secretly left our soldiers and attacked them by which the whole party came to grief.

On the 24th the army went back, taking with it the children and officers of Hadji Katang, altogether more than a hundred persons; they brought also a map of the country, a register of the population and a letter in golden characters presented by the king.

The Account of Shih-pi (Book 162) agrees with the above, but also adds some interesting details:

In the year 1292 he [Shih-pi] was made commander of the expedition to Java, whilst Ike Mese and Kau Hsing were appointed to assist him […]. In the 12th month he joined the other troops with 5,000 men and departed from Ch'üan-chou: the wind was strong and the sea very rough, so that the ships rolled heavily and the soldiers could not eat for many days. The passed the Sea of Seven Islands (the Paracels Is.) and the Long Reef (Macclesfield Bank); the passed the land of the Giau-chi [northern Vietnam] and Champa, and in the first month of the next year they came to the Western Tung Islands (Anambas?), entered the Indian Sea (?) and consecutively arrived at the Olive Islands (?), Karimata and Kau-lan (Billiton), where they stopped and cut timber to make small boats for entering the rivers.

At that time Java carried on an old feud with the neighbouring country of Kalang, and the king of Java, Hadji Ka-ta-na-ka-la, had already been killed by the prince of Kalang, called Hadji Katang. The son-in-law of the former, Tuhan Pidjaya, had attacked Hadji Katang, but not overcome him;

he had therefore retired to Modjopait and when he heard that Shih-pi with his army had arrived, he sent envoys with an account of the rivers and sea-ports and a map of the country of Kalang, offering his submission and asking for assistance.

Shih-pi then advanced with all his forces, attacked the army of Kalang and routed it completely, on which Hadji Katang fled back to his dominions.

Kau Hsing now said: "Though Java has submitted, still if it repents its decision and unites with Kalang, our army might be in a very difficult position and we do not know what might happen." Ship-pi therefore divided his army into three parts, himself, Kau Hsing and Ike Mese each leading a division, and marched to attack Kalang. When they arrived at the fortified town, Daha, more than a hundred thousand soldiers of Kalang came forward to withstand them. They fought from morning till noon, when the army of Kalang was routed and retired into the town to save itself. The Chinese army surrounded the town and soon Hadji Katang came forward to offer his submission; his wife, his children and officers were taken by the victors, who then went back.

Tuhan Pidjaya asked permission to return to his country, in order to prepare a new letter of submission to the Emperor and to take the precious articles in his possession for sending them to court; Shih-pi and Ike Mese consented to this and sent two officers with 200 men to go with him. Tuhan Pidjaya killed the two officers on the way and revolted again, after which he availed himself of the circumstance that the army was returning, to attack it from both sides. Shih-pi was behind and was cut off from the rest of the army; he was obliged to fight his way for 300 *li* before he arrived at the ships; at last he embarked again and reached Ch'üan-chou after a voyage of 68 days.

Of his soldiers more than 3,000 had died. (Groeneveldt 1876, pp. 25–27)

5. Conclusions

The various pieces of the story are like a jigsaw puzzle. Moreover, we do not have all the pieces, and some overlap. And, importantly, the pieces are qualitatively diverse. The nature of the different sources has been alluded to above, so that if one dares to draw conclusions on the actual history, this point can be borne in mind.

At least the time-frame appears to be firm, as the inscription and the Chinese reports are explicit, and (in the case of the Chinese) even the exact months and days are mentioned. So all the events being described occurred within the years 1292–1294. It is just the relations between them that are hard to fit together.

The time-line for the Chinese is as follows:

1292 2nd month: order given to prepare expedition to Java
    9th–11th months: troops collected
1293 1st month: expedition arrives
    3rd month: troops assembled, battles
    4th month: expedition comes to grief, returns to China.

From the Javanese viewpoint, we have the date 1292 (from the inscription of Gajah Mada) for the death of Krtanagara, that is, the attack on Singhasari and it defeat by Jayakatwang. The actual foundation of Majapahit, following the (temporary) reconciliation of Raden Wijaya and Jayakatwang, must have followed very soon, because Raden Wijaya was already well established in his new capital when the Tatars arrived in early 1293. By the fourth month it was all over, and by the next year, 1294, the new king was already in a position to reward the headman of Kudadu for his help, as recorded in the inscription.

It is obvious that the wealth of detail concerning Raden Wijaya's flight from his enemies as recorded in the inscription of Kudadu cannot be confirmed, but the account gives the impression of faithfully relating events (and follows them by only about two years), and it may also be possible to locate a number of the places mentioned. Similarly, the detailed account of the hostilities contained in the Chinese reports also give the impression of objectivity and accuracy, even including an admission that the expedition was actually defeated and had to withdraw in a hurry.

However, there are other elements that can also be considered. What about the role of the Madurese? Could Wiraraja have played such a prominent part in the foundation of Majapahit? The inscription of Kudadu already points in this direction, where it says '...as far as the district of Rěmbang in order that His Majesty could escape from there to Madura as he wished to.' The Madurese are prominent in the Javanese literary sources, but not present in the Chinese reports. They were unaware or not interested in a detail like this.

On the other hand, the Chinese do seem to be well informed on the political situation in Java. They are aware of the distinction between 'Java' (that is, Singhasari and its line) and Kalang (Kadiri) and its line. On arrival they go straight to Majapahit and make contact with Raden Wijaya: 'The officers of the Office of Pacification soon reported that the son-in-law of the prince of Java [the late Kṛtanagara], called Tuhan Pidjaya, wished to make his country submit...' The second Chinese report quoted is even more explicit: 'At that time Java carried on an old feud with the neighbouring country of Kalang [how true!], and the king of Java, Hadji Ka-ta-na-ga-la, had already been killed by the prince of Kalang, called Hadji Katang. The son-in-law of the former, Tuhan Pidjaya, had attacked Hadji Katang, but not overcome him...'

Raden Wijaya wastes no time in taking advantage of the situation. He knows that he is facing an attack from Kalang, and so 'Messengers came from Tuhan Pidjaya, telling that the king of Kalang had pursued him as far as Modjopait and asking for troops to protect him'. And within days soldiers from Kalang do indeed arrive; they are in turn pursued back to their city, where there is another battle, in which they are defeated. So Raden Wijaya has now succeeded in eliminating his enemies. The only remaining step is to turn on the Chinese: 'On the 19th Tuhan Pidjaya secretly left our soldiers and attacked them by which the whole party came to grief.' In this manner he had cleared the way to be set up as the undisputed king of Java, with his capital in Majapahit.

The Javanese literary sources stand apart, with their own preoccupations. They make no mention of Kudadu at all. They are not interested in the Tatars. It is most unlikely that they had any contact with the Chinese reports, and yet there is a curious detail in which the two concur. We recall that Raden Wijaya was escorted back to Majapahit by two Chinese officers and 200 men; the Kidung Panji-Wijayakrama (8.121) says, 'The Chinese indeed quickly sent out envoys to remind the Javanese of their promise, and two *mantri anom* [junior officers], Sudarsana, the son of Janapati, and Suryanasa, the son of Taru-Janaka, accompanied by 200 men...' Clearly the names are not Chinese, but the numbers tally — a mere coincidence, or a surviving tradition?

The justification for the Chinese expedition is given in the Chinese report that 'the Imperial Government has formerly had intercourse with Java by envoys from both sides and has been in good harmony with it, but that they have lately cut the face of the imperial envoy Mêng Ch'i and that you have come to punish them for that'. According to Rockhill (1914), this alludes to an event that occurred in 1281, so that retribution for the insult was long in coming, not arriving till 1292. It was not the result of an invitation from anyone in Java. Why did they take so long? 1281 was also the year of the destruction of the second Mongol fleet off Japan, and this may have discouraged an immediate move against Java. (See the Addendum.)

The Javanese literary sources are very interested in the daughters of Kṛtanagara, and have them play an important part in the conflicts of 1292–93. Apparently there were two, as we can read in the inscription of Kudadu, and one was married to Raden Wijaya and the other to Ardharaja, who was a son of Jaya Katwang. We cannot say exactly what happened to these two ladies in fact, but it is probable that they were important for guaranteeing the legitimacy of the new king. So having both was essential. The Pararaton tells that on the fateful night when Tumapĕl was attacked the two princesses, who 'were going to be married to Raden Wijaya' (no mention of Ardharaja here), were captured by the people from Daha. He managed to rescue one of them, the elder one, but was advised not to try to get the younger, as they were outnumbered, and so he carried the one princess off as he made his way northwards, fighting the enemy all the while. In this way, the younger princess arrived in Daha (where she may have been at home, if in fact she had been married to Ardharaja), and there was the object of Raden Wijaya's efforts to find and capture her during the attack on Daha with the help of the Chinese. The Chinese knew that he had been a son-in-law of 'the king of Java'. The Pararaton makes the princess(es) bait to induce the Chinese to join forces with Raden Wijaya, and to entice them to Majapahit to collect them as booty, with fatal results.

But the Chinese reports say nothing of this, although do say that when they withdrew, the army took with it 'the children and officers of Hadji Katang, altogether more than a hundred persons...'

Despite the disparate nature of the sources, the inscriptions, Chinese reports and the Javanese literary works, it is possible to get a reasonably clear picture of the history. The Javanese poems of the *kidung* genre, on the other hand, represent legend, in which the aim is not so much to record events for their own sake, or to support claims to legitimacy, but rather to celebrate heroic deeds on the part of individuals and to give a picture of the opulent court in which they lived. The poems have many links with the world of the arts of music and drama, which flourished in the 14th and 15th centuries.

The tale we have presented is one of machinations by various parties in Java, each vying for power and not hesitating to change sides or deceive each other in the process. The upshot was the continuation of the Singhasari dynastic line, but in a new location, Majapahit. The arrival of the Chinese expedition at the critical moment facilitated this — it was as if decreed by Fate. But despite its problematical beginnings, the capital, strategically situated at Majapahit between Kadiri and Singhasari, was within half a century the undisputed centre of a kingdom of remarkable prosperity and power, which extended its influence over a large proportion of the Indonesian Archipelago, with friendly relations with many of the other realms of east Asia — including China.

Equivalent names of persons and places

Raden Wijaya = Kṛtarājasa Jayawardhana = Tuhan Pidjaya = Dyah Wijaya

Kṛtanagara = Bhatāra Śiwabuddha

Jayakatwang = Jaya Katong = Jaya Katyĕng = Aji (Hadji) Katang

Tumapĕl = Sing(h)asari

Daha = Kadiri = Gĕlanggĕlang = Kalang

Majapahit = Modjopait

Addendum

Java was not the only place that Kublai Khan had to send an army to. Japan was also disinclined to accept his overlordship, and the pattern of events there forms an interesting comparison with Javanese history. The following passage has been translated from a standard textbook on Japanese history (*Nihonshi*, Vol. I: 314–17).[13] It is useful here, in that it offers a Japanese view of events.

Gan-kō no Sen – the Mongol Wars

In the 10th month of 1274 (Bunei 11) a Mongol division of 33,000 men, embarked in 900 ships, launched an attack. It was in the time of the Regent Tokimune. Before the attack was made two envoys had come from Mongolia but were sent away. Orders were given to every Constable and Steward in the land to send reinforcements to Kyushu. The enemy captured the islands of Tsushima and Iki (Nagasaki Prefecture) and made raids on the seacoast near Hakata. The Chinsei Bugyō (the Military Commandant at Dazaifu, = Kyushu HQ, near Hakata) in response to the news from Tsushima, sent an urgent message to the retainers of Kyushu to assemble at Hakata, and retainers from every district in Kyushu hastened to gather there and were assigned to its defence. The Mongol army landed on the 19th day of the 10th month at a place called Imazu, and our army fought fiercely but the enemy had poisoned arrows and firearms, and they acquitted themselves with great bravery. Moreover, as the enemy fought in close formation, the Japanese army, which was accustomed to single-combat fighting, was at a disadvantage. And so, on the 20th, abandoning the first line of coastal defence works, they retreated and took up a position in a higher place. That night a violent storm of wind and rain arose and the whole enemy fleet sank, so our army destroyed the enemy forces remaining at Shika-no-Shima. This is called the Bunei campaign.

As a result of this war the Bakufu [military government] found out that their control of the retainers was not satisfactory, and that the enemy's method of fighting was better than ours. So the next year the Bakufu greatly strengthened the defences on the seacoast of Nagato and at strategic points in Kyushu such as Hakata and sent an officer of Hōjō [the leading warrior family of the time] stock to take command. As the Bakufu lacked the confidence to establish and fight with a navy, they built defensive positions along the coast and called for troops to man them. In answer to this there were many who joined, and the population's enthusiasm increased greatly. While preparations were being made in this way, envoys came again from Mongolia. The first envoy was executed at Tatsu-no-kuchi ['Dragon's Mouth] (the Kamakura Bakufu's execution ground) and the second at Hakata. The Bakufu thus demonstrated how determined it was to people at home and abroad.

On the 5th day of the 6th month of 1281 Tsushima and Iki fell, and the Mongol host arrived off Shika-no-shima, Noko-no-shima and Hakata. Those who fought hard at the stone fortifications the check the enemy's landing were the forces from Ōtomo, Shōni, Shimazu, Akizuki, Kikuchi and Takazaki. Then the enemy removed the spearhead of their attack and made an assault on the coast of Nagato. Here too they were repulsed, so they retired to Takashima to await the arrival of the second army, coming from 'South of the Yangtse'. On this occasion men like Ōyano Taneyasu and Kōno Michi ari in our army made an attack in warships on the enemy ships, captured their general, and set fire to their ships. The enemy were very fearful, but as our army's losses were great this kind of attack ceased. The Bakufu received reports on the state of the war and strengthened the defences even more by making Hōjō Morotoki Constable of Nagato, and it decided to send Hōjō Naritoki to Harima and have him command the officers and men of the Inland Sea Coaatal Area. The Imperial Family prayed at the Ise Shrine for the surrender of the hostile forces and the repulse of the Mongol army. The second enemy army from 'South of the Yangtse' arrived at Takashima at the end of the 7th month and engaged in preparation for war, but on the night of the 29th on the 7th month a great storm arose and the whole enemy fleet sank. Their commander barely managed to return safely to his homeland; the remaining 2000 enemy soldiers were taken prisoner and the Japanese army raised a shout of triumph. This is known as the Kōan campaign. The gale which blew on this occasion was called a 'Divine Wind' (Kamikaze). Nowadays we would call it a typhoon. After that the Bakufu still secured the defences and awaited the coming of an enemy attack. Messengers came from Mongolia twice after that, but the Bakufu refused to deal with them and reinforced the defences. However, there was fortunately no third attack, but the Bakufu has exhausted its strength in national defence almost to the point of ruin.

Stuart Robson is Adjunct Associate Professor in the School of Languages, Cultures and Linguistics, Monash University.

Notes

1 To obtain Common Era dates we have to add 78 to Śaka, so here we get 1294. Full calendrical details follow here.

2 In the district of Pasuruan, East Java, and not to be confused with the Rembang in Central Java.

3 Aegle Marmelos, the bael tree.

4 Tatar is the name always given in Javanese for the Mongols.

5 Probably the Second Gate within the palace, see Deśawarṇana 9.2.

6 The river-port of Majapahit, located on the Brantas River.

7 In eastern Sumatra, probably Jambi.

8 Neither of these dates (1295 and 1296) is correct. Tumapel fell in 1293 and Aji Katong became king in 1293.

9 Although the title says 'Old Javanese', this work also covers Middle Javanese.

10 I am not in a position to verify this translation from the Chinese, and am not aware of any later attempts to correct or improve it. However, Groeneveldt's work has been reprinted several times.

11 However, see the Addendum on the Mongol expeditions to Japan.

12 The title Haji, found here and elsewhere, is Old Javanese *haji*, 'king', and has nothing to do with the Islamic title Haji.

13 This translation was kindly checked by the late Dr G.W. Sargent, formerly lecturer in Japanese at the University of Sydney.

References

Berg C.C.

1927 *De Middeljavaansche Historische Traditie.* Leiden dissertation. Santpoort: Mees.

Berg, C.C.

1930 *Rangga Lawe, Middeljavaansche historische roman.* Bibliotheca Javanica 1. Koninklijk Bataviaasch Genootschap van Kunsten en Wetenschappen, Weltevreden: Albrecht.

Berg, C.C.

1931 'Een nieuwe redactie van den roman van Raden Wijaya, Kidung Harsa-Wijaya, Middel-Javaansche Historische Roman, *Bijdragen tot de Taal-, Land- en Volkenkunde van Nederlandsch-Indie*, deel 88.

Blom, Jessy
1939 *The Antiquities of Singasari*. Leiden: Burgersdijk en Niermans.

Brandes, J.L.A.
1896 (2nd edn 1920) *Pararaton (Ken Arok), of Het Boek der Koningen van Tumapel en van Majapahit*. Verhandelingen van het Bataviaasch Genootschap van Kunsten en Wetenschappen, deel XLIX 1e stuk. Batavia: Albrecht & Rusche; 's-Gravenhage: M. Nijhoff.

Damais, L.-C.
1952 Etudes d'Epigraphie Indonésienne: III Liste des principales inscriptions datées de l'Indonésie, *Bulletin de l'Ecole française d'Extrême Orient* XLVI-2.

Groeneveldt, W.P.
1876 *Notes on the Malay Archipelago and Malacca, Compiled from Chinese Sources*, Verhandelingen van het Bataviaasch Genootschap van Kunsten en Wetenschappen, deel XXXIX.

Krom, N.J.
1931 *Hindoe-Javaansche Geschiedenis*. 's-Gravenhage: Martinus Nijhoff.
Nihon-shi [History of Japan] (4 vols.)
1955 Tokyo: Fukumura Shoten.

Robson, S.O.
1971 *Wangbang Wideya, A Javanese Panji Romance*. Bibliotheca Indonesica 6, Koninklijk Instituut voor Taal-, Land- en Volkenkunde, Leiden.

Robson, Stuart (transl.)
1995 *Deśawarṇana (Nāgarakṛtāgama) by Mpu Prapañca*. Verhandelingen KITLV 169. Leiden: KITLV Press.

Robson, Stuart
2000 'The Force of Destiny, or the Kidung Harsa-Wijaya Reread', *Indonesia and the Malay World* Vol. 28, No. 82, pp. 243–52.

Rockhill, W.W.
1914 'Notes on the Relations and Trade of China with the Eastern Archipelago and Coast of the Indian Ocean during the Fourteenth Century', *T'oung Pao* Vol. 14.

Zoetmulder, P.J.
1974 *Kalangwan, A Survey of Old Javanese Literature*. Translation Series 16, Koninklijk Instituut voor Taal-, Land- en Volkenkunde. The Hague: Martinus Nijhoff.

Yuan shi

I. Gaubil's abridgement

This selection is taken from pp. 217–20 of *Histoire de Gentchiscan et de toute la Dynastie des Mongous ses successeurs, conquérans de la Chine, tirée de l'histoire chinoise et traduite par le R.P. Gaubil de la Compagnie de Jesus, Missionnaire à Péking*. Translated from the French by David Bade.

After some time he [Khubilai] had sent to the King of *Kouaoua* an official named *Mengki* [for Gaubil's note, see Note 1 below]. It does not say what *Mengki* did, nor what was the incident that made the King of *Kouaoua* act so terribly. The king took *Mengki* and with a hot iron marked him on the face as was often done to common thieves. After being thus affronted *Mengki* was sent away. The Chinese were indignant at seeing a Great Mandarin of their nation dishonored by a Prince treating them like barbarians, and they implored Khubilai to exact vengeance. *Khubilai* made an uproar over the insult done to one of his envoys, and ordered a large flotilla of warships and others to assemble in *Tsuentcheou* in *Fokien*. The Provinces of *Kiamsi*, of *Fokien*, and of *Houkouang* furnished 30000 resolute men, and they had no trouble arming the flotilla, the Chinese being eager to furnish everything necessary, the Mandarins of the nation being much interested and resolved to make foreign lands see at least that they were very sensitive to a dishonor done to a Minister of the son of Heaven [Note 2].

In the 12th moon of the year 1292 the flotilla was ready; it had 1000 ships including the supply ships and others. There were 30000 soldiers not counting the sailors and provisions for a year. *Chepi*, a native of *Poyé* in the district of *Paotingfou*, had the general command, *Kaohing*, native of *Juningfou*, was general in command of the troops, and *Yehemiche*, a native of the country of the *Ygour*, was in command of the sailors, with *Yehemiche* and *Chepi* having made the trip to the Indes and understanding the language of *Kouaoua*.

The flotilla set sail in the 12th moon of the year 1292, and at first met with a rough storm. It proceeded along the coast of *Tongking* and of Cochinchine, passing by a mountainous coast and entering the sea of *Hoentun* [see Note 3] They then came to the *Kanlan, Yukia, Limata* and *Keoulang* mountains. They cut trees in order to make small ships, and in the 9th moon of the year 1293 disembarked by means of those small boats.

The Kingdom of *Kouaoua* is near to that of *Kolang. Tanaikialay* the King of *Kouaoua* had gone to war with *Hatchikafou* the King of *Kolang. Tanaikialay* was killed. *Touhanpitouye* the son of *Tanaikialay* futilely atempted to engage the King of *Kolang* in war, but all his efforts were thwarted. When he discovered that *Chepi* had arrived, and why he had come, he approached him and offered him all that he had. It was a deception by which he wished to triumph over the Chinese. He gave *Chepi* a Map of the country of *Kolang* and persuaded him to conquer it, promising him to join with his troops, thereby laying hold of measures for destroying the Chinese army. *Chepi* believed what *Touhanpitouye* had told him, left some officers to guard the ships, and went off with his troops in three sections to attack the main village of *Kolang* called *Tache*. The Chinese found an army of 100000 men ranged against them in the field; the battle lasted from dawn till midday, the troops of *Kolang* were beaten and retreated within the city to defend it. The King of *Kolang* did not wish to sustain a siege and came out with his wife and his children to surrender.

Touhanpitouye asked to return to his Kingdom. *Koahing* advised against this, but *Chepi* & *Yehemiche* were of the opposite opinion, and they killed the King of *Kolang*, his Queen and their children.

In 1293 *Touhanpitouye* went back on all he had promised, refusing to recognize the orders of *Chepi*, and attacked him with many troops, planning to cut off the Chinese on their retreat to their ships. Too late *Chepi* realized he had been betrayed, and defending himself with much valour he made his retreat with great discipline, and after 30 leagues found his way to the sea where he reembarked with everything he had, lifted anchor and after 68 days arrived in *Tsuentcheou*. During that expedition he lost 3000 men, and took much booty in gold and precious stones. The Emperor punished him and confiscated two thirds of his property for not having carried out his orders and having let *Touhanpitouye* escape; the same punishment was meted out to *Yehemiche*. Yet eventually they were pardoned, being good Officers, and the Mandarins had succeeded in doing what they had most wanted, that being to have shown the King of *Kouaoua* [Note 4] and the others that despite the distance they were powerful enough and determined enough to avenge any affronts that might be made to the Chinese.

Gaubil's notes:
Note 1. That is, one of his ministers.
Note 2. Title of the Emperor of China.
Note 3. The two Chinese characters express an immense chaos; I believe that it refers to a great ocean where one cannot see land and where one can sound no depth.
Note 4. Chinese geography books say that *Kouaoua* is a name given during the *Yuan* times, and that this is the country called *Toupo* in ancient times. *Toupo* is represented as a great Island in the sea that is to the south of China, and Geography under the Song knew very little about that island of *Toupo*. We add that *Kouaoua* is the country which the Bonzes of *Fo* call the Kingdom of the *Kouey*, or the Kingdom of Spirits, and that they say nothing about the situation in that country of the Spirits. Others understand that *Kouaoua* is not far from the Kingdom of Cambodge.

A large Map was made by order of the Emperor *Cambi* (I have seen this Map, which is carefully preserved in the Palace). Or rather a general Map on which the Emperor *Cambi* had written the names that the Chinese had given to the countries that they had knowledge of beyond their own, these characters of *Kouaoua* were over a good part of the Indian peninsula where *Cochin* is, but this could not be the *Kouaoua* which is in question here. I am led to believe that *Kouaoua* refers here to Borneo. A Chinese flotilla of 30000 men could go from Cochin to *Tsuentcheou* in *Fokien* in 68 days.

II. Groeneveldt's translation

This selection is taken from the English versions published in W.P. Groeneveldt's *Notes on the Malay Archipelago and Malacca compiled from*

Chinese Sources. Batavia: 1876 (*Verhandelingen van het Bataviaasch Genootschap van Kunsten en Wetenschappen*, v. 39) Groeneveldt's footnotes have not been reproduced here. It should be noted that Groeneveldt does not translate everything; for the full account it is still necessary to refer to the Chinese texts themselves.

A. From the History of the Yüan dynasty (1280–1367). Book 210. (beginning from p. 21 in Groenveldt's article)
When the emperor Shih-tsu (Kublai) pacified the barbarians of the four quarters of the world and sent officers to the different countries over the sea, Java was the only place he had to send an army to.

In the second month of the year 1292 the emperor issued an order to the governor of Fukien, directing him to send Shih-pi, Ike Mese and Kau Hsing in command of an army to subdue Java; to collect soldiers from Fukien, Kiangsi and Hukuang to the number of 20,000, to appoint a Commander of the Right Wing and one of the Left, as well as four Commanders of Ten Thousand; to send out a thousand ships and to equip them with provisions for a year and with forty thousand bars of silver. The emperor further gave ten tiger badges, forty golden badges and a hundred silver badges, together with a hundred pieces of silk, embroidered with gold, for the purpose of rewarding merit.

When Ike Mese and his associates had their last audience, the emperor said to them: "When you arrive at Java you must clearly proclaim to the army and the people of that country, that the imperial Government has formerly had intercourse with Java by envoys from both sides and has been in good harmony with it, but that they have lately cut the face of the imperial envoy Mêng Ch'i and that you have come to punish them for that."

In the ninth month some troops were collected at Ch'ing-yüan (old name of Ningpo); Shih-pi and Ike Mese went with the soldiers overland to Ch'üan-chou, whilst Kau Hsing brought the baggage with the ships. In the course of the 11th month the troops from the three provinces of Fukien, Kiangsi and Hukuang were all assembled at Ch'üan-chou and in the next month the expedition put to sea. In the first month of the year 1293 they arrived at the island Kô-lan (Billiton) and there deliberated on their plan of campaign.

In the second month Ike Mese and one of his subordinate commanders, taking with them their secretaries and accompanied by three officers of the Office of Pacification, who were charged to treat with Java and the other countries, and by a Commander of Ten Thousand, who led 500 men and 10 ships, went first in order to bring the commands of the Emperor to this country. The body of the army followed to Karimon (Karimon Java) and from here to a place on Java called Tu-ping-tsuh (Tuban), where Shih-pi and Kau Hsing met Ike Mese again and determined, together with the other leaders, that half the army should be sent ashore and the other half proceed at the same time in the ships. Shih-pi went by sea to the mouth of the river Sugalu (Sedayu) and from there to the small river Pa-tsieh (Kali Mas). On the other hand Kau Hsing and Ike Mese led the rest of the troops, being cavalry and infantry, and marched from Tu-ping-tsuh overland, one of the Commanders of Ten Thousand leading the vanguard. Three superior officers were sent in fast boats from Sugalu, with the order to go first to the floating bridge of Modjopait and then to rejoin the army on its way to the small river Pa-tsieh.

The officers of the Office of Pacification soon reported that the son-in-law of the prince of Java, called Tuhan Pidjaya, wished to make his country submit, but as he could not leave his army, order was given to three officers to go and bring his prime minister Sih-la-nan-da-ch'a-ya and fourteen others, who wanted to come and receive the army of the emperor.

On the 1st day of the 3rd month, the troops were assembled at the small river Pa-tsieh.

This river has at its upper course the palace of the king of Tumapan (Tumapel) and discharges itself into the sea called Pou-pên (the sea south of Madura); it is the entrance to Java and a place for which they were determined to fight. Accordingly the first minister of the Javanese, Hi-ning-kuan, remained in a boat to see how the chances of the fight went; he was summoned repeatedly, but would not surrender.

The commanders of the imperial army made a camp in the form of a crescent on the bank of the river and left the ferry in charge of a Commander of Ten Thousand; the fleet in the river and the cavalry and infantry on shore then advanced together and Hi-ning-kuan, seeing this, left his boat and fled overnight, whereupon more than a hundred large ships, with devil-heads on the stem, were captured.

Order was now given to a strong force to guard the mouth of the river Pa-tsieh and the body of the army then advanced.

Messengers came from Tuhan Pidjaya, telling that the king of Kalang had pursued him as far as Modjopait and asking for troops to protect him. Ike Mese and one of his lieutenants hastened to him, in order to encourage him and another officer followed with a body of troops to Chang-ku, for the purpose of assisting them. Kau Hsing advanced to Modjopait, but heard that it was not known whether the soldiers of Kalang were far or near, so he went back to the river Pa-tsieh; at last he got information from Ike Mese that the enemy would arrive that night, and was ordered to go again to Modjopait.

On the 7th day the soldiers of Kalang arrived from three sides to attack Tuhan Pidjaja, and on the 8th day, early in the morning, Ike Mese led part of the troops to engage the enemy in the south-west, but he did not meet them; Kau Hsing fought with the enemy on the south-east and killed several hundreds of them, whilst the remainder fled to the mountains. Towards the middle of the day the enemy arrived also from the south-west, Kau Hsing met them again and towards evening they were defeated.

On the 15th the army was divided into three bodies, in order to attack Kalang; it was agreed that on the 19th they should meet at Taha (Daha) and commence the battle on hearing the sound of the p'au [gun or rocket?]. A part of the troops ascended the river, Ike Mese proceeded by the eastern road and Kau Hsing took the western, whilst Tuhan Pidjaya with his army brought up the rear. On the 19th they arrived at Taha, where the prince of Kalang defended himself with more than a hundred thousand soldiers. The battle lasted from 6AM till 2PM and three times the attack was renewed, when the enemy was defeated and fled, several thousand thronged into the river and perished there, whilst more than 5000 were slain. The king retired into the inner city, which was immediately surrounded by our army and the king summoned to surrender; in the evening the king, whose name was Hadji Katang, came out of the fortress and offered his submission, on this the orders of the emperor were delivered to him and he was told to go back.

On the 2nd day of the 4th month Tuhan Pidjaya was sent back to his dominions in order to make preparations for sending tribute, two officers and 200 soldiers went with him as an escort. On the 19th Tuhan Pidjaya secretly left our soldiers and attacked them, by which the whole party came to grief.

On the 24th the army went back, taking with it the children and officers of Hadji Katang, altogether more than a hundred persons; they brought also a map of the country, a register of the population and a letter in golden characters presented by the king.

For further particulars see the account of Shih-pi.

B. Account of Shih-pi. History of the Yüan dynasty. Book 162.

Shih-pi, whose literary name was Chün-tso, and who was also called Tarhun, was a man from Po-yeh, district Li-chou, department Pau-ting, province Chih-li.

…

When the emperor Shih-tsu (Kublai) wanted to subdue Java, he said to Shih-pi: "Among my officers there are few who have my full confidence, therefore I want to entrust this affair of Java to you." The other replied: "If the Emperor deigns to command his servant, how could he venture to be afraid for his person."

In the year 1292 he was made commander of the expedition to Java, whilst Ike Mese and Kau Hsing were appointed to assist him. The Emperor gave him a hundred and fifty stamped badges and two hundred pieces of silk, in order to reward those who made themselves meritorious. In the 12th month he joined the other troops with 5000 men and departed from Ch'üan-chou; the wind was strong and the sea very rough, so that the ships rolled heavily and the soldiers could not eat for many days. They passed the Sea of the Seven Islands (the Paracels Islands) and the Long Reef (Macclesfield Bank), they passed the land of the Giau-chi and Champa, and in the first month of the next year they came to the Eastern Tung Islands (Natuna?), the Western Tung Islands (Anamba?), entered the Indian Sea (?) and consecutively arrived at the Olive islands (?), Karimata and Kau-lan (Billiton), where they stopped and cut timber to make small boats for entering the rivers.

At that time Java carried on an old feud with the neighbouring country Kalang, and the king of Java, Hadji Ka-ta-na-ka-la, had already been killed by the prince of Kalang, called Hadji Katang. The son-in-law of the former, Tuhan Pidjaya, had attacked Hadji Katang, but could not overcome him; he had therefore retired to Modjopait and when he heard that Shih-pi with his army had arrived, he sent envoys with an account of his rivers and seaports and a map of the country Kalang, offering his submission and asking for assistance.

Shih-pi then advanced with all his forces, attacked the army of Kalang and routed it completely, on which Hadji Katang fled back to his dominions.

Kau Hsing now said: "Though Java has submitted, still if it repents its decision and united with Kalang, our army might be in a very difficult position and we do not know what might happen." Shih-pi therefore divided his army into three parts, himself, Kau Hsing and Ike Mese each leading a division, and marched to attack Kalang. When they arrived at the fortified town Daha, more than a hundred thousand soldiers of Kalang came forward to withstand them. They fought from morning till noon, when the army of Kalang was routed and retired into the town to save itself. The Chinese army surrounded the town and soon Hadji Katang came forward to offer his submission; his wife, his children and officers were taken by the victors, who then went back.

Tuhan Pidjaya asked permission to return to his country, in order to prepare a new letter of submission to the Emperor and to take the precious articles in his possession for sending them to court; Shih-pi and Ike Mese consented to this and sent two officers with 200 men to go with him. Tuhan Pidjaya killed the two officers on the way and revolted again, after which he availed himself of the circumstance that the army was returning, to attack it from both sides. Shih-pi was behind and was cut off from the rest of the army, he was obliged to fight his way for 300 li before he arrived at the ships; at last he embarked again and reached Ch'üan-chou after a voyage of 68 days.

Of his soldiers more that 3000 men had died. The emperor's officers made a list of the valuables, incenses, perfumeries, textures etc. which he brought and found them worth more than 500.000 taels of silver. He also brought to the Emperor a letter in golden characters from the country Muli (or Buli), with golden and silver articles, rhinoceros-horns, ivory and other things. For more particulars see the articles on Kau Hsing and on Java.

On account of his having lost so many men, the Emperor ordered Shih-pi to receive seventeen lashes and confiscated a third of his property. In the year 1295 he was raised again to office and a memorial was presented to the Emperor, pointing out that Shih-pi and his associates had gone over the sea to a distance of 25.000 li, had led the army to countries which had never been reached in the last reigns, had captivated a king and awed into submission the neighbouring smaller countries, and that, for these reasons, mercy should be shown to him.

The Emperor then restored his goods which had been confiscated and raised him gradually to the highest ranks, until he died at the age of 86 years.

C. Account of Kau Hsing. History of the Yüan dynasty. Book 162.

Kau Hsing, styled Kung-ch'i, was a man from Ts'ai-chou.

...

When Java had marked the face of the imperial envoy Mêng-Ch'i, the Emperor appointed Kau Hsing, together with Shih-pi and Ike Mese, to take the command of an army and go to subdue this country. He also got a girdle adorned with precious stones, embroidered garments, a helmet, a bow and arrows, and a thousand mou of good land near a large town.

In the beginning of the year 1293 they reached Java; Ike Mese took command of the fleet and Kau Hsing led the infantry, at the small river Pa-tsieh they rejoined again. As the son-in-law of the late king of Java, Tuhan Pidjaya, had offered his submission, they marched to attack the country Kalang and subdued its king Hadji Katang. For further particulars see the article on Shih-pi.

They also awed into submission different smaller states and as Hadji Katang's son, Sih-lah-pat-ti Sih-lah-tan-puh-hah, had fled to the mountains, Kau Hsing went into the interior with a thousand men and brought him back a prisoner.

When he returned at the fortified town Taha (Daha), Shih-pi and Ike Mese had already allowed Tuhan Pidjaya to go back to his country, with an escort from the imperial army, in order to make preparations for sending tribute. Kau Hsing disapproved of this very much and indeed Tuhan Pidjaya killed the men sent with him and revolted again; he collected a large quantity of soldiers to attack the imperial army, but Kau Hsing and the others fought bravely with him and threw him back. After this they killed Hadji Katang and his son and returned to China.

By an imperial decree Shih-pi and Ike Mese, who had allowed the prince of Java to go away, were punished, but as Kau Hsing had taken no part in this decision and moreover greatly distinguished himself, the emperor rewarded him with 50 taels of gold.

D. Account of Ike Mese. History of the Yüan dynasty. Book 131.
Ike Mese was a man from the land of the Uigurs.

…

Next he was appointed governor residing at Ch'üan-chou and in 1292 he was called to court, on which occasion he presented to the emperor all precious articles in his possession. At that time an expedition against Java was contemplated and an army for the purpose formed in Fukien. Ike Mese, together with Shih-pi and Kau Hsing, got the command of it; the formation of the army was entrusted to Shih-pi, whilst Ike Mese had to provide for the transport over sea.

The Emperor gave them the following instructions: "When you have arrived in Java, you must send a messenger to inform me of it. If you occupy that country, the other smaller states will submit from themselves, you have only to send envoys to receive their allegiance. When those countries are brought to obeyance, it will be all your work."

When the army arrived at Champa, they first sent envoys to call into submission Lambri, Sumatra, Pu-lu-pu-tu, Pa-la-la and other smaller countries and in the beginning of 1293 they beat the country of Kalang and subdued its king Hadji Katang. Another envoy was sent to the different Malay states, who all sent their sons or younger brothers as a token of their allegiance.

The son-in-law of the prince of Java, Tuhan Pidjaya, submitted at first, but when he returned to his country he revolted again, for which see the account of Shih-pi.

The generals thought of carrying on the war, but Ike Mese wished to do as the emperor had ordered them and first send a messenger to court. The two others could not agree to this, therefore the troops were withdrawn and they returned with their prisoners and with the envoys of the different smaller states which had submitted.

The Emperor reprimanded Ike Mese as well as Shih-pi, because they had allowed Tuhan Pidjaya to escape, and confiscated one third of his property, but this was soon restored again.

APPENDIX 3

御批續資治通鑑綱目. 清康熙 46年
Yu pi xu zi zhi tong jian guang mu. Qing Kangxi 46 nian

I. *Yu pi xu zi zhi tong jian gang mu. Juan 3 (29th year of the Zhiyuan reign) (1292/93)* Translated by Geoff Wade

Emperor *Shi-zu* of the Yuan dynsty: 29th Year of the Zhi-yuan reign (1292)

In the second month [Feb/Mar 1292], Yi-hei-mi-shi, Shi-bi and Gao-xing were appointed as Managers of Governmental Affairs of the Fu-jian Branch Secretariat, and ordered to command troops in an attack on Java.

Earlier, Meng Hong, the Assistant of the Right had been sent as an envoy to Java, but [those of] Java had branded his face. When the envoy returned, the emperor was angered and ordered Yi-hei-mi-shi, Shi-bi and so on to lead 30,000 troops in a punitive expedition against them. At this time, the king of the country of Java had been killed by the neighbouring country of Ge-lang and his son-in-law Tu-han Bi-she-ye [Tuhan Wijaya] welcomed Shi-bi and sought their assistance. Bi and the others thereupon combined to capture the king of Ge-lang to take back. Then Tu-han Bi-she-ye again rebelled and Bi and the others engaged in fierce battle in order to defeat him and take him back. The dead numbered over 3,000 men and the officials estimated that the captured goods and valuables were valued at 500,000 [*liang* of silver]. However, as so many had died and they had failed to punish Tu-han Bi-she-ye's crimes, the Emperor ordered that one-third of the family assets of Shi-bi and Yi-hei-mi-shi be confiscated. Only [Gao] Xing was exempted as he had not been involved.

II. Mailla's version

My translation from Mailla's *Histoire de la Chine*, vol. 9, pp. 450–54. In this translation, Chinese names have been rendered in pinyin and Javanese names in the form in which I have used in the first part.

1292. In the year 1292, the first day of the first month, there was a solar eclipse. At the same time work on the Donghuei river canal which runs from Beijing to Dongjiu was finished.

The emperor had sent envoys to several kingdoms in order to urge them to put themselves under his protection and to pay him tribute. Meng Qi, who had been charged to go to Java, was not well received by them. The king of Java, shocked by Meng Qi's proposals, branded him in the face with a hot iron like a common thief and scornfully sent him away. Upon his return [to China], the emperor, indignant that some puny barbarian king had dared brand so ignominiously one of his high officials put together a flotilla with 30,000 men to avenge the insult and charged Yiheimishi and Shi-bi to lead it, with orders to bring him the head of the king of Java or to put him in chains and bring him on his feet before the throne to expiate the crime of which he was guilty.

The flotilla left Quanzhou the famous port of Fujian and sailed for Jiaoji; when they arived at Koulan of the kingdom of Zhenjing they weighed anchor and the two generals had small ships constructed with which they would cross the sea and enter the kingdom of Java. Haji Kertanagara who then governed that state was killed by Haji Jayakatwang the king of Kolang with whom he had been at war. Tuhan Wijaya, his son-in-law, had wished to avenge his death but he had been beaten and forced to retreat to Majapahit. At that point, learning that the Chinese had entered the country of Java, he sent one of his lords to present a map and detailed information on the kingdom of Java, and together with the map a request that the generals join him in his war against Jayakatwang, the enemy of Java, and to assist him with their troops.

The general Shi-bi, seizing upon an excellent opportunity to conquer both kingdoms, accepted the offer and promised his troops. He fought the king of Kolang and forced him to retreat to his own lands. Then dividing his army into three sections, they entered Kolang from three directions, reuniting near the capitol where the king Jayakatwang was with an army of 100,000 soldiers. On the morrow, the battle began, and lasted from daybreak until noon. The soldiers of Kolang, defeated, sought refuge in the town where they were surrounded by the Chinese and the Javanese together. Jayakatwang asked to surrender and submitted.

Wijaya who then ruled the kingdom of Java drew up a letter of submission for the emperor which he gave to Shi-bi along with the royal seal. He behaved toward the Chinese generals with whom he had come to Kolang as though he were a vassal of China, and having no doubts concerning his good faith, on his return to his capitol he was escorted by only 200 men. But when they had come within the limits of Java, he attacked these 200 men, killing many and readying himself to repulse the Chinese should they come to attack him.

The Chinese, indignant at his treason, retraced their steps in order to make him pay, but they fell into an ambush and were beaten. Shi-bi, in charge of the rear, was harassed during his retreat for 300 *li*, all the way to the sea where they boarded their ships and sailed back to China. He arrived in Quanzhou after a journey of 68 days and lost during this expedition more than 3000 of the best soldiers. He had gotten much booty in gold and precious stones, which were estimated at more than 500,000 taels of silver. Upon his arrival at the court, he turned over all these riches to be offered to the emperor, but the prince would not pardon him for having returned without fulfilling his orders and for allowing Wijaya to escape. He was condemned to receive 70 lashes and all of his possessions were confiscated.

Panji Wijayakrama
(Rangga Lawe, Part 1)

The English summary presented here is an abridged translation of Berg's Dutch summary which precedes his edition of the Middle Javanese text (*Rangga Lawe: middeljavaansche historische roman*. Bibliotheca Javanica, 1. Batavia: Kon. Bataviaasch Genootschap van Kunsten en Wetenschappen, 1930. Zoetmulder offers a brief summary and comments in his book *Kalangwan: a survey of Old Javanese literature* (pp. 415–17).

In Tumapel reigned a brave young ruler who was called prince Krtenagara, and given the name Shiva-Buddha after his enthronement. In those days there were two beautiful young princesses in Tumapel who were intended to become the wives of Wijaya, the king's young nephew. While Wijaya was a charming man, honoured and much loved by all, the king himself was bad, like a hot sun beating down mercilessly upon all.

Mpu Raganatha, the wise, old and prudent minister decided that since his advice was always disregarded he would resign. Kebo-Anengah and Panji-Agragani became prime ministers.

After he had overcome all dangers, Shiva-Buddha sent an expedition against Malaya. A great army departed, accompanied by the two ministers as far as Tuban. In Tumapel remained only a few soldiers.

While Shiva-Buddha was living a gay and carefree life, Banyak-Wide set to work to achieve his undoing. This man, later called Arya Wiraraja, had been forced out of his position in Singhasari and sent off to be the governor of East Madura. When he found out that Tumapel was empty of troops, his opportunity had come. He met with Jayakatwang, King of Kediri, and secretly advised him to march against Tumapel.

Jayakatwang followed his advice. He consulted with his men on how best to succeed against Tumapel. It was decided that his army would be divided into two groups: the worst troops would march against Tumapel along a northern route; the other, better troops would march silently along a southern route under the command of Kebo-Mundarang.

Shiva-Buddha received the news of the enemy's surprise attack but he did not believe it until the wounded were carried in from the battlefield. In great haste he sent Raden Wijaya with an army against the attack which was coming from the north. After Wijaya's departure the king once again gave himself over to carefree merry-making.

Unexpectedly the army which had gone the southern route fell upon Tumapel. The palace was captured and the king killed. A messenger brought to Wijaya the news of what had happened in Tumapel. At first Wijaya did not understand the situation; he said he had already won. The messenger made it clear to him that a second army had come to Tumapel silently under the command of Mundarang.

Wijaya debated with his companions what he should do. They finally decided they should quickly turn back to Tumapel. There they fell on troops from Kediri but they retreated. They had to flee with Kebo-Mundarang in pursuit. Wijaya fled into a rice field and Kebo-Mundarang followed after him. Just when Mundarang was standing over him ready to strike with his lance, Wijaya splashed his face with water from the furrow so that with mud in his eyes Mundarang had to retreat.

Wijaya rewarded his companions. Sora advised him to make another attack immediately since a new attack would be the least expected action. When they attacked the palace the troops from Kadiri were there amusing themselves and in fact had not taken any precautions to ensure their safety. Wijaya's attack was successful at the start: several warriors were killed. Other Kadiri warriors under the command of Mundarang hastened to help and suffered heavy losses. Nightfall saved Mundarang, for the battle had to stop.

Wijaya's enemies were now on the alert. The troops were stationed outside the palace but still not far away. Wijaya again attacked the enemy, first casting a sleep-mantra on them.

Because of the power of the sleep-mantra and their exhaustion many of the enemy troops fell into a deep sleep. Wijaya overcame them and killed them dead. Those who had been wakened by the noise could not move as a consequence of the enchantment. Finally, one of them, Sunti, understood what was happening and scooped up some earth with his hand and scattered it over the soldiers to break the spell. That night a fierce battle was fought in which Wiragati fell at Wijaya's side.

The older of the two princesses had found out that she was going to be carried away captive so she stopped and remained behind. When Wijaya undertook his night attack he found himself behind the enemy lines not far from a fire where he commanded his soldiers to warm themselves. By the light of this fire Wijaya unexpectedly saw the princess who had taken refuge there herself, and naturally immediately took her. Overjoyed at this stroke of good luck, Wijaya proposed to Sora to attack again and perhaps the younger princess would also be found, but Sora advised him to sooner strike out and march and take the princess and himself to safety. Wijaya followed his advice and the whole night they walked northward.

Early the following morning Mundarang's soldiers went in pursuit of them. Wijaya and his companions entered a forest to seek refuge and the soldiers from Kediri chased after them.

By turns carrying the princess, Wijaya and his companions marched on through the forest. When the trip had gone on a while Sora advised Wijaya to march to East Madura and call on Wiraraja for help. So they went, and further on came to Pandak where they were received with great hospitality by Macan-Kuping; Wijaya was offered a young coconut filled with pure white rice. The wounded hero Gajah-Pagon was left behind to recover.

After winning the battle, the troops of Jaya Katwang turned back to Kediri where the younger of the two princesses was handed over to him.

Towards evening, Wijaya and his men neared Madura and they had to stay the night in a rice paddy. Sora went and laid down on his stomache so the prince and princess would at least have a seat to sit on. The following morning they went on to Sumenep. When Wiraraja saw Wijaya coming he was at first frightened and went inside. Wijaya thought this was a bad sign, but it turned out otherwise. Wiraraja and his family soon came out to welcome the prince and princess and put Wijaya and his companions up for the night. Out of gratitude Wijaya promised that whenever he would become king, he would remember the help Wiraraja had given him.

Then Wiraraja advised Wijaya to try to enter into Jayakatwang's graces for which he would offer his mediation. Wijaya would keep his eyes open and whenever he considered that the time was best he would ask the king about the land of Trik; the Madhurese would clear the land prior to his arrival. Wijaya must then take the people of Tumapel there to his new settlement and bind the people of Daha to him with money and good words.

Wijaya went according to this plan and soon an envoy from Wiraraja departed for Kadiri with a letter in which Wijaya offered his submission and called upon the palace of Kadiri to accept it. Jayakatwang judged the plan to be good and Wijaya left Madura for Kadiri.

In Terung Wijaya separated from Wiraraja and with his men marched on to Jong Biru. Then Jayakatwang was informed that Wijaya was coming and he sent Sagara-Winotan and Jangkung-Angilo to go out to meet him and with a wagon on which he thought the princess of Tumapel would also come. However, she had been left back in Madura. The messenger met Wijaya under a tree and brought him the invitation from the king. Thereupon he marched to Daha. The king welcomed him heartily, accepting Wijaya's homage and the gift from Wiraraja which he had brought, sweet nyuman-spice from China, and let Wijaya sit down nearby him on the palimanan on the side of honour. When the audience was over, Jayakatwang gave Winotan orders to give lodging to Wijaya in Jong-Biru where there was a large camping place. A feast was ordered, and when Wijaya arrived at the feast it was overflowing. The guests gave themselves over to pleasure. Wijaya held himself aloof for he had vowed to be done with dainties and hard drinks until he had won back his other bride.

The following day the festival took place. First the king gave an audience at which appeared Ratna Sutawan, the charming young girl that Jayakatwang had adopted, in reality the younger Princess of Tumapel. Again as before Wijaya was seated next to the king. After a while Jayakattwang gave orders for his chief warriors to organize sword dances and war games and to pit Wijaya and his men against the men from Daha. So the competition began. They held races against one another and Wijaya's men won. After a break, a tournament followed. When Jayakatwang saw that his men were no match for Wijaya's, he pulled Wijaya from the fighting on the pretext that the men from Daha would refuse to fight their best against royalty like Wijaya. Wijaya obeyed, but even so the men from Daha lost the tournament.

During the festivities first Pamandana then Wijaya himself recognized Ratna Sutawan as the younger princess of Tumapel, while Sora had seen Madraka and Sodrakara, her two handmaids. Wijaya thought that he had now lost his beloved forever for she had become the property of Jayakatwang, but Pamandana thought that the wink the princess had given him had to be understood otherwise. Later, it also became evident that Jayakatwang was very much enamoured of Ratna Sutawan but that she had not permitted his love, instead threatening to kill herself rather than give herself to him. She had not slept a wink until the king's consort Sri Kirana took her herself and made her her own daughter, making it impossible for Jayakatwang to make plans for her.

Still he remained madly in love, and he was determined to remain by her side lest she try to take her life. Wijaya painted a picture of her prototype Sita and sent it to her through Sodrakara and she sent him gifts. When hearing of Wijaya's departure, the women, not knowing his plans, were overcome with grief.

Wijaya had in the meantime not sat still, but first had consulted with Wiraraja and had asked the king for the forest at Trik. The king had given it to him; the Madhurese had built the village of Majapahit, and then the new settlement itself developed quickly. Wijaya had asked to leave that he might go there, and Jayakatwang allowed his departure on the understanding that Wijaya not remain long, for he should still reside in Daha. So Wijaya travelled from Daha with his companions; it was a glorious exodus and he was admired by the people even as Jayakatwang himself was not admired. No one in Daha suspected Wijaya's plans, but suspicious signs and omens foretold that this exodus would not bring anything good for Daha.

Seven days later Wijaya arrived in Majapahit and installed himself there, granting audiences and declaring everyone an independent sovereign. In one of his first audiences he let those who had barely established themselves in Majapahit appear by themselves; the best of them were promoted in rank and received new names.

When Wijaya saw that all went well in Majapahit, he sent Mahisa Panagal to Madhura. When the envoy arrived in Madhura, Wiraraja had just prepared a ship to bring to Majapahit the Princess of Tumapel who had been left behind. He told the envoy from Wijaya that he himself would not yet come to Majapahit, but that he would send his son in his place; he was living in Tunjung in West Madhura, and his wife would accompany the princess. The company went on to Majapahit and came to Wirasabha, its northern district. While Wiraraja's son in the company of Banak-Kapuk remained in Wirasabhu, Mahisa-Wagal and the women went on into Majapahit, where he reported to Wijaya on their mission. Later Wiraraja's son brought the message from Wiraraja that the latter was busy preparing an embassy to go to Tatar, and would ask his friend the king of Tatar to give his help in the fight against Daha and promised him the princesses of Tumapel as a reward.

Wiraraja warned Wijaya that he must not be too hasty and attack Daha prior to the arrival of the Tatar troops. Wijaya promised he would act according to Wiraraja's wishes. Then Wijaya asked Wiraraja's son what his real name was, but he did not know. So Wijaya gave him the name Wenang, because he had such strength. In addition, he gave him the rank of rangga; consequently from then on he was officially called Rangga Lawe and stayed with Sora.

The following morning Wijaya consulted with Sora, Lawe and his other men about the way in which his men should lead the war against Daha, about the sending of spies and the difficulties that the troops might have in combat. Lawe suggested that he bring from Kore in Madhura the Bimaan horses, since Wiraraja had a right to ask this of Kore. Wijaya thought that was a good idea.

In the month of Waisakha Sgara-Winotan arrived in Majapahit as an envoy from Jayakatwang to Wijaya to remind him of his promise earlier after his departure from Daha that after having hunted a while in Majapahit, he would return and go hunting with the king. While Sagara-Winotan was in Wirasabha Lawe came back with the Bimaan horses. Winotan thought that Wijaya himself was coming with a hunting party and Wijaya did his best to reinforce that understanding in him that he was alone and they were waiting for the hunting equipment, that he would be pleased with the new men and whenever they arrived, they would journey to Daha. Winotan believed everything, but in his conversation with Lawe, Lawe thought he detected an insult to the Madhurese and asked Winotan what the difference was between these and the people of Daha; hinting at Wijaya's plans, he told Winotan in a threatening tone that he would soon see very well what the Madhurese could do. Winotan was not a little surprised over Lawe's outburst and asked how this impudent fellow could talk so injuriously. But Wijaya understood the great danger that lay in hostility between these two men, gave Sora a wink, and the latter skillfully diverted Lawe by instructing him to go make an inspection of the disembarking horses. Lawe stood up and went noisily and in an exaggerated manner as though he were not in audience. After his departure Sagara-Winotan was told that Lawe was a cousin of Sora's, a flat-lander from Tunjung in West Madhura who was uncultured and one must not be too severe with him. Winotan let himself be satisfied with this and soon set off back to Daha. The horses form Wiraraja, 27 of them, Lawe brought to Majapahit where they were distributed among the captains.

Then Wiraraja, his preparations complete, came with his troops and all his supplies to Majapahit; Wijaya himself fetched him at Wirasabha. In his next audience Wiraraja told about the result of his meeting with the king of Tatar. The two princesses from Tumapel were so renowned for their beauty that the Tatar king to whom Wiraraja promised them accepted the offer and promised to come to Java in the month of Waisakha, which fit in perfectly with Wijaya's plans. Lawe divided the army into two groups: one group which would march along the northern route, the long way via Linggasana; the other group would march along the southern route via Singhasari, Siddhabhawana and Lawor, over the same route that Kebo-Mundarang had taken earlier. The two groups would meet in Barebeg. Wiraraja went along with the plan and Wijaya instructed Wiraraja with command over the north and asked him besides to send messages along the way to the coast to the Tatar when they arrived to enlighten them about the situation; Wijaya himself would lead the southern army.

When it was reported to Jayakatwang that he was going to be attacked by Wiraraja, he immediately called his officers together to ask their advice about what he should do. The king was badly confused about the case and threatened his officers who were all quarreling. When Kebo-Rubuh blamed everything on Sagara-Winotan, that he had provided false information about Majapahit and therefore committed treason against the king, Winotan would not allow himself to be so insulted and drew his sword, but the king asked for silence. Suddenly a man came from Tuban to pay his respects; he brought the news that the King of Tatar — Tarulaksana — had arrived with a powerful army whereof one part had already landed at Dataran and that the rumour was that he had come at the request of Wijaya and Wiraraja. The troops had landed and set up along the coast and had destroyed Tuban, whereupon the inhabitants had fled in terror. Jayakatwang understood that there could be no delay. He divided the Daha army into three sections: a northern section over which Jayakatwang himself would lead; an eastern army under Sagara-Winotan and Janur and a southern army under Kebo-Mundarang and Pangelet; they would fight against the Tatar, Wiraraja and Wijaya respectively. Soon the troops pulled out; bad omens foretold Jayakatwang's defeat.

In the ensuing battle, Gajah-Pagon, the wounded soldier who Wijaya had left behind earlier now appeared and slaughtered a multitude. Pangelet was killed by Nambi, Mahisa-Rubuh by Mahisa-Wagal. Sora had a bad moment battling against Mundarang and Drawalika together, but even so he put Mundarang to flight.This all happened on the southern front where the Daha army after Mundarang's flight were completely defeated. Also on the eastern front the allies won after an exciting fight between Lawe and Sagara-Winotan in which Lawe from his horse Anda-Wesi leapt onto Winotan's wagon and by killing Winotan on the seat of his own wagon had proved to him how well the Madhurese could fight.

Only in the north were the forces of Majapahit suffering defeat and had begun a speedy retreat. The Tatar commanders Janapati and Taru-Janaka together with some Javanese held off the advance of the Daha troops in which Jaya-Katwang himself participated. In the following battle the Tatars and Javanese were both killed so that in the end the king of Daha and the King of Tatar came up against each other. The conclusion of this battle was that Jayakatwang was seized and that the King of Tatar ordered him temporarily placed in captivity; he would deliver him to Wiraraja when he went to ask for the two princesses from Tumapel. Mundarang also had to give up the fight in the end; he fled, was captured by Sora and brought onto the plain. Mundarang asked for his life and promised Sora his daughter, but Sora did not let himself be mollified and killed him. So the war ended in Wijaya's favour.

Then Wijaya immediately went to free the younger princess from the palace in Daha and brought her with Sodrakara and Madraka to Majapahit. At Majapahit, Wijaya's attitude towards the Tatars regarding the taking of the princesses is apologetic. Soon the Tatars sent envoys to the Javanese to remind them of their promise: two officers, Sundarsana the son of Janapati, and Suryanasa, the son of Taru-Janaka, accompanied by 200 men. Sora tells them truthfully that the princesses of Tumapel cannot bear the sight of weapons and so unarmed they must meet them; the envoys brought this news to the king of Tatar and the latter willingly let the Javanese envoys in. The king himself ordered the return to Tatar-land to make wedding presents for the princesses. When the procession that came to call for the princesses arrived in Majapahit, they were all guided to a ball, where they were entertained as guests. The men were obliged to remain behind while Wiraraja took the women further inside the palace. Sora and Lawe stayed with the men and when they had eaten their fill and were resting, unexpectedly they attacked them, killing many and taking the rest captive. Likewise, the Tatar ships which lay on the beach with all they contained were captured and brought to Majapahit. At the same time, from Daha an enormous booty and a great number of prisoners were brought to Majapahit, where all were distributed among the captains; above all Wiraraja received a large portion. Jayakatwang was shut up in Jung-Galuh and in his imprisonment wrote the *Kidung Wukir-Polaman*, dying shortly thereafter.

Kidung Panji-Wijayakrama
(Raffles' version)

This account is taken from Raffles' *History of Java*, 2nd ed., 1830, v. 2, pp. 110–16. I am assuming that it is a summary, whether summarized by Raffles or at his request.

The history of the kingdom of *Tumápel*, being an account of the origin and rise of the kingdom of *Majapáhit*, written on the day of *Respáti* (Thursday,) the 10th of the fifth season. Date *wisaya rasa toya wasitan* (literally 1465.)

In the kingdom of *Tumápel* there reigned a king, named and styled *Rátu Sri Jáya Purúsa*, who in his demise was succeeded by his son, known by the name and title of *Sri Láksi Kirána*, who on dying left two sons, the elder named and styled *Sang Sri Síwabúda*, who succeeded to the throne; the younger *Ráden Wijáya*, who was remarkable for the beauty of his person.

During the reign of *Sáng Srí Síwabúda* the state had very much declined. Every district was going to ruin, in consequence of which the *páteh*, named *Mángku Rája Náta*, addressed himself to the prince, reminding him of the manner in which his forefathers used to treat the people, and which the welfare of his kingdom required of him to follow. To this, however, the prince would not listen, and as a punishment to the *páteh* for his presumption, he immediately ordered him to quit *Tumápel*.

Sang Sri Síwabúda had a man in his service named *Wíra Rája*, whom, in consideration of his useful services, he had made ruler over the eastern part of *Madúra* called *Súmenap*. On being informed that the king intended to accuse him of a crime of which he was innocent, and considering himself in danger, he sent a messenger to *Sri Jáya Kátong*, sovereign of *Kedíri*, to say, 'that as the kingdom of *Tumápel* was almost in a state of confusion, he might attack and conquer it without difficulty'.

Sri Jáya Kátong, on hearing the intelligence, was very much delighted, and accordingly he ordered his *páteh*, *Kébo Mundárang*, to make preparations for the purpose of invading *Tumápel*.

When every thing was ready the king gave orders to his *páteh* that he should march with a considerable force to *Tumápel*, and attack the southern part of the kingdom, while himself and his followers began the attack on the west.

Sri Síwabúda being informed that his kingdom was invaded by the sovereign of *Kedíri*, appointed his younger brother, *Ráden Wijáya*, to command the forces, and meet the enemy coming from the west. Instead of marching out himself to meet the attack from the south he remained in his *kadáton*, and amused himself with his concubines. This enjoyment, however, was soon interrupted; for *Mundárang* having reached the *kadáton* obliged him to come out and meet him, and on his making his appearance, *Mundárang* and his followers lost no time in deciding his fate. *Sri Síwabúda* was accordingly killed before the palace gate. *Ráden Wijáya* and *Jáya Kátong* had by this time fought several battles, as well as skirmishes, in which a great number of men were killed on both sides.

They continued to oppose each other when *Mundárang* came up and attacked *Wijáya* in the rear. This soon determined the victory in favour of *Kedíri*, and obliged *Wijáya* to fly to *Súmenap* for the safety of his person, where he remained in the house of *Wíra Rája*, to whom he gave a full account of all the circumstances.

Among the spoils which *Mundárang* had taken from the palace was the beautiful wife of *Wijáya*, who was afterwards delivered to the sovereign of *Kedíri*. He was very much struck with her beauty, and proposed to make her his lawful wife.

This proposal was however refused, and the king, instead of being offended by the refusal, adopted her as his daughter.

Ráden Wijáya had by this time remained a good while with *Wíra Rája* at *Súmenap*, and was then advised by him to repair to *Kedíri*, that *Jáya Kátong* might forgive him, and employ him in some way or other. He accordingly went over to *Jáya Kátong*, who received him very kindly; and he had not remained long at *Kedíri* when *Jáya Kátong* granted him an extensive forest, with which he might do as he liked.

Wijáya, with a view of making a large town in the forest, sent a messenger to *Wíra Rája* to get some assistance. *Wíra Rája* accordingly sent over a good many people to *Wijáya*, who, after procuring every thing necessary for such an undertaking, began to cut down the forest. While they were at work they found a large *mája* tree loaded with fruit, but when they tasted the fruit they found it quite bitter; whence the place was called *mája páit*, (literally the bitter *mája*.)

Ráden Wijáya, after making *Májapáhit* a very large town, assumed the title of *Bopáti Sang Browíjáyá*, having for his *Páteh* a son of *Wíra Rája*, whose name and title was *Kiaái Pateh Ráng'ga Láwé*.

The population of *Májapáhit* increasing very rapidly, *Browíjáyá* thought, that with the aid of *Wíra Rája* he should be able to invade *Kedíri*.

Jáya Kátong, on being informed that a considerable force from *Májapáhit* was coming to invade his kingdom, immediately sent out a band of fighting men to meet the enemy. Several battles were fought in which many fell on either side.

Jáya Kátong, previous to the invasion of *Browíjáyá*, had promised his guest, the King of *Tátar*, whose name and title was *Srí Laksemána*, to give him his adopted daughter (wife to *Browíjáyá*) in marriage. This was however delayed. Several times did *Laksemána* press *Jáya Kátong* to fulfil his promise, but he never received a positive answer.

Laksemána therefore being informed that *Browíjáyá* of *Májapáhit* had attacked *Kedíri*, forthwith sent a letter to him, saying that he would co-operate with the people of *Májapáhit*, provided *Browíjáyá* would be on good terms with him.

Browíjáyá on receiving this intelligence was very much delighted, and accordingly returned a letter of approbation to *Laksemána*.

Laksemána and his followers then joined *Browíjáyá*, and fought several battles with *Jáya Kátong*, in which a great number of men, as well as chiefs, were killed on both sides.

In the heat of the action *Jáya Kátong* and *Laksemána* met, and a fierce encounter took place between these chiefs. *Jáya Kátong* threw his javelin at *Laksemána*, but missed him; and *Laksemána*, in return, struck him on the breast with his poisoned spear, and killed him on the spot.

Páteh Mundárang, and the whole force of *Kedíri*, perceiving that their king was fallen, immediately surrendered.

Browíjáyá then eagerly went into the *kadáton*, and was received by his faithful wife. They embraced with tears of joy; and *Browíjáyá* was so enraptured at recovering her, that without taking further notice of the *kadáton*, he returned with his wife to *Májapáhit*. He invited the King of *Tátar* to visit him. On his arrival *Browíjáyá* received him with every attention, and made him a present of a beautiful virgin.

Laksemána remained for some time at *Májapáhit*, during which *Browíjáyá* gave him two or three grand entertainments. He afterwards embarked on board of his own vessel and returned to his kingdom of *Tátar*.

[Raffles summarizes the remainder of the text as follows: "The story concludes with stating that *Browíjáyá*, with his *Páteh, Rang'ga Lawé*, reigned at *Májapáhit*, and governed the whole of the island of Java, and his people were very happy."]

APPENDIX 6

Kidung Harsawijaya

The English summary below is in large part a translation of Berg's Dutch summary which precedes the Middle Javanese text published by C.C. Berg (*Kidung Harsa-Wijaya. Tekst, inhoudsopgave en aanteekeningen door C.C. Berg. 's-Gravenhage: Martinus Nijhoff, 1931*). I have omitted and condensed a few passages, and incorporated additional material taken — sometimes directly — from Zoetmulder's English summary (in *Kalangwan: a survey of Old Javanese literature*, pp. 409–15).

Over Java and the surrounding lands there ruled king Narasingha of Singhasari from the family of Hari. This king had a relative who held the rank of *arya*, named Kertanagara. His Prime Minister was *mpu* Raganatha, his *demang* (Chamberlain) Wiraraja, his *tumenggung* (Commander-in-chief) Wirakrti, and his chief brahmin was Cantasmrti.

To Narasingha and his *prameswari* (first wife and queen) a son is born, who receives the name of Harsawijaya. The dignitaries sent their sons to the court and these became the inseparable friends of Harsawijaya: Lawe, Nambi, Sora, Pedang, Dangdi, Gajah-Pagon and Lembu-Peteng.

When Narasingha felt his end was near Cantasmrti, Harsawijaya, Kertanagara and the other ministers came to his sick bed. The king asked Kertanagara to take Harsawijaya as his son; Kertanagara did, since he was sure that he would succeed him as king and rule over Harsawijaya himself. The king died and was cremated with his consort who followed him in death. Kertanagara now became king. Under his rule Wijaya grew up, and when he got older he received his own residence together with his companions. Harsawijaya is especially handsome in appearance; all the women fall in love with him. He grows up as the personification of every quality required in a prince, being handsome, clever and valiant, and excelling in every branch of art.

The new king did not pay much attention to the words of his Prime Minister; the latter therefore quit his office; he was succeeded by Rangga Nengah. Also, Wirakrti quit his office, as did the Chamberlain who was appointed to the governour of East Madhura. Cantasmrti was also unable to reconcile himself with the state of affairs under the new regime; he left Singhasari and became a hermit at Meru.

After he had reigned for a number of years Kertanagara formed a plan for his two daughters who he had from his queen, Puspawati and Pusparasmi, to give them in marriage to Harsawijaya; he would retire as a *bagawan* (royal ascetic) while Harsawijaya ruled the kingdom. He summoned Harsawijaya to a private audience during which he would tell of his plan and make his proposal.

Harsawijaya was with his companions when the messenger came to him and invited him to proceed to the audience with the king. He got himself ready and set on his way. Rangga Wenang (=Rangga Lawe) carried his betel paraphernalia, Nambi his fan, Gajah-Pagon the sweets; Sora, Pedang, Dangdi and Lembu-Peteng carried other things. When they passed by, the girls of the city expressed the love they felt in their hearts. Harsawijaya arrived at the place where the audience was to take place and was welcomed there by the former patih Raganatha and Wirakrti, who expressed the wish that Wijaya would soon succeed Kertanagara.

At the audience Kertanagara gave both his daughters to Harsawijaya and said that he himself would now retire. Against Kertanagara's plan, however, Prime Minister Nengah proposed another plan, bringing to his attention that the sovereign of Malayu also had two beautiful daughters, Dara-Petak and Dara-Jingga, and he thought that, first an expedition against Malayu should be undertaken, so that this land itself would become subject to Singhasari, and the two princesses would be offered as a sign of their subjection to Singhasari. So Java would come to seem all the greater in foreign lands and Wijaya would then make them his *mahadewi* [co-spouses of inferior rank, and thus complete the number of four wives].

The king fell for this plan. He asked his former prime minister Raganata and Wirakrti their opinions on this proposal. The former answered the king that he did not have a very high opinion of it, that he was in danger of being threateneed by Jayakatwang of Kediri who from of old had been the king's enemy, had not paid homage for some time, and who now knowing that everyone will not be back in Singhasari for a long time is waiting to make himself king; perhaps, so the former prime minister thought, Jayakatwang harboured a plan for avenging the defeat inflicted upon the previous king, Jayakatwang's ancestor Dangdang-Gendis. Anengah disagreed saying that Jayakatwang was just too young when Dangdang-Gendis was overthrown, and that through the king's death itself he had reached the pleasant life as king of Daha.

The other ministers who were opposed to the Prime Minister's plan ventured to express their opinions. The advice of Raganatha was ignored and the expedition was sent off.

The story continues with a description of the royal women of Singhasari of whom the chief and secondary consorts with the two princesses are elaborately described. The king and the prince go to the women's quarters, where the queen, her co-spouses and two daughters are diverting themselves with *gamelan* practice, to convey the news of the decision taken in the assembly. While the queen listens to the gamelan they enter. The king reveals the plan, including the two extra brides for Harsawijaya, after hearing which the two princesses leave crying for shame. The prince asked the king to see the troops off as far as Tuban, but the king refused, saying that the Prime Minister had that responsibility. Then Kertanagara handed over to Harsawijaya the royal jewels and kris [a dagger with special powers]. The youth then went away. He had fallen in love with the two princesses and went to the palace to express himself in poetry.

The troops who had set off for Malayu embarked from Tuban 10,000 strong. After seeing them off the prime minister returned to Singhasari. Every day the king kept drinking hard. Wiraraja, the Governor of Madhura, was so very hurt that he had lost his position. He understood that an army from Singhasari had left for Malayu and now thought that the opportunity was good to revenge himself over the indignity of having been moved to Madhura. He gave his son Wirondaya orders to secretly go to Jayakatwang and tell him that Singhasari was empty of its troops and that Jayakatwang should make plans now to make the most of the opportunity. Wirondaya cautioned him about Peteng, Nambi and above all Harsawijaya, for the king in his danger had not sent everyone away. Upon hearing this his father answered that one must take the opportunities which are presented, and gave him his plan to help Harsawijaya later attain the throne. Wirondaya went with a letter from his father and with a considerable retinue and journeyed across Terung and Canggu to Daha.

Jayakatwang of Kadiri was in many respects an excellent king who had distinguished himself from the previous king Dangdang-Gendis. His three main officials were: Prime Minister Mundarang, his Chamberlain Wirasandhi, and his Commander-in-Chief Mrgapati.

In the morning the queen of Daha told the sovereign of her dream of the previous night: people were on a hunt and the princess of Daha was given to a friendly white deer. The king did not atach any value to the dream since only bad dreams are fulfilled. The queen went off to the volcanoe Wilis to seek advice on the matter of her dream.

Wirondaya had come to Daha for a meeting with the prime minister, to whom he made known the purpose of his coming. He was escorted to Jayakatwang and a learned scholar read the letter in front of them. Its contents went as follows:

> I have to inform His Majesty you are comparable with a hunter, who has to make use of every good opportunity and place. The right time has just come. Please make use of it. At this moment the field is dry, no grass grows. The leaves are falling down, scattered all over the ground. The hills are small and the ravines are not dangerous occupied by one lonesome, tame tiger, that is not to be feared. The buffaloes, the cows and the rees are hornless. It is good to hunt on them while grazing. Of course there is no danger. The only tiger staying there, is an old and toothless one: he is Mpu Raganata. (Slametmuljana, 1976, p. 27)

The king asked Wirondaya to tell him of the particulars of the current situation in Singhasari, and he replied that there was general dissatisfaction with the government since the resignation of the previous prime minister.

The king hesitated and asked his prime minister what he thought about the matter. The minister asked if the king did not know that the land belonged to a family from Pangkur, Ki Angrok, son of Ndok, and that he was later called king Rajasa, the previous ruler of Daha, his father, the last suzerain of Daha. Furthermore, that he was defeated and subjected by Krtanagara's ancestor, and advised him not to miss the opportunity of regaining his former independence and punishing Singhasari for the humiliation it had inflicted on his house. The king doubted his words but the priests confirmed his statement and also told him of his duty regarding this hereditary enemy.

Jayakatwang mastered his anger when he heard how insultingly Daha was offended and humiliated, and he wanted to march against Singhasari himself. The prime minister advised him to wait and consider that the king should leave such activities to him and the army. He proposed that two armies should march out, one via the northern route, visible to all and with as much noise as possible, the other silently making its way through the forest of the south. The officers who were asked to lead the army enthusiastically approved the plan and the king set the departure date for the following day; after leaving Wirondaya in the care of the prime minister he ended the meeting.

While his queen, her companions and Ratna Kesari were discussing the meaning of her dream and whether it would come true, Jayakatwang arrived and announced that he had decided to attack Singhasari.

Preparations for the march to Singhasari were made and the troops departed. The strength of the troops going along the southerly route was 10,000 men. After the departure of both armies, the king went to meditate for the success of the expedition. After a march of seven days the southern army reached Jurang-Angcoka in the kingdom of Singhasari; towards nightfall they came to Kali-Tura where they made camp.

That night the king of Singhasari, Kertanagara, dreamt that the kingdom was ravaged by a tidal wave by which all were killed except Harsawijaya, who with his companions and his jewel (bride-to-be) were brought safely to the top of Mount Meru where all of Java bowed respectfully before him. The king thought that the dream referred to a disaster, that the troops sent to Malayu were threatened, and decided, worried about their fate, to give orders to the priests to exorcise the evil.

At the audience the king asked if perhaps a report about the *Pamalayu* had arrived; the prime minister answered that he had heard that the army had won and that the ruler of Malayu himself had submitted. However then came word by the ex-prime minister that a boat from Madhura had brought a report about a surprise attack by Jayakatwang. Kertanagara doubted the truth about this last report for he had always been on good terms with Jayakatwang. The prime minister proposed that after the return of the troops from Malayu, they should take action against Kadiri and give the beautiful princess of Daha, the daughter of Jayakatwang, to Harsawijaya as another wife. The former prime minister was displeased about the bragging of the new prime minister, but said nothing. Then suddenly people came from the north with the news that an army from Daha was on the way to Singhasari and had already gotten as far as Memeling. Many had been killed, many captives had been taken, still many others had fled into the wilderness. The king was terrified; alarm struck the whole of Singhasari and stirred up great commotion. Harsawijaya came in great haste to wait upon the king and asked permission to go out and attack the enemy. Although the king and his prime minister preferred that they should remain together, Harsawijaya went off with his companions and an army.

Anxious over the fate of the young Harsawijaya, inexperienced in war, Kertanagara ordered the prime minister to follow him. In vain the former prime minister cautioned him about the danger of remaining behind alone, unprotected against any enemy strategies; Kertanagara did not listen to him and the new prime minister left with all the remaining soldiers.

The southern Daha army which had been hiding in the forest of Lawon, upon receiving the news that the capitol was empty, marched via Siddhabhawana up to the city. When Kertanagara heard about this second attack he was pretty upset and wanted to close the gates. The former prime minister and Wirakrti both reproved him for his cowardice and pointed out to him that a king who died in the women's quarters would end up in hell. So finally the king took courage and in a heated battle outside the palace the Kadiri invaders were first repulsed, but some Singhasari heroes were killed and the soldiers had to retreat. The king, the former prime minister and Wirakrti then attacked. Wirakrti battled with the chamberlain of Daha — Wirasandhi — and was defeated. The former prime minister shared his fate. In the end the king stood alone; his opponent was the *raden arya* from Daha and he it was who killed Kertanagara. The passing away of Singhasari's king was marked by many natural phenomena.

Nengah, who was following Harsawijaya, found himself right by Sawah-Miring when he noticed that something was happening in the city. Immediately he made an about face. When he reached the edge of the city he understood that the king, the former prime minister and Wirakrti had all been killed in battle with more troops from Kadiri. Angrily he dashed in and fell on the Dahanese soldiers. In the battle he came up against the Commander-in-Chief of Daha who defeated him. What troops he had left beat a retreat.

After Harsawijaya had defeated the northern army, he received the news of the attack upon Singhasari from the south. He quickly returned to the city and once more there was a fight. Harsawijaya and his men were no match for the superior enemy force. They were forced to retreat and were followed by Mundarang of Daha. They fled into a rice paddy and the enemy followed them there. Once again Harsawijaya and his men fought a heated battle. Just when Mundarang had his lance ready, Harsawijaya kicked up some muddy water into his face, temporarily blinding him. Rangga Lawe and Sora did the same to their opponents and the result was that the Dahanese fled head over heels back to Singhasari.

Harsawijaya and his men discussed what they should do. They concluded that by night they would attack again since the enemy would least expect it. When they attacked, the troops from Daha were thrown into complete confusion. By chance Harsawijaya happened upon the elder princess of Tumapel near a campfire. From her companions he learned that the younger princess had been staying by her father, and had wished to follow her father in death but he had not allowed her because Harsawijaya was still living. Then she was carried off captive by the enemy. Harsawijaya then wanted to make a new attack in order to look for the younger princess and rescue her from the hands of her captors but his men convinced him of the hopelessness of such an undertaking. They left with the one princess and were followed in the morning by the Dahanese. Southward to Talaga-Pager they again fought with the troops from Kadiri and while covering the retreat of the prince and princess Gajah-Pagon was wounded. The retreat was successful, even though the Danahese wanted to pursue them all the way.

Harsawijaya and his companions escaped from their enemies and sought a hiding place in the forest; there they wandered for a long time in wretched circumstances. They came to the conclusion that they could no longer continue like this. Rangga Lawe suggested that they look for the hermitage of Cantasmrti. Some considered that such an attempt was doomed to failure. To make matters worse, Gajah Pagon declared that he would stay behind because he was wounded and in no condition to walk further, especially if they were going into the mountains. Nevertheless, in the end they marched further after all. They went on a new and long road of suffering from whence they had a view of the busy North Sea and they appeared to be in the woods of the hermitage. They asked a hermit where Cantasmrti was and he pointed to where they should go.

In his residence Cantasmrti warmly welcomed them, and when he heard of the attack on Singhasari and the vicissitudes of Harsawijaya's life since then, he readily offered to help them. He put them up in the guesthouse. Harsawijaya wanted to drink some coconut milk but the half-ripe coconut which he was given contained pure white cooked rice; the hermit interpreted this as an indication of Harsawijaya's future coronation. Of the request of the prince to remain in the ashram and dedicate himself to the spiritual life Cantasmrti would hear none of it for he thought the prince was just too young. He advised him to go to East Madhura and approach Wiraraja, who was clever and tactfull and maybe he could figure a way out of his predicament. Harsawijaya approved of his advice, took his leave of the holy man, and proceeded with his company to Datara where he boarded ship.

At the same time the prime minister from Daha learned that Harsawijaya had crossed over to Madhura by ship and was much pleased. The spoils of war from Singhasari were gathered and brought to Daha. Great joy reigned because of the victory, tempered only by the sorrow of those who had lost relatives in the battle. The *raden arya* brought Jayakatwang his report from the campaign and informed him that Kertanagara and his officials had died and that Harsawijaya and his companions had escaped. Thereupon he presented him with the booty. Among the captives was the younger princess of Singhasari. Jayakatwang had pity on her and to make her situation less painful for her put her with his own daughter Ratna Kesari. The queen of Daha became very fond of her. The other spoils of war were divided among Jayakatwang's officials. The whole of Java was now under the rule of Daha.

Harsawijaya and his companions arrived in Madhura. In the morning when Wiraraja was holding audience suddenly he saw his son Nambi appear. Having asked the reason for his unexpected arival Nambi told his father what had happened in Singhasari and how things had gone with Harsawijaya and his folks. Wiraraja let nothing of his satisfaction over Kertanagara's downfall be noticed, but showed him pity, going with his whole family to welcome Harsawijaya and the princess. He brought them into the palace and set prince Harsawijaya in a place of honor where everyone paid him their respects. After Wiraraja provided for Harsawijaya the latter told him of all that had happened recently. Grateful for Wiraraja's aid, Harsawijaya promised him half of the kingdom whenever he should again return as ruler.

After some time Wiraraja advised Harsawijaya to curry favour with Jayakatwang, and when the prince had gotten the sympathy of the officials of Daha, he should ask the king for the forest at Trik. If the king were amenable to his request, then he should establish himself there and the Madhurese would clear the area and build a settlement there. In agreement with the plan Harsawijaya with the princess sailed to Terung and after a while arrived in Canggu. The prince then sent Rangga Lawe to Daha to ask Jayakatwang to allow him to come to court.

Arriving in Daha, Rangga Lawe was introduced to the prime minister. The prime minister brought the news that Harsawijaya was in Canggu and wished to see Jayakatwang. Harsawijaya's request was considered from all sides: the possiblilty of a quest for vengeance, the difficulties that could arise, etc. Against that it was argued that the heavens stand open for those who practice virtue but the wicked will fall into hell. The king was convinced by this last argument and sent news to Rangga Lawe that Harsawijaya could come to Daha. Rangga Lawe asked for the pleasure garden of Bagenda as a residence for the prince and princess and the king granted his request. Rangga Lawe returned to Canggu and told Harsawijaya about the result of their trip.

Harsawijaya received the news of his permission and made preparations for his audience with Jayakatwang. The king and his ministers were greatly impressed by the beauty and manners of Harsawijaya and the court brahmin foretold that a man with the appearance of Vishnu would become king. All went well except that the elder princess was saddened at the impossibility of seeing her younger sister even though she was living so near her.

The troops from the *Pamalayu* then returned with the two Malay princesses. They heard what happened in their absence and so did not return to Singhasari, sailing instead towards Canggu and marching on to where Harsawijaya was staying. Harsawijaya was overcome with joy when he heard that Malayu had submitted and that two beautiful princesses with their retinue and many valuables had been carried off to Java. The newly arrived army offered their support to Harsawijaya in any eventual attack on Daha. Harsawijaya was to go the next day to Daha for the *Galangan* festival and so had a long conversation with Puspawati, the elder princess of Singhasari.

At the audience the king announced a tournament between the men of Daha and those of Harsawijaya. Everyone was pleased with the idea. The Dahanese were excited about the opportunity to see the two princesses from Malayu; Harsawijaya and Puspawati were glad that they would again get to see Pusparasmi, the younger princess who had been captured by the troops from Daha and who at that time was staying at the court of Jayakatwang. The day of the festival came. There is a long description of the royalty present, including descriptions of the daughters of Kertanagara and Jayakatwang. At the great audience the two princesses spotted each other.

The king ordered the tournament to begin. Harsawijaya looked so fine in his knight's outfit that Jayakatwang had an impulse to rise before him in spite of his low birth, so resplendent he appeared. The Dahanese lost the first contest because Harsawijaya participated. Therefore Jayakatwang insisted that Harsawijaya must leave the tournament. The tourney began again; the prime minister from Daha faced Rangga Lawe, Commander-in-Chief Mrgapati stood against Sora, Chamberlain Wirasandhi fought Nambi, and other high officials from Daha were set against Pedang and Dangdi; Mahisa-Rubuh was against Gajah-Pagon and Mahapati faced off against Lembu-Peteng. Still the Dahanese lost. Playing down the defeat, Harsawijaya said that the Dahanese had intentionally let them win out of sympathy, while the prime minister from Daha blamed the loss on the old age of the Dahanese champions who were no match for the youth and strength of the prince's men. So the tournament ended.

Now the question arose as to where Harsawijaya and all the newly arrived soldiers and people from Malayu would live. The king objected to allowing a resettlement of Singhasari and on the advice of his prime minister he decided that Harsawijaya should resettle his people in the forest of Trik. Harsawijaya agreed with the plan and was pleased. The king thought that the best thing would be for Harsawijaya to leave the following day with his men and go to their new settlement. Harsawijaya and his company returned to Bagenda where a great feast was held and a long discussion concerning what would become of Jayakatwang's daughter Ratna Kesari took place.

The following day Harsawijaya sent Wirondaya to Madhura for Wiraraja. After arriving in Trik Harsawijaya immediately began the work of reclaiming the wasteland, the work was made easier by the arrival of Wiraraja who came with his men and they with their tools to help with the work. Harsawijaya asked Jayakatwang if he could remain there for good and he granted his wish. Jayakatwang knew well the danger that now threatened him, but he accepted it with the words "Nothing is permanent in life with its alternation of fortune and misfortune."

Wiraraja then returned to Madhura. Quite a while passed and Harsawijaya remained on good terms with Daha, though all the while trying with gifts etc. to win the Dahanese officials to his side.

One morning he asked Rangga Lawe if the time had not now come to make his move against Daha. Rangga Lawe was of the opinion that they should not fight withhout reason: that would be ingratitude towards Jayakatwang. He proposed sending a messenger to Jayakatwang asking that he send to him Pusparasmi, the younger princess of Singhasari; if

Jayakatwang were unwilling, then Harsawijaya would have cause to make war. Sora argued for an attack without further ado, for he was certain Jayakatwang would be unwilling to give up such a stunning beauty; in his opinion, the earlier actions of Jayakatwang were sufficient cause for making war. Gajah-Pagon and Lembu-Peteng agreed with Sora, while Nambi made his plea for a sensible course of action: first convince Jayakatwang's officials to defect. Harsawijaya's other companions offered their opinions and finally Rangga Lawe suggests that before they take any action they should ask Wiraraja's advice. Harsawijaya followed Rangga Lawe's suggestion and sent Lembu-Peteng to Madhura.

When Wiraraja learned what was happening, he proposed an even better plan: he was a friend of the king of Tatar and would ask him for his help against Daha. As a reward, he would offer him the princess of Daha, Ratna Kesari, the daughter of Jayakatwang. He asked Lembu-Peteng to request Harsawijaya to wait for the Tatar and Madhurese soldiers one month before beginning his campaign against Daha. With this message Lembu-Peteng returned to Majapahit and Harsawijaya agreed to go along with Wiraraja's plan. While waiting for the Tatars, Harsawijaya and Puspawati celebrated their marriage and what a fine party it was!

After a while Wiraraja and his men arrived in Majapahit and the Tatars landed in Canggu. Jayakatwang received news that the Tatars had landed and were marching on Daha. He called his officials and informed them that the Tatars had landed and erected fortifications west of Canggu in Janggala. He proposed that they march against the enemy. The prime minister advised against this for the reason that the Tatars would bring destruction upon them. The Chamberlain, like the king, wanted an immediate attack, yet other ministers argued against this; they had learned that Majapahit and the whole of the east from Bobot-Sari were coming to attack, backed by Wiraraja and his Madhurese; thus the earlier prophecy came to pass. Mrgapati insisted that they must attack anyway: Jayakatwang knew he must do his duty and follow his calling. This argument convinced the king: he would accept whatever the divine will decreed. Seven generations had now ruled over Kadiri and now it was time for another house, in this case Majapahit, to rule. So the conclusion was to march into battle himself the next morning and proceed to Bobot-Sari.

Jayakatwang let the palace women know what had happened and told them that he had decided to march into battle the following day and had resolved to die in battle; they expressed their indignation at Harsawijaya's ingratitude. Likewise, Pusparasmi was very distressed over this betrayal. The queen comforted her and asked her to remain faithful to her and to Ratna Kesari.

In Majapahit Harsawijaya was engaged in conversation with Puspawati who suggested that he take the two princesses from Malayu as additional wives when he was informed by Raganurida that Wiraraja and the Tatar official wanted to speak to him. The Tatar official informed him of the fact that the Tatars were at Jung-Galuh, that they had built fortifications north of Bobot-Sari and that the region around Canggu was in their hands. They again agreed that the princess from Daha would be given to the Tatar Khan, and also decided that their three armies would march on Bobot-Sari from three directions.

The Majapahit troops were in high spirits, and there was eating and drinking all through the night. Harsawijaya made Dara-Petak his wife and spent the night first with Dara Petak, and then with Dara Jingga. After saying farewell to Puspawati he set out for Bobot Sari at the head of the Majapahit army. The army of Majapahit marched to battle and met the armies of the Tatars and of Wiraraja at Bobot-Sari. There they waited for the arrival of Jayakatwang and his army.

Jayakatwang did not join in the battle and his armies lost on all three fronts. When the news of their defeat reached him, he decided to enter the battlefield himself. When he appeared on his elephant before the Majapahit warriors, they were unwilling to kill him on account of his royalty, and Harsawijaya himself hesitated to kill the king who had been his friend and benefactor. Sitting on the elephant Jayakatwang began to meditate, and then vanished into the air. After the king's dissappearance, his soldiers fought till their deaths. The survivors fled or begged for their lives.

Under a large banyan tree Harsawijaya, his companions and Wiraraja, weary from the battle, rested and considered what to do next. Wiraraja advised Harsawijaya first of all to go as quickly as possible to rescue the younger princess of Tumapel who still remained in Daha. Harsawijaya sent a messenger to the Tatar Khan requesting him to return to his fortifications while in the meantime he would cremate the dead. He then went to Daha where all was in an uproar. When he arrived at the inner palace gate he saw that the whole place was covered with corpses: upon hearing of the death of Jayakatwang the palace women, including Ratna Kesari, had committed suicide. Pusparasmi alone remained alive; the queen and Ratna Kesari had not allowed her to kill herself, since Harsawijaya yet lived. Harsawijaya was then reunited with his beloved princess and asked Lembu-Peteng, Jaran-Waha and Panji-Amarajaya to bring her to Majapahit. To Siddhi he gave charge over the removal and cremation of the palace women. Harsawijaya himself returned to Bobot-Sari and looked for Wiraraja.

The Tatar khan learned that Harsawijaya had taken a princess from Daha to Majapahit and thought that this meant that their earlier agreement had been broken. Therefore he sent his Prime Minister, his Chamberlain and his Commander-in-Chief to meet Harsawijaya in order to recover the princess(es) and bring them back. They came up to Bobot-Sari and brought the message to their Javanese allies. When Harsawijaya did not know what to say in reply, the messenger got angry and accused him of breaking his promise. He said rather than leave the field empty-handed they would return with their army. Wiraraja interrupted and explained that Harsawijaya had not broken his promise, for the princess and all the palace women had killed themselves. The mesenger reported this news back to the Tatar Khan. The Khan was frustrated because the taking of the princess had been the main purpose of the entire campaign. When a spy later reported to the Khan the truth of how Harsawijaya had Pusparasmi taken to Majapahit, his dissappointment turned to anger and he ordered his army to march immediately against Majapahit.

His Prime Minister arranged to delay the departure until the next day, when they also decided to march to Bubat, from where the Prime Minister would proceed to Harsawijaya's palace to demand once again the promised princess.

In the meantime Harsawijaya and Wiraraja arrived in Majapahit. There Puspawati had heard reports of the outcome of the battle; in addition she was told by her handmaidens that Pusparasmi was on the way to Majapahit;

she proposed a feast to welcome the victorious armies. Dara-Petak welcomed her proposal but Dara-Jingga was still crying from longing to be with her father. Puspawati tried to console Dara-Jingga, saying that Harsawijaya would surely be willing to permit the king of Malayu to come to Majapahit whenever she desired. Then Pusparasmi arrived, very distressed at the deaths of Ratna Kesari and the queen of Daha. The others expressed their sympathy with her fate.

When Harsawijaya and Wiraraja arrived in Majapahit with all the spoils of war, Harsawijaya wanted to give a great part of the booty to the Tatar Khan on the following day. Wiraraja advised the prince to invite the Tatar Khan to come to Majapahit as proof of his friendship. Rangga Lawe then shared the news that he had learned that the Tatar Khan was very angry over Harsawijaya's reported breaking of his promise, and that he was on his way to Majapahit to destroy the palace if his demand for the extradition of the princess was not met. Harsawijaya was indignant; he would have kept his promise but the princess of Daha was dead before he got to her and Pusparasmi had already become engaged to him while he was still a prince in Singhasari; he would rather die than give her up again. Sora and Nambi proposed to destroy the Tatars' reinforcements, but Wiraraja urged caution. He wanted first to try to convince the Tatars that the promised princess was indeed dead and that the princess who was brought to Majapahit was no part of the agreement at any time. Nonetheless, for safety's sake, Harsawijaya must put the troops on alert. When he came to the palace Harsawijaya was welcomed by the four princesses, and he and Pusparasmi were wedded.

In the palace at Majapahit the special troops were posted. They received orders not to attack immediately, but to wait to see if the Tatars would maybe give signs of ill-will. The Tatars meanwhile marched from Canggu to Bubat. From there the Prime Minister, the Chamberlain and the Commander-in-Chief were sent to Majapahit.

When Harsawijaya heard the Tatar war cries he became frightened: Majapahit was in big trouble now. He told Pusparasmi that the king of Tatar wanted her and asked her if she wouldn't rather marry the Tatar Khan. She rejected the proposal.

The Tatar soldiers with great fanfare entered Majapahit calling out their demand loudly: the delivery of the princess from Daha. The people of Majapahit remained calm at first, only attacking when the Tatars entered the walled area. The battle was fierce and in the end the Tatars were defeated. Those who fled were pursued, surrounded in Bubat and most of them killed. The Tatar Khan himself died according to the dharma in the shadow of a white lotus. After the cremation of the dead, messengers were sent to Cantasmrti to come to Majapahit and perform the necessary rites for the new king. After completing the rites he discoursed on the duties of kingship and returned to his hermitage. At his consecration Harsawijaya received the sacral name of Krtarajasa and under his wise reign the empire prospered and the other islands – Bali, Tatar, Tumasik ... — recognized him as their suzerain.

APPENDIX 7

Pararaton

The Pararaton: a study of the Southeast Asian chronicle. Translated from the original Kawi text by Dr. I Gusti Putu Phalgunadi. New Delhi, Sundeep Prakashan, 1996. I have revised and edited the relevant portion of his English version found on pp. 97–115.

Chapter V

King Rangawuni was survived by his son Sri Krtanagara. Mahisa-champaka also had a son, Wijaya. Sri Krtanagara was crowned as the king, with the consecration title of Bhattara Siva-Buddha. He had an officer who was the son of the chief of Nanka village. His name was Banak-wide and his title was Arya Wiraraja. Apparently the king did not trust him, so he was removed and sent to East Madhura to serve as the governor of Sumenep province.

When Sri Krtanagara was consecrated, the Prime Minister was Mpu Raganatha. Although he had always served the king well and devotedly, the king did not think much of him and demoted him to an inferior position. His place was given to Kebo-tenah and Panji Aragani. Mpu Raganatha was transferred as a Superintendent (or Supreme Judge) in Tumapel. An important event of the regime was that king Krtanagara killed the villainous (Kalana) Bhaya. Then he sent an expedition to attack Malayu. While this expedition to Malayu was in progress there were fewer guards in Tumapel. Panji Aragani accompanied the invading army up to Tuban region and then returned to Tumapel, as it was his duty to supervise king Krtanagara's household. There was rivalry between king Krtanagara and King Jayakatwang the ruler of Daha. He was the enemy of king Krtanagara. He did not pay any heed to a possible surprise attack from his enemy. He did not realise his error.

Banak-wide was forty-three when king Krtanagara launched his expedition to Malayu. He was a close friend of king Jayakatwang. Jayakatwang had sent a message to Banak-wide, also known as Arya Wiraraja of Madhura. Then Wiraraja sent a letter to Jayakatwang in reply.

The letter said: "My lord, I respectfully tell you, if His Majesty has any consideration and desire to hunt in the former field, now His Majesty has the chance to so hunt. It will be the best and the most opportune moment. There is no danger. There are no tigers, wild buffaloes, or snakes even. There is only one tiger, but it is toothless."

The old Prime Minister Mpu Raganatha was called a toothless tiger because he was already too old. So king Jayakatwang set out to attack Tumapel. The armed forces guarding the north of Tumapel were attacked ruthlessly. Banners were raised and war-drums were beaten all over the area. The northern region of Tumapel was conquered and many wounded soldiers were captured by the invaders. The armed forces of Daha had marched through the north and halted at Memelin.

King Krtanagara Bhattara Siva-Buddha was then merrily absorbed in enjoying palm wine. When he was informed about the attack on Tumapel by Daha, he could not believe it and repeatedly uttered "How is it possible that king Jayakatwang has acted like this towards me, when he has always been on friendly terms with me?"

When the wounded army appeared before the king, only then would he believe it. So prince Raden Wijaya was instructed to face the enemy, who had come through the northern region of Tumapel. He was accompanied by the Commanders-in-chief Banak-Kapuk, Rangga Lawe, Pedang, Sora, Dangdi, Gajahpagon, Peteng, Wirot and Nambi the son of Wiraraja. All of them were chosen to lead the army. They attacked the Daha army in great numbers and repulsed them in the north. The army of Daha fled away, chased to the north by Raden Wijaya. Immediately afterwards, a large contingent of the Daha forces which had been stationed quietly near the southern border at Aksa began its march silently towards Lawor. The soldiers were not allowed to make any noise, especially while carrying the royal banner, and war-drums were not allowed to be played. After reaching Siddhabhavana, they marched together to Singhasari directly. The army of

Daha was led by its ministers Kebo-Mundarang, Pudot and Bowong. They marched straight into Tumapel from the south.

At the time King Bhattara Siva-Buddha was drinking palm-wine along with his Prime Minister in the palace. All of them were taken by surprise, vanquished in combat and finally killed. Kebo-tenagh tried to flee so that he might later avenge the defeat but he was also caught and killed at Manguntur.

Chapter VI

Raden Wijaya in the north was informed that king Bhattara Siva-Buddha had been killed by an army of Daha that had come from the south. Even the old Prime Minister had been murdered. All of them had followed their king. Hearing this, Raden Wijaya hurried back to Tumapel along with his soldiers. On arriving at Tumapel they wanted to restore the former order, but did not succeed. On the contrary they had to flee from the enemy. Raden Wijaya was then chased by Kebo-mundarang. Raden Wijaya went upwards in the direction of the irrigated rice fields that then stretched by the wayside. When Kebo-mundarang was about to pierce him with his lance, Raden Wijaya threw the earth and raised up such a storm of dust and mud, that Kebo-mundarang was smeared from his chest upwards to his face. Kebo-mundarang recoiled with horror and exclaimed: "Wow! God is certainly with you, nobleman!"

Then Raden Wijaya tore away some of his clothes and distributed the pieces among his followers, Sora, Rangga Lawe, Pedeng, Dangdi and Gajah Pagon. Then they planned a formidable attack wherein Sora attacked the army of Daha and killed many of them. He then respectfully said: "His Highness, you have to attack now. It is the right time."

Raden Wijaya then attacked the armed forces of Daha. Many fell on the battlefield. The army of Daha retreated for nightfall, retiring to their camps. When they were in deep sleep, Raden Wijaya launched a furious attack on them. The army of Daha was scattered and most of the soldiers were hit with the lances of their own companions in the confusion, while fleeing in the darkness. King Bhattara Siva-Buddha had two daughters. Both of them were to be united in wedlock with Raden Wijaya by King Bhattara Siva-

Buddha. Both princesses had been taken captive by the army of Daha. That night the army of Daha had a bonfire in the camp. In the radiance of the fire, Raden Wijaya saw the elder princess there and recalled that she was his sister, the elder princess. The younger princess got separated from the eldest one, as they had to run away in different directions. This happened because of the confusion in Daha's army caused by Raden Wijaya's sudden ruthless attack. The eldest princess was then brought back by Raden Wijaya. Then he commanded Sora: "Sora, come on! Attack! Run wild again, so that I can find my sister, the younger princess!"

Sora respectfully said: "Do not do so my Lord! Your sister, the elder princess, has been found, but how many of your followers are left now!"

Raden Wijaya answered: "I do agree with you!"

Then Sora spoke again: "The right thing to do, my Lord, is that you should retreat. But if you insist on a fierce attack and it turns out to be successful, that would be the best thing. You can get your sister, the younger princess back. But if it is unsuccessful, it will be like the white-ants flying to the flame."

Then Raden Wijaya retreated and carried his sister in his arms. Throughout the night they moved forward to go to the north. Later on in the morning, they were chased again by the army of Daha. They met them to the south of Talaga-pager, where some of his followers were kept waiting to fight and stop the army of Daha from chasing thenm. Gajah-Pagon was stabbed in his thigh. Even then he forced himself to move. Raden Wijaya asked him: "Gajah-Pagon, can you walk? If you cannot do so, well, let us go wild and hit back!"

"I will force myself to walk, my Lord, but slowly." The army of Daha did not have any further intention to follow them.

Finally they returned to Talaga-pager. Raden Wijaya penetrated deep inside the forest and roamed. He was followed by a number of his followers. They all carried the elder princess on their arms in turns. There his followers discussed the situation, and after arriving at a conclusion, all of them together came and said to Raden Wijaya respectfully: "My Lord, all your servants would like to know what orders you have now for us? We are just going to and fro wandering in the trackless wood. We would suggest that it is better if you go to East Madhura. There you may take refuge with Wiraraja. It is proper for you to seek his protection. How can he refuse to help you? He became a great man only due to your father, who is no more."

Raden Wijaya answered: "It would be so only if he is sympathetic to me. If he is not, I will be put to shame."

Sora, Rangga Lawe and Nambi forcefully said: "My Lord, how can Wiraraja lift his head before you?"

Then Raden Wijaya followed the suggestion of his followers. He left the jungle and came to Pangakan. There he met Machan-kuping, the chief of Pandakan village. Wijaya asked for a green coconut. He was offered the water of a green coconut, but when it was broken open it was found to be filled with white cooked rice. The on-lookers were amazed. They said: "It is really extraordinary because there is never a raw coconut with cooked rice inside it."

Gajah-Pagon had no strength to walk. Raden Wijaya said: "Chief of Pandakan, I request you to keep one of my followers. Gajah-Pagon is not strong enough to walk. Let him be here."

The chief of Pandakan said: "Oh, it would be unfortunate, my Lord, if Gajah-Pagon is found out here. It is not possible. Your subjects in Pandakan would not agree. They would rather have him confined in the wood. In the centre of the park we will make a hut for him, clearing the grass. It is a secluded place and nobody would pay any attention to it. The servants of Pandakan will serve him food every day."

Then Gajah-Pagon was left there, and Raden Wijaya went to Datar. The army of Daha had gone back home and the younger princess had been carried away to Daha. She was offered to king Jayakatwang. He was very happy to know that king Bhattara Siva-Buddha had been killed.

Raden Wijaya took a boat to cross the sea to go northwards. When he got to the other side, it was night. So he had to stay in the middle of the irrigated rice fields on the borders of Sumenep. He spent the night on a narrow edge of a small dike enclosing irrigated rice fields, which had just been harrowed. There Sora laid himself on the ground facing downwards. Raden Wijaya and the princess sat on his back.

Next morning they went direct to Sumenep. They took rest in the long pavillion outside of the palace. He asked his followers to find whether Wiraraja was there. The messenger returned and informed him that

Wiraraja was in his audience hall. Then Raden Wijaya moved towards the audience hall.

Wiraraja saw Raden Wijaya as the latter approached the hall. He was surprised, and suddenly went back into his residential quarters inside the palace. The people who had assembled there dispersed. Raden Wijaya's heart stopped. He spoke to Sora and Rangga Lawe: "Well, what was I saying? He made me feel ashamed. It was perhaps better if I had died when I had gone wild in the battle."

Then suddenly Wiraraja appeared before him and approached him together with his family and the chief queen all standing in a line. All of them carried betel-vine on their palms. Rangga Lawe respectfully said: "My Lord, it is now as it ought to be, since Wiraraja comes to appear before you."

So Raden Wijaya was pleased. The chief queen offered betel-leaves to the princess and Wiraraja offered the same to Raden Wijaya. Then Raden Wijaya was requested to go to the chamber in which the governor resided. The princess was made to ride the wagon. The wives of Wiraraja walked on foot to escort the princess. Wiraraja walked by the side of Raden Wijaya. Both were taken inside the residence of the governor and were led ceremoniously to one of Wiraraja's bed chambers. Wiraraja again appeared before Raden Wijaya in the pavillion in the second courtyard and then they recalled the death of king Bhattara-sang-lumah-ring-pandahan-sajeng ["The King Who Had Been Killed While Drinking Palm-Wine", i.e. Kertanagara]. Thereafter they talked of his fierce attack against the army of Daha.

Wiraraja respectfully said: "Now, what do you want my Lord?"

Raden Wijaya answered: "I would like your assistance, if you are willing to help me."

Wiraraja answered: "Do not be anxious. Whatever are our feelings, they must be controlled."

Then Arya Wiraraja requested him to proceed further toward the innermost part of the palace. There Raden Wijaya was offered clothes and a sash. These were carried on the palms of his wives and the chief queen. Raden Wijaya said: "Father Wiraraja, I am greatly indebted to you. If I succeed in achieving my goal, I will divide the land of Java: you will have one half to govern, while I shall govern the other half."

Wiraraja respectfully said: "As you wish, my Lord. In any case, you will be the ruler." Such was the promise of Raden Wijaya as given to Wiraraja. After that Raden Wijaya was served in an exceptional manner by Arya Wiraraja. Each day delicacies as in feasts were prepared for him and offered to him along with palm-wine.

For a long time, Raden Wijaya remained at Sumeneb. One day Arya Wiraraja said: "My Lord, I have got an idea. You have to pretend to apologise and act so as to draw Jayakatwang's attention. If the king shows no objection to receiving you, you should stay in Daha for some time. If you succeed in getting his confidence, then request king Jayakatwang to grant you the forest belonging to the people of Trik. That will be used to establish a new settlement. The servants of Madhura will clean that forest. It will be a resting place for you where the servants of Madhura will appear before you. The object of your service under the king is to carefully observe the activities of the army of king Jayakatwang; whether his soldiers are really sincere, brave, fearless and skilled. Particularly the intelligent ways of Kebo-mundarang. When you find all that out and everything is ready and in proper shape, then you have to request the king to allow you to dwell in Trik forest cleared by the servants of Madhura. There is one thing: perhaps if there happens to be any of your servants from Tumapel willing to serve you, accept them, that the army of Daha may be controlled by you. Now I shall send a message to king Jayakatwang.

A messenger was ordered to carry the secret letter. He departed and, after crossing the sea, went southwards. After reaching Daha, he forthwith appeared before king Jayakatwang and delivered the letter to him. The letter read: "My Lord, your servant informs you that your grandchild wants to beg pardon and to apologise. He wants to surrender to your Highness. This is my prayer to you. Now it is up to you to decide your action, if it will be favourable or not."

King Jayakatwang said: "How could I not be happy if my grandchild Harsa Wijaya wants to pay me obedience!"

Then the emissary was ordered to go back to inform them of the King's command. Upon arriving, the emissary handed over the king's letter. The letter was read out before Raden Wijaya and Wiraraja. Arya Wiraraja was very happy. Then Raden Wijaya returned to Java. He was escorted by his followers and the army of Madhura. Wiraraja accompanied him up to the region of Terung. Then he returned.

After coming to Daha, Raden Wijaya pleased king Jayakatwang by his devoted service. The king became sympathetic. He reached Daha exactly on the day of the Galungdan Festival. His followers were ordered to appear on the stage to fight in the arena bouts. Not one of the high officials of Daha was prepared to face them since all of them were so fit. Prominent among Raden Wijaya's men were Sora, Rangga Lawe, Nambi, Pedang and Dangdi. They all jumped onto the stage to participate in the armed bout in the Manguntur of Daha. Now it was the turn of the high officials of Daha such as Panglet, Mahisa-rubuh and Kebo-mundarang. All of them were defeated by Sora and Rangga Lawe in the race.

Later on, King Jayakatwang hit upon the idea of a spear bout, saying: "Harsa Wijaya, come on! Take part in the spear fighting! I want to see you fight. My high officials will play against you!"

Raden Wijaya answered respectfully: "Yes my Lord!"

Then they engaged in mock spear-fights. The sound of the clash of weapons was exceedingly loud. Many spectators had come to watch. The soldiers of King Jayakatwang were exhausted in chasing Raden Wijaya. Jayakatwang commanded: "Tell the honourable Harsa Wijaya to take part no more in the game. Who has the courage to have this master as his opponent!"

Raden Wijaya stopped playing the game, so that the soldiers who were engaged in the spear fighting were equals in rank. They chased and attacked each other. Sora ran straight to Kebo-mundarang, Rangga Lawe to Panglet and Nambi to Mahisa-rubuh. At last the high officials of Daha were put to flight by the men of Raden Wijaya. They did not come back into the arena. Thus it all ended. So, Raden Wijaya assessed that the high officials of Daha were inferior in fighting to his men. And then he sent a letter to Wiraraja. Arya Wiraraja replied asking Raden Wijaya to request the king to grant him the forest belonging to the people of Trik. Raden Wijaya acted upon his advice and King Jayakatwang granted Raden Wijaya's prayer. This is how the forest which belonged to the people of Trik came to be cleared.

When it had just been cleared by the men from Madhura, there was a hungry man, who having no adequate provision of food to eat, plucked a Maja-fruit from there and ate it. Its taste was very bitter. Then he threw away the Maja-fruit. It was spoken of far and wide that there was a Maja-fruit in that forest with an extremely bitter taste. Hence the forest was called Maja-pahit (the bitter bael).

Meanwhile Raden Wijaya had been cautiously watching the state of affairs in Daha. The Majapahit forest had already been cleared and turned into a settlement. The men of Wiraraja had spread widely in Daha. Majapahit served as the central place for their activities. Then Raden Wijaya was instructed by Wiraraja now to request king Jayakatwang to allow him to stay in Majapahit. King Jayakatwang agreed, because he had considerable regard for Raden Wijaya for his ability to serve him so sincerely.

Thus Raden Wijaya succeeded in settling at Majapahit. Then he informed Wiraraja that the ministers and dignitaries of Daha, including their followers, had already been brought under his control. Raden Wijaya invited Wiraraja to attack Daha. Arya Wiraraja sounded a note of caution, and told the emissary: "Do not be in a hurry! I will chalk out yet another strategem again. Hey! Ki Panalasan! Tell your master that the emperor of Tatar is a friend of mine. I will take the princess, you go back to Maja-pahit Kaki Panalasan! After your return I shall send a letter to Tatar, through the boat from Tatar which is here for trade. I have a boat too, and I will order it to get prepared to join them on their way to Tatar. I will invite the Tatar Emperor to attack Daha. If the king of Daha is defeated, the beautiful princess of Tumapel whose beauty has no equal all over the land of Java, will be offered to the Emperor of Tatar. That will be my trap for the Emperor of Tatar. Tell this to your master. Then I will join him in attacking Daha."

Then Panalasan went back to Maja-pahit. Raden Wijaya was very happy on being informed about the instructions of Wiraraja. Arya Wiraraja and all of his family followed after Panalasan to Maja-pahit. He brought also his army from Madhura. And the selected Madhuranese fighters with their weapons had also accompanied Wiraraja.

Only after the arrival of the emissary from Tatar did he attack Daha. The army from Tatar came from the north and the Madhuranese and the Maja-pahit army attacked from the east. King Katon was bewildered. He did not know which one should be faced. Then the Tatar army marched to attack him from the north. Kebo-mundaran, Panlet and Mahisa-rubuh faced the army which came from the east. Panlet was killed by Sora, and Mahisa-rubuh by Nambi, while Kebo-mundaran had to run away. He was chased and finally killed by Ranga-Lawe at the Trinipanti valley after telling Ranga-Lawe "Ki Ranga-Lawe, I have a daughter. Please give her to Sora as a reward for his bravery."

King Jaya-katon took his Dadap shield and went to the north. The Tatar army attacked him furiously. Consequently he was caught and imprisoned by the Tatar army. Raden Wijaya quickly entered the inner part of the Daha royal palace and took away the younger princess to Maja-pahit. Later on the Tatar army came to Maja-pahit and demanded the princesses as promised by Wiraraja, who had said that the two princesses would be given to them after the fall of Daha. This issue bewildered all the ministers. Sora said: "Well I will fiercely attack the Tatar army if they come here!"

Arya Wiraraja answered: "It is right dear Sora. But I shall devise another alternative." Then they discussed various options open before them.

Sora asked: "What will happen if I attack the Tatar army?"

In the evening when the sun had already set in the west, the Tatar army came to take the princesses.

Wiraraja spoke: "Hey all of you in the Tatar army! Do not be in a hurry. The princesses are in a state of shock because they have undergone some shattering experiences at the time when Tumapel was defeated and particularly while Daha was being destroyed. They will really be frightened if they see all your pointed weapons. Tomorrow I will hand them over to you. They will be put in a box decorated with clothes. They will be brought and escorted to your boat. The reason to put them in the box is that they do not like to see the sharpness of the weapons. Moreover, whosoever from the Tatar army comes to take the princesses should be clean and have a comely bearing and he should not have too many companions. The princesses have clearly stated that if they see any weapon, they will jump into the sea as they reach the boat. So, all the risks which you have taken in battle will go in vain if the princesses jump into the sea. Will it not be all futile then?"

The Tatar army believed this while in truth they were being deceived. The commander of the Tatar army answered: "Your observations are quite correct."

The Tatar army came hurriedly at the fixed time in great numbers to demand the princesses. Many of them did not bring arms. When they entered the gate, the guards closed and locked the gate from inside and outside. Sora tied his kris (sacred dagger) in his thigh and fiercely attacked the Tatars. The Tatar army suffered great losses. Ranga-Lawe attacked from outside the audience-hall. He chased away the Tatar army up to their camps. As the Tatars ran away to the Changu harbour, Ranga-Lawe still followed them. In the end they were all killed.

About ten days later, the expedition to Malayu returned. They had brought two princesses. One of them was married to Raden Wijaya; she became his queen. Her name was Dara-Petak. Dara-Jinga, the elder princess was given to the prince in marriage. She gave birth to a son, Tuhan Janaka, who was to become the king of Malayu. He was given the title Sri Marmadeva. He was coronated with the title of King Mantrolot.

The expedition to Malayu and the events in Tumapel coincided at the same time in the Saka-era Rsi sana-samadhi 1197 (1275 A.D.). King Katon had been enthroned as king in the Saka-era Naga mukha-dara-tungal 1198 (1276 A.D.). After reaching Jun-galuh and being released by the Tatar king Katon had composed a poem, the Wukir-polaman. After completing his works there he died.

Chapter VII

Raden Wijaya was crowned in the Saka-era Rasa-rupa-dvi sitansu 1216 (1294 A.D.). Raden Kalagemet was his son from Princess Dara-Petak. The two daughters of King Bhattara Siva-Buddha, who were involved in deceiving the Tatar troops, were also married to Raden Wijaya. The elder princess ruled over the Kahuripan province and the younger reigned at the Daha province. When Raden Wijaya was installed as the king, he was given the consecrated name of Sri Krtarajasa. He suffered from a carbuncle and died in the Saka-era 1257 (1335 A.D.). He was enshrined at Antapura.

APPENDIX 8

Babad Majapait

The latest edition of the Sundanese text was published as: *Babad Majapait*. Anggitan Kadir Tisna Sujana. Jakarta 1979. The following selections in English are my translations based on the Indonesian translation: *Babad Majapahit*. Translated by Rusman Sutiasumarga. Jakarta 1987. The pagination refers to the 1979 Sundanese version. The Indonesian translation omits some of the verses found in the Sundanese text.

[concerning Meng Qi (pp. 16–18)]

Then the nation of Singosari
befriended the nation of the Tartars
from the land of the Chinese Empire,
asking for the favor of the Ruler of the Tatars
whose renowned name was Khubilai
since in fact from the earliest of times
of previous kings they enjoyed
a close relationship of unceasing friendship.

Yet these two kingdoms
were not of the same mind
because Khubilai Khan
beheld Tumapel as a subject
since such was the opinion of his heart
[Kertanagara] felt unsatisfied to accept the
Khan's wishes to

immediately come across to surrender
himself properly as a subordinate.

When He did not send his representative
with an official messenger
then Khubilai Khan
sent a messenger immediately
carrying orders for Kertanagara
he went to the land of Java
appeared before the honourable King
bringing the command from his Khan
directly before His Majesty of Singasari
the sovereign Lord Kertanagara.

But the King of Singasari
did not feel himself under orders to serve Khubilai
would not consider subjection.
Often in their correspondence
presents from Java
were offered in friendship
without the proper submission
which Khubilai desired
and thus were not accepted.

The Tartar Khan would not accept
nonfulfillment of his wishes
and again He sent
more delegations
and several envoys
yet still He was not pleased
until finally the King,
the Lord King Kertanagara
because of the repeated delegations
responded in a fit of rage.

When the envoy named Meng Ki arrived
he was seized and branded
prominently on his forehead
then ordered to go back
to turn back towards home again.
When he arrived
he appeared before the Great Khan,
reported the whole matter
and the Khan could not bear his anger
when he saw the branded forehead.

"The king's words were barbaric
King of Java you are truly ill-bred
because of your audacious arrogant behaviour
your land will certainly be smashed
destroyed by our army
there will be no safety
there will be no pardons
all will be destroyed
just wait for our response
to your disrespectful attitude!"

The Tartar Khan prepared himself
amassed his strong army
intending to attack Tumapel
for revenge against the king
but the soldiers' departure was delayed;
before they could leave
troubles broke out elsewhere,
rebellion in his own land.
Only after putting down the rebellion
would they make ready again.

[Concerning the invitation of the Tartar soldiers to fight with Wijaya (pp. 42–44)]

Wijaya was determined
the time to act would soon arrive
he began to make plans
the way was already open
he quickly sent a letter
straight to Sumenep
In the letter he wrote:

I ask your judgement noble sir
the moment has arrived to attack the soldiers,
seizing the palace
is all which remains to be done
the easy capture of Tumapel is not impossible
yet this matter I submit
to the honourable governor's judgement

From Wiraraja came the reply:
"Thank God if His Majesty the Prince is certain
of the excellent possibilities of war in the interior
yet there is an opinion
your uncle hopes the Prince will agree
your uncle does not insist,
submitting to the Prince's person

"I make no obstacles
the Prince's plans are as good as done
I only make a proposal:
Increase your strength
even if in order to easily drive away the enemy

victory may be won
with few soldiers.

"To make war with a whole army
its methods your uncle cannot fathom,
I will quickly send a delegation
to the Tartar Khan
requesting His agreement
to fight with us together
we'll make war against Singasari.

"He is sure to agree
for He bears a grudge within
against your late father-in-law
the Lord Kertanagara
for His envoy's forehead was branded
He will not be expecting events such as these.

"Since the kings have changed
He will not wish
to be drawn out
unless in addition
we entice him with a beautiful princess.
The princess remaining in the palace
we will promise Him as a guarantee."

Wiraraja was a master schemer
knowing how to arrange his purposes so neatly
that no one would know.
Thinking everything was proper
no one suspected that all was deception
enclosed in beautiful language
hidden from intelligence.

His Majesty Khubilai the Tartar Khan
was intensely sastisfied and joyful;
already there was a plan
and now there was a way.
He accepted the plan and now would be of help,
one who knew the details,
the necessities of soldiers and war.

[arrival of the Tartar ships in Java (pp. 46–48)]

With adequate supplies
again they departed quickly
not straight for Java
but stopping briefly on Karimun Java,
to plan their strategy
military methods and soldiers tactics.

The battle plan finished
the soldiers each understood their mission.
They formed two groups,
part of the army
headed for Tuban to anchor there
to back up those who were to attack,
ready all along the beach.

The larger group came by sea
arrived in Surabaya
stopping first in Sedayu.
Three messengers
went directly to Majapahit
picked up reinforcements;
together they would go to war.

Wijaya rejoiced
at the arrival of the Tartars
they conferred and discussed
which way next
the war was planned
whatever the Tartar soldiers needed
for a quick victory.

An agreement was reached:
after Majapahit soldiers triumphed
they would swear allegiance to the Tartars
a token of submission
every year tribute would be sent
after Wijaya had become King
ruling over Singasari.

Messengers were sent
to Jayakatwang as well
to explain that relations were severed;
no longer in his service,
this was a challenge to war
in answer to his father-in-laws' distress
to make right his inheritance.

They say that Lord Jayakatwang
after hearing the purpose of the message
could not contain his anger
his face turned beet red
crude words leapt from his mouth
"That ill-bred Wijaya
is a real son of the Devil!"

"He has no character;
to love and pity he responds with envy;
proud, arrogant and conceited.

Prime Minister Senapatya
make ready an army big enough
to quickly capture that Wijaya,
attack Majapahit and destroy it!"

The Prime Minister respectfully replied
"I am ready to carry out your order, my Lord,
but I also have information:
Just now there was a report
a spy on duty by the seashore
spied the arrival of a Chinese army
complete with all the weapons of war.

"Perhaps for this reason
Wijaya has emboldened himself
made himself an enemy of your Excellency
and has joined China
Otherwise, how could he challenge You?"
The Lord King's anger increased;
passionately he spoke again:

"Wijaya that child of Satan
he will find out what I will do later.
Come on my man, do not be confused.
Be alert,
fortify the harbor."
The Prime Minister paid his respects and took his leave
to assemble the troops.

[the battle between the Mongols and Jayakatwang's soldiers at Surabaya
(pp. 50–53)]

Ever nearer came the Tartar soldiers
from land and sea
upon seeing them

the Javanese soldiers
were not slow to challenge
then, being attacked
they did not stand silently.

Quickly responding to the enemy's movements they fought
soldiers' voices rumbled
the noise of their shouting
shook Surabaya
against an enemy equally courageous
without ceasing
the attackers came one after another

Their canon thundering
bullets sprayed like buckshot
many exposed ships
were struck and destroyed
the boats
together with their contents
completely wrecked

The roar of shouting shook the whole of Surabaya
together with the blasts
of gun and canon
and martial music
the soldiers hastened their advance
the battle field darkened
by clouds of gunsmoke

From the barrel of the blunderbuss
from the mouth of canon
burst the flash of fire like lightning
the enemies raced
none lacking courage

growing ever louder
they fell upon one another

Dead soldiers by the hundred spread all round
corpses piled one atop the other
in the ocean and on land
bodies so broken
the blood smeared dead
and countless more
with smashed-in head

More besides were limbless bodies
lost their hands or feet
some whose eyes were smashed
those whose faces peeled
their liver sliced to shreds
blood pouring out
the ocean turned blood red.

The Tartar soldiers battle
completely undaunted, straight forward;
the Javanese soldiers stood their ground
but after a while
in spite of their bravery
they could not endure
the enemy's never ending assault.

The Javanese soldiers began to lose their spirits
feeling overwhelmed by the enemy
hopeless
from in front and from behind
they were destroyed:
"There is no chance"
the chief minister groaned.

They had thought that the opposition
would not be strong;
the leaders fled
paying no attention to the soldiers
their ranks further decimated
with no one to lead
the remaining soldiers
at last ran away.

The Tartar soldiers were overjoyed
with Surabaya hemmed in
they would loot
cargo boats and ships
with not a few weapons
carry off what remained
after the attack was over

After putting Surabaya in order
they set off again
this time for Daha
to seize Kertanagara
still unaware
that His Majesty
had already been killed.

Already dead and succeeded by Jayakatwang,
tricked by the deceitful cunning
of the crafty Wiraraja,
they were met along the way
by messengers
all together three of them
who came from Majapahit.

They reported that Wijaya, son-in-law of the King
would surrender himself

as their subject to subordinate himself
indeed he had even now
been about to meet them
but he was delayed
because of the war.

For their aid in the war against the King of Daha
he delegated the ministers
to meet together
and deliver the agreement
promise to pay tribute
and assign soldiers

The Tartar soldiers even happier
they passed on
but not long after
another messenger arrived
also from Majapahit
Prince Wijaya
again requested aid

At that moment his soldiers
had the feeling
they were being defeated by Daha
by treasonous acts.
The Tartar soldiers were ready
and left quickly to go help Majapahit.

When they arrived in Daha there was heavy fighting;
Majapahit was fortunate
to get reinforcements
but not so Kediri.
Daha-Singasari was broken,
forced to surrender
to Majapahit superiority.

[the capture of Jayakatwang and the plot to deceive the Mongols (pp. 56–60)]

Because the soldiers of Majapahit and the Tartars
in their three divisions
pressed forward
there was no refuge in Daha
in the end, disordered and confused
the army was destroyed
innumerable the dead.

Those still living fled from the field
escaped to desolate places
paying no attention to ravines,
stones, rocky ground they leapt over
looking for hidden places
in the valleys
alone, remote, isolated.

The Lord Jayakatwang was left behind; confused,
he entered then the palace
his soldiers destroyed
many of the royal family
had also been killed
he had no hope
of being safe himself.

Suddenly the Tartar soldiers arrived
entered the palace
inside the guards were brave
but all too few;
the Tartar leader,
the one named Shih-bi,
was now rejoicing

Lord Jayakatwang was forced to surrender
could no longer deny
his powerlessness,
submitted to his fate as prisoner.
All the people of the palace were carried off
except the princesses
for they were not there.

Previously Wijaya
had thought to remove the princesses
brought both of them to Majapahit;
Shih-bi did not guess they had been taken

Instead King Jayakatwang
the usurper who became the ruler
was alone in the horrible battle
and he escaped from the field
when he realized
he could not win;
the battle was certainly lost.

But alas! His aim was not achieved
for he was followed immediately by Wijaya
unobserved by the Tartar soldiers;
after the capture
he returned to Majapahit.

They say that the Tartar soldiers
having successfully siezed the palace of Kediri
also that night
came straight to Majapahit
to demand fulfillment of Wijaya's earlier promise
concerning the princesses.

Already having won the war
and about to offer tribute
in the custom of a vassal
he heard the report:
there were messengers with Tartar soldiers following.
Wijaya was confused
not yet having hit upon a plan.

Because he was worried
he discussed with those in the palace
what means would be good.
He sought a strategy
yet no one had any answers;
only one man, Sora,
voiced his opinion:

"I implore my Lord not to worry
your servant is responsible for the Tartar soldiers.
When it becomes clear that they are about to advance
Your servant will set his face against them."
At that moment Wiraraja interrupted
"Indeed your uncle is also ready
you have no need to worry."

Soon the messenger arrived
voiced his demand for the fulfillment of the promise
calling for the beautiful princesses.
Wiraraja replied:
"Listen, messenger, we beseech you, be not hurried
we have come together
to meet with ceremony.

"In order that the celebration not be voided
should we not make our way carefully

lest its result turn out badly?
Now the princesses
are still completely confused
the atmosphere of war
makes not for peaceful hearts.

"In disturbing times of war
worries arise in the princesses hearts
making them nervous
thus are the princesses of Java.
If you desire to take the beautiful princesses
there is no obstacle
yet we make these requests.

"To those of you
who will pick up and accompany the princesses
on land and on the ocean
you should not bring your weapons
better leave them that the princesses be not disturbed
and those who pick them up
will have no need of an escort.

"Our greatest wish
two things we demand, that is all,
what we propose will hopefully come to pass;
yet if you do not agree
we cannot guarantee what may happen,
we cannot be responsible
for the princesses' suicides.

"They will sacrifice their souls,
they are not reluctant to choose death,
to throw themselves into the sea
or by some other means

to kill themselves or end their years;
here such a custom
is already common."

The reply was such that the messenger
did not feel deceived
but thought it all true and proper,
the words of a knowledgeable person,
because Wiraraja was experienced in crafting speech
in varnished words and attitudes
to charm suspicious hearts.

"Your words ring true
I thank you for giving me knowledge of this custom.
We do not intend
to refuse your requests
and hope they be sincerely granted.
Do not be sorry now
that we take our leave.

"We intend to return to our headquarters
then tomorrow make the decision
and according to the previous promise
to carry out our task."
Immediately after the departure of the messenger
those who remained behind rejoiced
at the result of their strategy.

Banjaran Singhasari

Banjaran Singhasari was performed from June to November 1992 by the East Java Ballet at the Amphitheatre Taman Candra Wilwatikta in Pandaan, Pasuruan Regency. The synopsis of this dance drama was published in a trilingual edition — English, Indonesian and Javanese. *Banjaran Singhasari*. Surabaya: Dinas Pariwisata Daerah, Propinsi Dati I Jati, 1992. In the selection presented here I offer an edited version of the English texts found on pp. 43–65.

Performance of Saturday, September 26, 1992, 7:30 P.M.
VIII. Kertanegara's effort to unite the Indonesian Archipelago.

After Shri Wisnuwardhana died in 1268, his son, Kertanegara succeeded him as king. The kingdom of Singhasari expanded for even though he was young, he was always victorious in war. Singhasari had truly entered a glorious era; it was easy to get clothing and food, and people lived secure.

The people embraced the Hindu and Buddhist religions and were obedient to them.

The unification of the countries beyond Java began under Panji Gula Kelapa. Swarnabumi in the western part, Nusa Cendana in the eastern, Seram, Ambon, and Kalimantan Islands in the northern part were now ruled by Shri Baginda Maharaja Kertanegara.

Narrated: Shri prabu Kertanegara was not happy to see foreign Chinese merchants come in and out of Nusantara without heeding the sovereignty of the state which they visited and they were unwilling to pay tax. They ignored his sovereignty, and that is why King Kertanegara ordered Ki Kebo

Anabrang to meet Prabu Darmasaraya in Palembang to invite him to stop the Chinese merchants who would try to come through Malaka Strait. Prabu Darmasaraya agreed with the idea of prabu Kertanegara to close Malaka Strait, and that made Shri Khan, the King of China disappointed.

> Shri Wisnuwardhana is dead,
>> His son named Kertanagara succeeds him as king,
>> A noble whose supernatural powers
>> are without equal.
>> Though he is very young,
>> He is a capable ruler,
>> Solving every problem,
>> He never makes mistakes.

> The whole world was astonished,
>> A true appreciation of Singhasari
>> Would take too long to tell,
>> Striving for generosity,
>> Orderly and safe,
>> Crime never appears.
>> Nayaka is well-known to all the people,
>> His virtue maintains the nation's fame.

> No religious discrimination,
>> All are practiced without interference,
>> Hindu and Buddhist alike,
>> Are harmoniously nurtured,
>> All worship God
>> Without exception,
>> For blessed prosperity;
>> No wonder, for there are good leaders.

> His majesty and authority
>> Are not yet fully realized,

Due to the Chinese merchants' attitudes,
Sailing wherever they like,
Without permit,
Shri Baginda,
The honoured ruler of Nusantara,
Is the disappointed and downhearted Shri Kertanegara.

The king orders Kebo Anabrang immediately,
To go across the island,
To Palembang,
To meet Shri Darmasaraya,
In order to
Return to the state its sovereignty,
United by this strong desire.

Stop all merchants
Coming from China,
Close the gate
Of Malaka Strait,
They may enter the region
When they pay the tribute,
A fixed tax.

Those who are sailing are surprised,
Tax has to be paid.
No more wheeling and dealing;
If they cannot pay,
They can substitute wealth,
Gold and pearl;
Just don't try to avoid it.

On Saturday, August 17, 1992 at 7:30 P.M.
IX. Meng Khi, the Tartar envoy
Shri Khubilai Khan was disappointed by Prabu Kertanegara, who did

not allow the foreign merchants to come through Malaka Strait. That's why Shri Khan ordered Meng Khi, an envoy, to meet Shri Kertanegara in Singhasari.

Meng Khi, accompanied by his guard reached Java and after landing in Tuban went straight to Singhasari by land. Meng Khi met and asked Shri Kertanegara to acknowledge his power and submit to his authority. He had to allow foreign merchants to come in Malaka Strait again. Due to the arrogance and impoliteness of Meng Khi, Shri Kertanegara was angry and unsheathed a sword to kill him. Meng Khi screamed and ran away accompanied by Ki Sora and Ki Nambi. Other noble families were disappointed by the actions of Shri Kertanegara.

> Shri Khan is shocked to hear that
>> The merchants may not voyage anymore.
>> He quickly asks his envoy Meng Khi
>> Accompanied by his soldiers
>> To meet king Shri Baginda Kertanegara,
>> The King of Nusantara.

> Their voyage went smoothly,
>> They arrived in Java
>> Where they met the King,
>> Prabu Kertanegara.
>> Impolite and arrogant,
>> Bare-chested and speaking loudly,
>> Meng Khi shocked and astonished those who heard him.

> Shri Kertanegara's face
>> Reddened like a wora-wari flower.
>> Red like fire,
>> Unable to restrain his anger,
>> Wild-eyed and sweaty,
>> As if his chest had been kicked,
>> His chair trembled.

He quickly went to the weapons store,
　　Where his sword hung,
　　It flickered when drawn from its sheath,
　　Like a hungry tiger,
　　He attacked the envoy,
　　Meng Khi the anger maker.

Suddenly Shri Kertanegara,
　　Jumped like a flash,
　　Seized his neck,
　　Kicked him onto the floor.
　　His face was broken,
　　Scratched and cut up;
　　Blood stained the floor.

Quietly, not saying a word
　　Because of the prestige
　　Of the king who is angry and
　　Speaking loudly,
　　Challenging Shri Khan, the ocean's king.
　　Without asking permission,
　　Meng Khi goes out painfully.

Immediately, Ki Nambi and Ki Sora,
　　Asked for permission to leave the palace,
　　To supervise the journey.
　　Of the injured envoy,
　　For none thwarts him.
　　He returns to the waiting boat,
　　And sails back to his country.

On Saturday, October 31, 1992 at 7:30 P.M.
IX. Singhasari's total defeat.

　　One of the noble families who disagreed with King Kertanegara for torturing the envoy was Banyak Wide, the Minister of Foreign Affairs.

However, Shri Kertanegara refused his advice and even became more angry and decided to degrade Banyak Wide's position from the minister of Foreign Affairs to Regent of Sumenep, renaming him Wiraraja.

The King's decision disappointed the officers who thought it unjust. To avenge himself secretly, Wiraraja cooperated silently with Jayakatwang and the Prime Minister of Kadiri called Mundarang to stage a rebellion. When there were no guards in Singhasari as most of them were sent to abroad, the defences of Singhasari were very weak. Shri Kertanegara was considered to be an old toothless tiger. This situation was relayed to Jayakatwang by Wiraraja.

Jayakatwang instructed his soldiers to attack Singhasari and he won easily. In the battle Shri Kertanegara was killed and he was cremated at Jawi Temple.

> The king's word is heard,
>> Slow, but full of pride,
>> "Shri Khan" meet the bravest one:
>> This is Shri Kertanegara from Singhasari,
>> I don't fear a fight,
>> To match our supernatural power.

> They say that
>> The Minister of Foreign Affairs,
>> Came respectfully,
>> Ki Banyak Wide,
>> Reminded the King,
>> Not to be angry,
>> At the envoy.

> The customs there,
>> In China,
>> Are very different,
>> From those in our country,
>> So I hope,
>> You do not create conflicts.

The king's anger did not abate,
  Banyak Wide was considered disloyal.
  Demoted from Minister of Foreign Affairs,
  To regent of Sumenep
  On the island of Madura,
  Henceforth called Arya Wiraraja.
  He was shocked,
  Hearing the king's sudden words.

Arya Wiraraja immediately said goodbye,
  The king left the meeting,
  His voice echoed,
  Full of sadness;
  The King's punishment was decided.
  As for Arya Wiraraja,
  Some people agreed,
  Some others disagreed;
  The king was considered unjust,
  And broke the friendship.

Then Regent Wiraraja,
  Appeared to accept the punishment sincerely,
  But he was very disappointed,
  At the king who was so angry.
  He drew up a plan,
  To meet Jayakatwang.

Wiraraja quickly wrote a letter
  To Jayakatwang,
  The aim of the letter:
  To let him know Singhasari was empty.

"The king is like a tiger with no teeth,
  His soldiers all abroad,
  There is no danger:
  It is a good time to hunt a tiger."

The noisy troops,
>   Left for Singhasari,
>   Which was unguarded,
>   They attacked without opposition.
>   The Singhasari troops were shocked,
>   Overwhelmed by the enemy,
>   Many of them were killed.

Unaware of the danger,
>   The king was unprepared.
>   There were so many enemies to attack;
>   The king was killed in the fight,
>   The battle stopped immediately.
>   Kadiri had won,
>   Jayakatwang would now be king.

On Saturday, November 14, 1992 at 19:30
X. The aggression of Tartar soldiers.

Finally, the envoy Meng Khi arrived back in his country and met the King Shri Khubilai Khan to report what had happened. After hearing his report the King became angry and commanded the soldiers to attack Singhasari. They sailed the ocean to seek out Shri Kertanegara for they would punish him.

They say that when Kadiri attacked Singhasari, one of the king's family R. Wijaya, a son in law of Shri Kertanegara, was not killed during the battle. It was because of Regent Wiraraja's help and he even got an area of land in the Tarik forest. Then he cleared the field and built a village named Majapahit.

Although Raden Wijaya seemed obedient and loyal to Jayakatwang, actually he was waiting for the right time to regain the glory which he had before. So, he took a chance on the arrival of the Tartar soldiers from China that this was the time to achieve his aim. Therefore, before the soldiers came and spread out he quickly met the commander to express his willingness to help them destroy Kadiri. The two powers of Majapahit and Tartar soldiers defeated Jayakatwang and he was killed. The soldiers stood in rows like wild buffalos and dragon, and together exterminated 'lion' Jayakatwang in a big war between the 'lion' and the 'wild buffalo' Raden Wijaya with the 'dragon' from across the sea. In the end, Kadiri was completely destroyed by the two united powers. The loud cheering of the Tartar and Majapahit soldiers who won the fight was deafening. After Jayakatwang died the battle was over.

The envoy Meng Khi,
    He faced the King,
    Reported to him,
    Leaving out nothing.
    Shri Khan looked at his favorite envoy,
    He saw the injured face,
    The reason for which,
    The envoy tells truthfully:
    The reason for his injury,
    He was tortured by the Javanese King.

His chest was heaving as though he had been kicked,
    His face glowing red,
    He called the officer of the troops,
    To prepare the army,
    To sail across the ocean,
    To go abroad,
    To the land of his powerful enemy,
    Kertanegara,
    The Great King of Singhasari,
    Ruler of Nusantara.

A story has been spread,
    Of the son in law of King Kertanegara,
    Named Raden Wijaya,
    Spared of danger,
    When Singhasari was ruined,
    He cut down the forest of Tarangwulan,

At the village of Tarik,
Changed it into cultivated land,
In charge of his elite soldiers,
Who overpower whomever they face.

Raden Wijaya heard about
The coming of the Tartar soldiers,
From China,
Complete with weapons.
Raden Wijaya quickly went into action,
Joined with the foreign soldiers,
Changing their plans
To attack Jayakatwang,
Who replaced the King of Singhasari:
Events are better than he had expected.

Together they attack Jayakatwang,
The Regent of Kadiri,
Who has a lot of enemies,
The battle can't be avoided,
Most are killed,
In the battle,
The blood pours out of corpses on the ground.

The soldiers of Kadiri are defeated,
The rest retreat,
King Jayakatwang,
Died in the battle,
His soldiers surrendered,
And put their weapons down:
The battle was over.

On Saturday, November 28, 1992 at 7:30 P.M.
XII. The glory of Raden Wijaya.

The Tartar and Majapahit soldiers celebrated their victories by having fermented palm wine. Many of the Tartar soldiers got dead drunk. Their behaviour was quite different from that of the Majapahit soldiers. Although they attended the party, they were always on guard. Wherever they went they were ready with their sword and sharp lance. Seeing the Tartar soldiers were drunk, Raden Wijaya gave a code to his sister Dyah Pamasi to attack the Tartar. Dyah Pamasih knew what Raden Wijaya wanted, instructed her troops to fight against Tartar soldiers. Raden Wijaya and his soldiers attacked the Tartar soldiers and like wild buffaloes broke the unfortunate dragon. Raden Wijaya who was assisted by Dyah Pamasi, Ki Sora, Ki Nambi and Rangga Lawe defeated the Tartar soldiers. They ran helter-skelter and the survivors got on the boat back to their country.

It was dawn, the red glow in the east revealed tomorrow's spirit. Majapahit had appeared as the sun for tomorrow morning.

The glorious happy soldiers who won the battle,
    They were Tartar soldiers,
    Who drank palm wine,
    Until drunk,
    Let down their guard,
    Paid no attention,
    To the danger that was coming.

Seeing the off-guard Tartar soldiers,
    Raden Wijaya quickly called,
    His sister Dyah Pamasi,
    And all the officers,
    Attacked immediately
    The Tartar soldiers.

The Tartar troops are dispersed,
    Destroyed in the battle,
    They ran separately,
    To their boat,

Those left would die.
Wijaya won the fight.

All the soldiers of Majapahit
Paying respect to the Creator,
After winning the battle,
Nursed the injured soldiers,
In religious teachings,
To become the country's heroes.

The sun rises,
Filling the earth with light,
The peacocks also sing,
Escorting the Majapahit,
Which has been born,
To rule the world.

APPENDIX 10

Banjaran Majapahit

This dance drama was performed at Candra Wilwatikta Amphitheater Pandaan, Pasuruan, from June to November 1993. The illustrated synopsis was published in a trilingual edition — English, Indonesian and Javanese. *Banjaran Majapahit*. Surabaya: Dinas Pariwisata Daerah, Propinsi Daerah Tingkat I Jawa Timur, 1993. In the selection presented here I offer an edited version of the English text.

Episode 1. [Prose introduction]
It is a story written on an inscription. After Regent Jayakatwang's attack on Singhasari, he crowned himself king. Based on history, it happened in 1292.

What a story! The son-in-law of King Kertanegara, Raden Wijaya, was defeated in the battlefield, escaped from his country safely, sailed across the sea and sought protection under Wiraraja, Regent of Sumenep. Because of Wiraraja's cunning diplomacy, Raden Wijaya got a pardon from Jayakatwang, and was even granted a piece of land in Tarik. Tarik was a large jungle with big trees. The jungle was dark in the morning, and got even darker at night. There was a part of the jungle that had no trees anymore. So when the moon shone brightly, the moonbeam illuminated the forest, going through the forest trees. Therefore the land was called Tarang Wulan or Trowulan, which means the full-moon.

Soon, the big trees in the forest were cut down, and the land cultivated. Then it became a small village called Majapahit. The new land was called Majapahit because Raden Wijaya, together with his troops were suffering life's bitterest days. Besides, in the forest there were many Maja trees which have bitter fruit.

Raden Wijaya appeared to submit to Shri Jayakatwang, but actually he was planning to take revenge. He wanted to get back the throne since by having it, Raden Wijaya wished to unite Nusantara (Indonesian Archipelago) which had been the dream of the late King Kertanegara.

Meng Khi, the Tartar envoy, went back to his country to meet King Shri Khubilai Khan and reported what had happened hastily. Hearing his report the king became angry. Then he ordered the troops to attack Kertanegara, the king of Java. Knowing that Tartar soldiers were coming to attack Kertanegara, Raden Wijaya made plans to join with them. Raden Wijaya convinced the Tartar soldiers of his allegiance and they changed their plans. They failed to meet with Kertanegara, but led by Raden Wijaya, they attacked Jayakatwang who claimed to be the king of Java.

The long rows of Tartar soldiers, like a dragon ready to bait his enemies, allied with Raden Wijaya and his soldiers destroyed Kadiri completely. Kadiri was destroyed like sugar cane flowers trod by elephants. Jayakatwang was defeated and killed on the battlefield.

The war over, the Tartar soldiers celebrated their victory by drinking palm wine, many of them getting dead drunk. Raden Wijaya took advantage of the situation to turn on the Tartars. They ran in disorder and the rest got on the boat and sailed back to their country.

Soon afterward Raden Wijaya was crowned the king of Majapahit and given the title Shri Narpati Kertarajasa Jayawardhana. Historically, the story took place in 1293.

The cocks crow in the morning, announcing the coronation of Raden Wijaya, the noble knight from the east.

Beginning with Dhandhanggula song,
    Let us narrate an ancient history,
    This is the story
    About ancient Nusantara,
    United by Majapahit,
    Under Gula Kelapa's flag,
    The scattered became united,
    In the best manner,

Bhineka Tunggal Ika (Unity in Diversity),
Tan Hana Dharma Mangrua.

When Singhasari was destroyed,
    By Regent Jayakatwang,
    The kingdom's soldiers,
    Ran dispersedly,
    Leaving the battlefield,
    Shri Kertanegara was killed,
    Singhasari was ruined,
    Jayakatwang won,
    And crowned himself King,
    Respected like a God.

They say,
    There was a soldier,
    Named Raden Wijaya,
    Loved by the Lord,
    Away from danger,
    He crossed the sea,
    Sailed to Madura Island,
    Seeking refuge,
    He was accepted by Regent Wiraraja,
    Who spoke softly and tenderly.

"Oh, it is the Lord's will
    Hope for God's mercy.
    Don't be so sad,
    Because God's will
    Makes us happy.

"The brave King
    Knows what happens
    Cannot be avoided,

His strong desire,
Is to be certain
Of God's will.

"If the king wants
   To get back the kingdom,
   It is better now
   To wait for a good chance,
   And being careful,
   Plan the strategy."

The happy Raden Wijaya,
   Helped by Regent Wiraraja,
   Went to Kadiri,
   Asked forgiveness
   And received a piece of land
   In the north-east
   Named Tarik.

The Maja trees grew in a row,
   Grew in such dense forests,
   But helped by the people
   Of Madura
   Who cut down the forest,
   They cultivated the land
   And named it Majapahit.

The name Majapahit
   Is a reminder that
   At that time
   There was a tree of Maja
   Which had bitter taste.
   This became a story,
   Written on an inscription.

There was a part of the forest
  With no trees anymore,
  Allowing the moonbeam
  To shine through the forest,
  Opening up the new founded land.
  It was named Tarangwulan
  (the full moon).

The Tarangwulan developed,
  Became nicer and nicer.
  A small village
  Named Majapahit,
  Sheltered by banyan trees,
  In the middle of the square.
  Beside it was a pool called Refreshment,
  Surrounded by colourful flowers,
  The water rippled.

That is then,
  The story on an inscription.
  Raden Wijaya payed his respects
  To King Jayakatwang
  As a means only
  To wait for the right time,
  To get back the kingdom,
  Singhasari.
  He wanted to unite Nusantara.

The time came,
  Indeed a good time came,
  Together with the coming of
  Tatar soldiers from China.
  Regent Wiraraja
  Was brilliant enough to be the Spokesman,

To change the enemies' plans
So they would attack Kadiri.
Majapahit and Tartar solders attacked together.

The soldiers departed speaking boastfully,
    Attacked Kadiri,
    King Jayakatwang,
    And his soldiers were defeated,
    On the battlefield,
    The dust flew,
    So thick no one could see.

Arrows flew and swords stabbed.
    Like the sound of lightning,
    continuously among the soldiers' screams,
    The cry of pain was heard.
    Shri Jayakatwang was killed,
    On the battlefield.

Kadiri's soldiers were in disorder,
    Some sought for help.
    Corpses scattered,
    The Tartars won the battle.
    The Majapahit soldiers too,
    Feeling happy and gay,
    Celebrated the victory.

Ready to stop,
    The soldiers on the battlefield
    Put down their weapons,
    Rescued the wounded,
    And the victims,
    Friends and enemies,
    Were all carried indifferently.

The soldiers of Majalengka
   Carefully tended the wounded,
   Unlike the Tartar soldiers
   Who cheered happily
   And ignored the wounded.

The arrogant Tartar soldiers,
   Laughed and cheered,
   While drinking palm wine,
   Until drunk,
   Paid no attention at all,
   But fought for beautiful ladies,
   Forced them to make love.

Raden Wijaya was alerted
   To the Tartars' movements,
   He was astonished,
   And asked his younger sister,
   To quickly prepare the troops,
   Attack the arrogant Tartars,
   Scatter them in chaos.

Unaware of the danger,
   The Tartar soldiers,
   Were all destroyed,
   Most were killed,
   By Majapahit soldiers,
   Stricken with swords,
   Stabbed by the sharp spears.

On the battlefield Dyah Pamasi
   Followed by Lembu, Sora and Nambi,
   Fighting together with Rangga Lawe
   They attacked the enemies.

If you are brave in the battle,
    You are the man
    Chosen by God.
    Raden Wijaya
    Triumphed over the Tartar soldiers.

The troops cheered:
    The battle was won.
    From Majalengka
    The Tartars were defeated,
    Running, seeking safety,
    They boarded their boats
    And set sail for their country.

Joyfully
    He became King,
    In the country of Majalengka.
    Raden Wijaya celebrated,
Living happily in the great castle.

It is narrated in a song
    That the King changed his title,
    Becoming Narpati Kertarajasa,
    Jayawardhana,
    Supported by his officers,
    Loved by the people.

Glowing brightly,
    The Kingdom of Majapahit,
    Rises like the sun in the morning,
    Shining over the world;
    The cocks crow,
    Singing beautifully.

All the people and the leaders,
    Made a firm decision,
    To unite Nusantara,
    Unity in Diversity.

Bibliography

I. Primary texts and translations

A. Java and Bali

Babad Majapait

Sudjana, Kadir Tisna (1935; 1940). *Babad Madjapait*. Bale Poestaka, 1ˢᵗ printing, 1935. 2ⁿᵈ printing, 1940.

Sujana, Kadir Tisna. *Babad Majapait*. (New orthography) Jakarta, 1979.

Sujana, Kadir Tisna (1987). *Babad Majapahit*. Translated into Indonesian by Rusman Sutiasumarga. Jakarta.

Banjaran Majapahit

Banjaran Majapahit. Surabaya, 1993.

Banjaran Singhasari

Banjaran Singhasari. Surabaya, 1992.

Desawarnana by Mpu Prapanca

Brandes, J.L.A. (1902). *Nagarakretagama*. Batavia (*Verhandelingen van het Bataviaasch Genootschap van Kunsten en Wetenschappen*, deel 54:1).

Kern, H. (1922). *Het oud-Javaansche lofdicht Nagarakertagama* / van Prapantja (1365 A.D.); de vertaling en bespreking van H. Kern met aanteekeningen van N.J. Krom; populair bewerkt ten behoeve van de Commissie voor de Volkslectuur. Weltevreden: Drukkerij Volkslectuur, 1922. Dutch translation.

Pigeaud, Theodore G.Th. (1960). *Java in the 14ᵗʰ century: a study in cultural history: the Nagara-Kertagama by Rakawi Prapañca of Majapahit, 1365 A.D.* 3ʳᵈ ed. The Hague 5 vols. Texts, translation, commentaries.

Robson, Stuart (1995). *Desawarnana: (Nagarakrtagama)*/by Mpu Prapañca; translated by Stuart Robson. Leiden (*Verhandelingen van het Koninklijk Instituut voor Taal-, Land- en Volkenkunde*, v. 169).

Kidung Harsawijaya

Berg, C.C. (1931). *Kidung Harsa-Wijaya*. Tekst, inhoudsopgave en aanteekeningen door C.C. Berg. 's-Gravenhage: Martinus Nijhoff. Summary in Dutch.

Alih aksara lontar Kidung Harsa Wijaya. Denpasar: Unit Pelaksana Daerah, Pusat Dokumentasi Kebudayaan Bali, Propinsi Bali, 1989. 72 p. This manuscript contains only the events narrated in the first two *demang* of the Berg edition and ends prior to Wiraraja's request sent to the King of Tatar.

Kidung Panji Wijayakrama (Rangga Lawe)

Berg, C.C. (1930). *Rangga Lawe: middeljavaansche historische roman: critisch uitgegeven.* Batavia: Kon. Bataviaasch Genootschap van Kunsten en Wetenschappen (*Bibliotheca Javanica*, 1) Summary in Dutch.

Raffles' manuscript. A brief but very different text based on the *Kidung Panji Wijayakrama*, in English, is printed in his *History of Java*, 1st ed. 1817, pp. 103–08 and 2nd ed. 1830 v. 2, pp. 110–16 (see below, section II of bibliography).

Kidung Panji Wijayakrama, Grya Pidhadha, Klungkung. Copy of typescript, 8 Desember 1984. Balinese Manuscript Project. Balinese Transcripts, nr. 5603. Department of Manuscripts and University Archives, Cornell University Libraries.

Wirawangsa, R. Rangga. (1979) *Serat Ranggalawe: babon serat basa jawi kina tengahan.* Alih aksara Singgih Wibisono, terjemahan Hardjana HP. Jakarta. Javanese and Indonesian.

Kidung Sunda

Berg, C.C. (1927). *Kidung Sunda.* Inleiding, tekst, vertaling en aanteekeningen door C.C. Berg. 's-Gravenhage. (*Bijdragen tot de taal-, land- en volkenkunde van Nederlandsch-Indië*, deel 83) Javanese text in transcription with translation into Dutch.

Pararaton

Brandes, J. (1897). *Pararaton (Ken Arok) of Het boek der koningen van Tumapel en van Majapahit.* Batavia (*Verhandelingen van het Bataviaasch Genootschap van Kunsten en Wetenschappen*, deel 49) 314 p. Javanese text and Dutch translation.

Brandes, J. (1920). *Pararaton (Ken Arok) of Het boek der koningen van Tumapel en van Majapahit.* 2. druk bewerkt door N.J. Krom. Batavia (*Verhandelingen van het Bataviaasch Genootschap van Kunsten en Wetenschappen*, deel 62) 314 p. Javanese text and Dutch translation.

Padmapuspita, Ki J. (1966). *Pararaton: teks bahasa Kawi, terdjemahan bahasa Indonesia.* Jogjakarta. Javanese and Indonesian.

Phalgunadi, I Gusti Putu (1996). *The Pararaton: a study of the southeast Asian chronicle.* Translated from the original Kawi text. New Delhi. Javanese text, English translation, historical introduction.

B. Chinese

Gaubil, Antoine (1739). *Histoire de Gentchiscan et de toute la dinastie des mongous, ses successeurs, conquérans de la Chine; tirée de l'histoire chinoise, et traduite par le R.P.*

Gaubil... A Paris, chez Briasson et Piget, M.DCC.XXXIX. A combination of the two principle sources — the *Yuan shi* and the *Yu pi xu zi zhi tong jian gang mu* — translated into French, with much interpolation and explanation added.

Rockhill, W.W. (1914–1915). "Notes on the relations and trade of China with the Eastern Archipelago and the coast of the Indian Ocean during the fourteenth century." Parts I and II. *T'oung Pao* v. 15, pp. 419–47; v. 16, pp. 61–159, 236–71. Rockhill translates and comments on the relevant passages in the *Yuan shi*, *Xingcha shenglan*, *Yingyai shenglan* and *Daoyi zhilüe*.

Fei Xin

Mills, J.V.G. (1996). *Hsing-ch'a sheng-lan: The overall survey of the star raft by Fei Hsin.* Translated by J.V.G. Mills, revised, annotated and edited by Roderich Ptak. Wiesbaden: Harrassowitz.

Ma Huan

Mills, J.V.G. (1970). *Ying-yai sheng-lan = 'The overall survey of the ocean's shores' [1433].* Translated from the Chinese text edited by Feng Ch'eng-Chün with introduction, notes and appendices by J.V.G. Mills. Cambridge: Published for the Hakluyt Society at the University Press. [other editions available].

The relevant passage was also translated by Groeneveldt and appears on p. 47 in his article of 1880, for which see below under **Yuan shi**.

Ming shi

English translation of the brief note about the campaign may be found in Groeneveldt's *Notes on the Malay Archipelago and Malacca compiled from Chinese sources.* Batavia, 1880, p. 34.

Wang Dayuan

汪大淵 (1981). 島夷誌略校釋. 汪大淵原著; 蘇繼廎校釋. 北京: 中華書局 (中外交通史 籍叢刊).

汪大淵 (1996). 岛夷志略. 沈阳市: 辽宁教育出版社.

I have relied on translations of the relevant portions which I have found in several works, in particular Rockhill (1914 and 1915).

Yu pi xu zi zhi tong jian gang mu (御批續資治通鑑綱目)

御批資治通鑑綱目全書: [一百九卷]. [北京]: 内府, 清康熙 46年 [1708]

(The relevant section has been translated into English by Geoff Wade and appears in an appendix in this book.)

Mailla, Joseph-Anne-Marie de Moyriac de (1777–1785). *Histoire générale de la Chine, ou Annales de cet empire, traduits du Tong-kien-kang-mou...* Paris. In large part an abridged translation of the Kangxi edition above. Volume 9 contains the account of the Javanese expedition.

Yuan shi

Numerous editions. The Chinese texts of the relevant portions are reprinted in Niwa Tomosaburo (1953).

I have quoted the English translations found in the relevant selections of the following publications:

Groeneveldt, W.P. (1876). "The expedition of the Mongols against Java in 1293, A.D." *The China review, or, Notes and queries on the Far East* v. 4, pp. 246–54.

Groeneveldt, W.P. (1880). *Notes on the Malay Archipelago and Malacca compiled from Chinese sources*. Batavia (*Verhandelingen van het Bataviaasch Genootschap van Kunsten en Wetenschappen*, deel 39:1) x, 144 p. Includes same material as the previous, with much more on other matters. Later reprinted under the title *Historical notes on Indonesia and Malaysia*.

Schurmann, Herbert Franz (1956). *Economic structure of the Yüan Dynasty: translation of chapters 93 and 94 of the Yüan shih*. Cambridge, Massachusetts: Harvard University Press.

C. Other sources on the Mongols

Grigor of Akanc' (1949). "History of the nation of the archers (the Mongols) by Grigor of Akanc' hitherto ascribed to Maghak'ia the Monk." The Armenian text edited with an English translation and notes by Robert P. Blake and Richard N. Frye. *Harvard Journal*, v. 12, no. 3/4, pp. 269–443.

Ibn Battuta (1958–2000). *The travels of Ibn Battuta, A.D. 1325–1354*. Translated by H.A.R. Gibb. London (v. 4, 1994).

Odoric of Pordenone (1989). "Journal of Friar Odoric" in *Contemporaries of Marco Polo* edited by Manuel Komroff.

Onon, Urgunge (tr.) (1993). *Chinggis Khan: the golden history of the Mongols*. Translated and with an introduction by Urgunge Onon, revissed by Sue Bradbury. London.

Onon, Urgunge (tr.) (2001). *The secret history of the Mongols: the life and times of Chinggis Khan*. Richmond, Surrey.

Polo, Marco (1930). *The travels of Marco Polo*. New York.

Spuler, Bertold (1988). *History of the Mongols based on eastern and western accounts of the thirteenth and fourteenth centuries*. Translated from the German by Helga and Stuart Drummond. New York.

Wassaf. Quotations in this volume are taken from Spuler (1988) and Judith Pfeiffer, *Conversion to Islam among the Ilkhans in Muslim narrative traditions: the case of Ahmad Tegüder*. Thesis (Ph.D.), University of Chicago, Department of Near Eastern Languages and Civilizations, December 2003.

II. Studies on the Mongols in Java

Note: items mentioned in passing in Part II (Historiography) are not included here, since they were mentioned only to note their lack of significant discussion of the topic.

Amiot, Joseph Marie (1776–1791). "Introduction a la connaissance des peuples qui ont été ou qui sont actuellement tributaires de la Chine: Du royaume de Koua-oua" *Mémoires concernant l'histoire, les sciences, les arts, les mœurs, les usages, &c. des Chinois par les missionaires de Pékin*. Paris. v. 14 (1789), pp. 101–11. Reprinted in: Schlegel, Gustaaf. "Iets omtrent de betrekkingen der Chinezen met Java, voor de komst der Europeanen aldaar." *Tijdschrift voor Indische taal-, land- en volkenkunde*, deel 20, 1873, pp. I–XI following p. 31.

Berg, C.C. (1950). "Kertanagara, de miskende empirebuilder" *Orientatie* July 1950 pp. 1–32.

Berg, C.C. (1951a). "De geschiedenis van pril Majapahit. I: Het mysterie van de vier dochters van Krtanagara" *Indonesië* v. 4 nr. 6 mei, pp. 481–520.

Berg, C.C. (1951b). "De geschiedenis van pril Majapahit. II: Achtergrond en oplossing der pril-Majapahitse conflicten" *Indonesië* v. 5 nr. 3 nov., pp. 193–233.

Berg, C.C. (1952). "De Sadeng-oorlog en de mythe van Groot-Majapahit" *Indonesië* v. 5, nr. 5 Maart, pp. 385–422.

Berg, C. C. (1953). *Herkomst, vorm en functie der middeljavaanse rijksdelingstheorie*. Amsterdam: N.V. Noord-Hollandsche Uitgevers Maatschappij (Verhandelingen der Koninklijke Nederlandse Akademie van Wetenschappen, Afd. Letterkunde, Nieuwe reeks, deel LIX, no. 1).

Berg, C.C. (1965). "The Javanese picture of the past" in Soedjatmoko et al. editors. *An introduction to Indonesian historiography*. Ithaca, pp. 87–117.

Bokshchanin, A.A. (1970). Бокщанин А.А. "Попытки монголо-китайского вторжения в страны юго-восточной Азии" in *Татаро-монголы в Азии и Европе: сборник статей*. Москва pp. 294–310.

Bosch, F.D.K. (1956). "C.C. Berg and ancient Javanese history." *Bijdragen tot de taal-, land- en volkenkunde* deel 112, 1e afl., pp. 1–24.

The Cambridge history of China. Vol. 6: Alien regimes and border states, 907–1368. (1994) Edited by Herbert Franke and Denis Twitchett. Cambridge.

Campbell, Donald MacLaine (1915). *Java: past & present: a description of the most beautiful country in the world, its ancient history, people, antiquities, and products*. London.

Cœdès, G. (1944; 1968). *Histoire ancienne des états hindouisés d'extrême-orient*. Hanoi. An English translation of the 3rd edition was published in Honolulu: *The indianized states of Southeast Asia*.

Dalai, Chuluuny (1973). Далай, Ч. *Юан гурний уеийн монгол (XIII зууны II хагасаас XIV зуун).* Улаанаатар: БНМАУ Шинжлэх Ухааны Академи Туухийн Хурээлэн. Russian translation published as *Монголия в XIII–XIV веках.* Москва: Наука, 1983.

Damais, L.C. (1957). "L'expédition à Java des troupes de Qubilai Qagan et la date de fondation de Majapahit (summary)" in *Proceedings of the Twenty-second Congress of Orientalists, held in Istanbul, September 15th to 22nd, 1951.* Leiden, pp. 322–23.

Darmosoetopo, Riboet (1993). "Sejarah perkembangan Majapahit" in *700 tahun Majapahit (1293–1993): suatu bunga rampai.* Surabaya, 2nd ed., pp. 47–63.

Delgado, James P. (2008). *Khubilai Khan's lost fleet: in search of a legendary armada.* Berkeley and Los Angeles: University of California Press.

Din Ta-san, José and Francisco F. Olesa Muñido (1965). *El poder naval chino desde sus orígenes hasta la caída de la Dinastía Ming.* Barcelona.

D'Ohsson, C. (1834). *Histoire des Mongols depuis Tchinguiz-khan jusqu'a Timour Bey ou Tamerlan.* La Haye et Amsterdam. Tome II.

Flecker, Michael (2003). "The thirteenth-century Java Sea wreck: a Chinese cargo in an Indonesian ship" *The mariner's mirror,* v. 89 no. 4 (November), pp. 388–404.

Franke, Otto (1930–1952). *Geschichte des chinesischen Reiches.* Berlin v. 4, 1948; v. 5, 1952.

Friederich, R. (1850). *Voorloopig verslag van het eiland Bali.* Batavia (*Verhandelingen van het Bataviaasch Genootschap van Kunsten en Wetenschappen;* deel 22).

Groeneveldt, W.P. (1876). "The expedition of the Mongols against Java in 1293, A.D." *The China review, or, Notes and queries on the Far East* v. 4, pp. 246–54

Hall, D.G.E. (1964). *A history of South-East Asia.* 2nd ed. London.

Heng, Derek (2009). *Sino-Malay trade and diplomacy from the tenth through the fourteenth century.* Athens: Ohio University Press (Ohio University Research in International Studies. Southeast Asia Series no. 121).

Howorth, Henry H. (1876). *History of the Mongols from the 9th to the 19th century. Part I. The Mongols proper and the Kalmuks.* London: Longmans, Green, and Co.

Ishzhamts, N., et al. (1995). Н. Ишжамц, С. Дашцэвэл, М. Хурметхан. *Монголын эээнт гурний гадаад харилцаа.* Улаанбаатар: Дорнодахин, олон улс судлалын х ээлэн.

Komandoko, Gamal (2009). *Sanggrama Wijaya: babad ksatria agung pendiri Majapahit.* Jogjakarta: Diva Press. (Historical novel).

Kramp, F.G. (1903). "De zending van Meng K'i naar Java en de stichting van Madjapahit" in *Album-Kern: opstellen geschreven ter eere van Dr. H. Kern hem aangeboden door vrienden en leerlingen op zijn zeventigsten verjaardag.* Leiden, pp. 357–61.

Krom, N.J. (1931). *Hindoe-Javaansche geschiedenis.* 2. druk. 's-Gravenhage. *The legacy of Majapahit.* Singapore, 1995.

Lombard, Denys (1990). *Le carrefour javanais: essai d'histoire globale. Tome II: Les réseaux asiatiques*. Paris.

Nakada Kozo (1969). 仲田浩三."元のジャワ進討" 第三十七輯" 東方学 (Tohogaku) No. 37 昭和44年3月刊行, pp. 101–25. English summary, pp. 8–9: The military expedition of the Mongols against Java.

Niwa Tomosaburo (1953). 丹羽友三郎.中国・ジャバ交渉史.東京:明玄書房 // メイゲンショボウ. Colophon title: 元代における中国・ジャバ交渉史.

Niwa Tomosaburo (1954). 丹羽友三郎."元世祖ジャバ遠征雑考"史学研究 nr. 53 pp. 57–63. English summary: Notes on the numbers of the armed forces sent to Java by Khubilai Khan.

Niwa Tomosaburo (1990). 丹羽 友三郎. "『元史』爪哇伝に関する諸問題" 三重法経, v. 85–86, pp. 1–38.

Phalgunadi, I Gusti Putu (1996). *The Pararaton: a study of the southeast Asian chronicle*. Translated from the original Kawi text. New Delhi.

Pigeaud, Theodore G.Th. (1960). *Java in the 14th century: a study in cultural history: the Nagara-Kertagama by Rakawi Prapañca of Majapahit, 1365 A.D.* 3rd ed. The Hague. 5 vols.

Ptak, Roderich (1995). "Images of maritime Asia in two Yuan texts: *Daoyi zhilue* and *Yiyu zhi*" *Journal of Sung-Yuan Studies* v. 25, pp. 47–75.

Dr. Purwadi and M. Hum (2004). *Nyai Roro Kidul dan ligitimasi politik Jawa*. Yogyakarta: Media Abadi.

Raffles, Sir Thomas Stamford (1817; 1830). *The history of Java*. 1st ed. London, 1817. 2nd ed. London. 1830.

Reid, Anthony (1996). "Flows and seepages in the long-term Chinese interaction with Southeast Asia" in Anthony Reid and Kristine Alilunas Rodgers, eds., *Sojourners and settlers: histories of Southeast Asia and the Chinese in honour of Jennifer Cushman*. St. Leonards, NSW: Asian Studies Association of Australia in association with Allen & Unwin, pp. 15–49.

Robson, Stuart (1962). *The history and legend of the foundation of Majapahit*. Unpublished B.A. Honours thesis, University of Sydney.

Robson, Stuart (1979). "Notes on the early Kidung literature" *Bijdragen tot de Taal-, Land- en Volkenkunde*, v. 135, no. 2/3, pp. 300–22.

Robson, Stuart (2000). "The force of destiny, or the Kidung Harsa-Wijaya reread" *Indonesia and the Malay World*, vol. 28, no. 82, pp. 243–53.

Rockhill, W.W. (1914). "Notes on the relations and trade of China with the Eastern Archipelago and the coast of the Indian Ocean during the fourteenth century. Part I." *T'oung Pao* v. 15, pp. 419–47.

Rockhill, W.W. (1915). "Notes on the relations and trade of China with the Eastern Archipelago and the coast of the Indian Ocean during the fourteenth century. Part II." *T'oung Pao* v. 16, pp. 61–159, 236–71.

Rossabi, Morris (1988). *Khubilai Khan: his life and times*. Berkeley.

Rossabi, Morris (1994). "The reign of Khubilai khan" in *Cambridge history of China. Vol. 6: Alien regimes and border states, 907–1368*. Cambridge, [pp. 414–89].

Scheltema, J.F. (1912; 1985). *Monumental Java*. 1912 (repr. 1985, New Delhi).

Schlegel, Gustaaf (1873). "Iets omtrent de betrekkingen der Chinezen met Java, voor de komst der Europeanen aldaar." *Tijdschrift voor Indische taal-, land- en volkenkunde*, deel 20, pp. 7–31 (includes Amiot's "Introduction a la connoissance des peuples qui ont été ou qui sont actuellement tributaires de la Chine: Du royaume de Koua-oua" as an appendix).

Shaub, A.K. (1992). Шауб, А.К. *"Нагаракертагама" как источник по истории раннего Маджапахита (1293–1365)*. Москва.

Slametmuljana (1976). *A story of Majapahit*. Singapore.

Stuart-Fox, Martin (2003). "Mongol expansionism" in *A short history of China and Southeast Asia: tribute, trade and influence*, Crows Nest: Allen and Unwin, pp. 52–72. Reprinted, pp. 365–78 in volume 1 of *China and Southeast Asia*, edited by Geoff Wade (Routledge Library on Southeast Asia).

Татаро-монголы в Азии и в Европе: сборник статей. Москва, 1970.

Tan Ta Sen (2009). *Cheng Ho and Islam in Southeast Asia*. Singapore: Institute of Southeast Asian Studies.

Terwen-De Loos, J. (1971). "De Pandji-reliefs van oudheid LXV op de Gunung Běkěl Pěnanggungan" *Bijdragen tot de Taal-, Land- en Volkenkunde*, deel 127, 3e aflevering, pp. 321–30.

Tregonning, Kennedy (1957). "Kublai Khan and south-east Asia." *History today* v. 7 nr. 3 March, pp. 163–70.

Walckenaer, Charles Athanase, baron (1842). "Mémoire sur la chronologie de l'histoire des Javanais, et sur l'époque de la fondation de Madjapahit" *Mémoires de l'Institut royal de France, académie des inscriptions et belles-lettres*, t. 15, pp. 224–50.

Yamaguchi Hiroko (2003). 山口裕子. "ウォリオの歴史の語り方―ブトン社会の起源からスルタネイト初期までを中心に = Historical narrative of the Wolio: from the origin of Buton society to the early period of the Sultanate," アジア・アフリカ言語文化研究 = *Journal of Asian and African Studies*, no. 66, pp. 75–116.

Yamin, Muhammad (1962). *Tatanegara Madjapahit*. Jakarta, 7 vols.

Zahari, Abdul Mulku (1977). *Sejarah dan adat fiy Darul Butuni (Buton)*. Jakarta: Departmen Pendidikan dan Kegudayaan Indonesia. 3 v.

Zoetmulder, Petrus Josephus (1974). *Kalangwan: a survey of Old Javanese literature*. The Hague.

III. Secondary and related literature

Arps, Bernard (1992). *Tembang in two traditions: performance and interpretation of Javanese literature*. London.

Barfield, Thomas J. (1981). "The Hsiung-nu imperial confederacy: organization and foreign policy" *Journal of Asian Studies,* v. 41, no. 1, Nov. pp. 45–61.

Barrett, T.H. (1999). "Qubilai Qa'an and the historians: some remarks on the position of the Great Khan in premodern Chinese historiography" in *The Mongol Empire & its legacy.* Leiden, pp. 250–59.

Berry, Wendell (1989). "The Futility of Global Thinking." *Harper's Magazine,* Sept. 1989, pp. 16–22.

Bira, Sh. (1999). "Qubilai Qa'an and the 'Phags-pa bLa-ma" in *The Mongol Empire & its legacy.* Leiden, pp. 240–49.

Charbonneau, Bernard (1991). *Nuit et jour: science et culture.* Paris: Economica.

Christie, Jan Wisseman (1998). "Javanese markets and the Asian sea trade boom of the tenth to thirteenth centuries A.D." *Journal of economic and social history of the Orient* v. 41, nr. 3, pp. 344–91. Reprinted, pp. 261–97 in volume 1 of *China and Southeast Asia,* edited by Geoff Wade (Routledge Library on Southeast Asia).

Cleaves, Francis Woodman (1979–1980). "The biography of the Empress Cabi in the *Yüan shih*" *Harvard Ukrainian studies* v. 3–4, pt. 1, pp. 138–50.

Conlan, Thomas D. (2001). *In little need of divine intervention: Takezaki Suenaga's scrolls of the Mongol invasions of Japan: translation with interpretive essay.* Ithaca: Cornell.

Cook, Theodore F. (2001). "The Mongols in the making of Japan's national identity: invasion from across the sea and the legend of the Kamikaze" in *The Chinggis Khan Symposium in Memory of Gombojab Hangin.* Ulaanbaatar, pp. 45–76.

Crawfurd, John (1856). *A descriptive dictionary of the Indian islands & adjacent countries.* London.

Creese, Helen (1991). "Balinese *babad* as historical sources: a reinterpretation of the fall of Gèlgèl." *Bijdragen tot de taal-, land- en volkenkunde.* deel 147, 2e en 3e afl., pp. 236–60.

Creese, Helen (2000). "Inside the inner court: the world of women in Balinese Kidung poetry" in *Other pasts: Women, gender and history in early modern Southeast Asia,* edited by Barbara Watson Andaya. Honolulu: Center for Southeast Asian Studies, University of Hawai'i at Manoa, pp. 125–46.

Dabringhaus, Sabine (1997). "Chinese emperors and Tibetan monks: religion as an instrument of rule" in *China and her neighbours: borders, visions orf the other, foreign policy, 10th to 19th century.* Edited by Sabine Dabringhaus and Roderich Ptak. Wiesbaden, pp. 119–34.

Damais, Louis-Charles (1958). "Études d'épigraphie indonésienne: V. Dates de manuscrits et documents divers de Java, Bali et Lombok" *Bulletin de l'Ecole française d'Extrême-Orient.* Tome 49, pp. 1–257.

Dars, Jacques (1979). "Les jonques chinoises de haute mer sous les Song et les Yuan" *Archipel* nr. 18, pp. 41–55.

DeWeese, Devin (1978–1979). "The influence of the Mongols on the religious consciousness of thirteenth century Europe" *Mongolian studies: journal of the Mongolia Society* v. 5, pp. 41–78.

DeWeese, Devin (1994). *Islamization and native religion in the Golden Horde.* University Park, Pennsylvania.

Fang, Jun (1994). "Yuan studies in China: 1980–1991" *Journal of Sung-Yuan studies* nr. 24, pp. 237–54.

Fisher-Smith, Jordan Fisher (1993). Field observations: An Interview with Wendell Berry. *Orion,* 12 (Autumn 1993), pp. 50–59.

Fletcher, Joseph (1986). "The Mongols: ecological and social perspectives" *Harvard journal of Asiatic studies* v. 46, nr. 1, pp. 11–50.

Fletcher, Joseph (1979-1980). "Turco-Mongolian monarchic tradition in the Ottoman Empire" *Harvard Ukrainian studies* v. 3–4, pt. 1, pp. 236–51.

Franke, Herbert (1974). "Zum Legitimitätsproblem der Fremddynastien in der chinesischen Historiiographie" in *Geschichte in der Gesellschaft: Festschrift für Karl Bosl zum 65. Geburtstag* hrsg. Von Friedrich Prinz, F.-J. Schmale, Ferdinand Seibt. Stuttgart, pp. 14–27.

Franke, Herbert (1978; 1994). *From tribal chieftain to universal emperor and god: the legitimation of the Yüan Dynasty.* Munich (*Bayerische Akademie der Wissenschaften, Philosophisch-Historische Klasse, Sitzungsberichte;* 2) Reprinted in his *China under Mongol rule.* Aldershot, Hampshire, UK and Brookfield, Vt., 1994.

Franke, Herbert (1989). "Pax Mongolica" in Heissig and Müller. *Die Mongolen.* Innsbruck, pp. 54–57.

Gonda, Jan (1976). "Old Javanese literature" in *Handbuch der orientalistik, 3. Abteilung: Indonesien, Malaysia und die Philippienen unter Einschluss der Kap-Malaien in Südafrika. 3. Band: Literaturen, Abschnitt 1.* Leiden: Brill, pp. 187–245.

Halperin, Charles J. (1985). *Russia and the Golden Horde: The Mongol impact on medieval Russian history.* Bloomington.

Hamashita Takeshi (1988). "The tribute trade system and modern Asia" *Memoirs of the Research Department of the Toyo Bunko (The Oriental Library)* no. 46, pp. 7–25.

Hamann, Johann Georg (2007 [1784]). "Golgotha and Sheblimini!" in Johann Georg Hamann, *Writings on philosophy and language,* translated and edited by Kenneth Haynes. Cambridge: Cambridge University Press, pp. 164–204.

Harris, Roy (2004). *The Linguistics of History.* Edinburgh: Edinburgh University Press.

Hirth, F. (1896). "Chao Ju-kua, a new source of mediæval geography," *Journal of the Royal Asiatic Society of Great Britain & Ireland,* pp. 57–82.

Hirth, F. and W.W. Rockhill (trans. and eds.) (1966). *Chau Ju-kua: his work on the Chinese and Arab trade in the twelfth and thirteenth centuries, entitled "Chu-fan-chi."* New York: Paragon (reprint of original St. Petersburg edition of 1911).

Hobart, Mark (1997). "The missing subject: Balinese time and the elimination of history" *RIMA: Review of Indonesian and Malaysian Affairs*, v. 31, nr. 1, June, pp. 123–72.

Hutton, Christopher (2009). *Language, meaning and the law*. Edinburgh: Edinburgh University Press.

Irwin, Richard Gregg (1974). "Notes on the sources of de Mailla, *Histoire générale de la Chine*," *Journal of the Royal Asiatic Society Hong Kong Branch*, v. 14, pp. 92–100.

Kotwicz, Wladyslaw (1950). "Les Mongols, promoteurs de l'idée de paix universelle au début du 13e siècle" *Rocznik orientalistyczny*, v. 16, pp. 428–39.

Kumar, Ann (1979). "Javanese historiography in and of the 'Colonial period': A case study" in Reid and Marr, eds. *Perceptions of the past in Southeast Asia*. Singapore, pp. 187–206.

Kumar, Ann (1984). "On variation in babads." *Bijdragen tot de taal-, land- en volkenkunde* deel 140: 2-3, pp. 223–47.

Kuwabara Jitsuzo (1928; 1935). "On P'u Shou-keng, a man of the Western Regions, who was the Superintendent of the Trading Ships' Office in Ch'üan-chou towards the end of the Sung dynasty, together with a general sketch of trade of the Arabs in China during the T'ang and Sung eras." *Memoirs of the Research Department of the Toyo Bunko* no. 2, 1928, pp. 1–79 (continuation); no. 7, 1935, pp. 1–104.

Lo Jung-Pang (1955). "The emergence of China as a sea power during the late Sung and early Yüan periods." *Far Eastern Quarterly*, v. 14, no. 4, pp. 489–503.

Michaud, J. Fr. and Louis Gabriel Michaud (1811–1828). *Biographie universelle, ancienne et moderne; ou, Histoire, par ordre alphabétique, de la vie publique et privée de tous les hommes qui se sont fait remarquer par leurs écrits, leurs actions, leurs talents, leurs vertus ou leurs crimes. Ouvrage entièrement neuf, redigé par une société de gens de lettres et de savants*. Paris: Michaud.

The Mongol Empire & its legacy (1999). Edited by Reuven Amitai-Preiss & David O. Morgan. Leiden.

Mori Masao (1981). "The T'u-chüeh concept of sovereign" *Acta Asiatica* v. 41, pp. 47–74.

Nordholt, Henk Schulte (1992). "Origin, descent, and destruction: text and context in Balinese representations of the past" *Indonesia* no. 54 (*Perspectives on Bali*) pp. 27–58.

Patocka, Jan (2002). *Plato and Europe*. Stanford.

Pfeiffer, Judith (2003). *Conversion to Islam among the Ilkhans in Muslim narrative traditions: the case of Ahmad Tegüder*. University of Chicago, PhD dissertation.

Ptak, Roderich (1996). "Glosses on Wang Dayuan's Daoyi zhilüe (1349/50)". In *Récits de voyages asiatiques: genres, mentalités, conception de l'espace. Actes du colloque EFEO-EHESS de décembre 1994*. Édités par Claudine Salmon. Paris: École française d'Extrême-Orient, pp. 127–42.

Ptak, Roderich (1998). "Südostasiens Meere nach chinesischen Quellen (Song und

Yuan)" in *L'horizon nousantarien: mélanges en homage à Denys Lombard* (*Archipel*, vol. 56), v. 1, pp. 5–30.

Rachewiltz, Igor de (1973). "Some remarks on the ideological foundations of Chingis Khan's empire" *Papers on Far Eastern history*, no. 7, March, pp. 21–36.

Richard, Jean (1972). "Ultimatums mongols et lettres apocryphes: l'Occident et les motifs de guerre des Tartares" *Central Asiatic journal* v. 17, pp. 212–22.

Ricklefs, M.C. (1972). "A consideration of three versions of the *Babad tanah Djawi*, with excerpts on the fall of Madjapahit." *Bulletin of the School of Oriental and African Studies, University of London* v. 35, pt. 2, pp. 285–315.

Rosenstock-Huessy, Eugen (1938; 1993). *Out of revolution: autobiography of western man*. Providence.

Ruotsala, Antti (2001). *Europeans and Mongols in the middle of the thirteenth century: encountering the Other*. Helsinki (Sarja-ser. Humaniora, nide-tom. 314).

Sagaster, Klaus (1973). "Herrschaftsideologie und Friedensgedanke bei den Mongolen" *Central Asiatic journal* v. 17, pp. 223–42.

Salmon, Claudine; Lombard, Denys (1979). "Un vaisseau du XIIIème s. retrouvé avec sa cargaison dans la rade de "Zaitun"" *Archipel*, nr. 18, pp. 57–67.

Saunders, J.J. (1977). "Nomad as empire builder: A comparison of the Arab and Mongol conquests" in *Muslims and Mongols: essays on medieval Asia*. University of Canterbury, pp. 37–66.

Schlegel, Dietlinde (1968). *Hao Ching (1222–1275), ein chinesischer Berater des Kaisers Kublai Khan*. Bamberg.

Schrieke, Bertrand (1957). "Ruler and realm in early Java" in *Indonesian sociological studies: Selected writings of B. Schrieke, Part Two*. The Hague and Bandung: W. van Hoeve Ltd. (Selected studies on Indonesia by Dutch scholars, v. 3).

Sedyawati, Edy (1993). "Majapahit: fakta atau fiksi?" *Matra* no. 80 (Maret 1993); pp. 35–39.

Sidharta, Myra (2008). "Soyfoods in Indonesia", in *The world of soy*, edited by Christine M. Du Bois, Chee-Beng Tan and Sidney W. Mintz, Urbana and Chicago: University of Illinois Press, pp. 197–207.

Solovyov, Vladimir (1883; 1953). *Великий спор и христианская политика*. 1883 (*Собрание сочинений*, 1911, t. 4) French ed.: *La grande controverse et la politique chrétienne (Orient-Occident)* Paris, 1953.

Supomo, S. (1979). "The image of Majapahit in later Javanese and Indonesian writing." in Reid and Marr, eds. *Perceptions of the past in Southeast Asia*. Singapore, pp. 171–85.

Turan, Osman (1955). "The ideal of world domination among the medieval Turks" *Studia islamica* v. 4, pp. 77–90.

Vining, Joseph (1986). *The authoritative and the authoritarian*. Chicago: University of Chicago Press.

Voegelin, Eric (1940–1941). "The Mongol orders of submission to european powers" *Byzantion* v. 15, pp. 378–413.

Vries Robbé, A. de (1987). "The structure of the landscape in Javanese art" *Annali* (Istituto Universitario Orientale), v. 47, fasc. 2, pp. 181–208 + 8 p. of plates.

Wada Sei (1929). "The Philippine Islands as known to the Chinese before the Ming period" *Memoires of the Toyo Bunko* 4, pp. 121–66.

Wang Gungwu (1958). The Nanhai trade: a study of the early history of Chinese trade in the South China Sea. Kuala Lumpur. (*Journal of the Malayan Branch of the Royal Asiatic Society*, v. 31, pt. 2).

Wilson, Ian Douglas (2002). T*he politics of inner power: the practice of Pencak Silat in West Java*. Ph.D. thesis, School of Asian Studies, Murdoch University, Western Australia. Available at http://wwwlib.murdoch.edu.au/adt/pubfiles/adt-MU20040210.100853/02Whole.pdf.

Worsley, P.J. (1991). "Mpu Tantular's kakawin Arjunawijaya and conceptions of kingship in fourteenth century Java" in *Variation, transformation and meaning: studies on Indonesian literatures in honour of A. Teeuw*/edited by J.J. Ras and S.O. Robson. Leiden, pp. 163–90.

Zhao Rugua (1966 [1225]). *Chau Ju-kua: his work on the Chinese and Arab trade in the twelfth and thirteenth centuries, entitled "Chu-fan-chi."* Hirth, F. and W.W. Rockhill (trans. and eds.) New York: Paragon (reprint of original St. Petersburg edition of 1911).

Zoetmulder, Petrus Josephus (1982). *Old Javanese-English dictionary*. s-Gravenhage.

Index